In Kashmir

In memory of
Anna Politkovskaya
(1958–2006)

In Kashmir

Gender, Militarization &
the Modern Nation-State

SEEMA KAZI

Cover design by Benjamin Shaykin
Cover from *Blind Desire,* Mixed Media on Canvas (2008) by Priyanka Lahiri
Interior design by Tulika Print Communications & the South End Press collective

Library of Congress Cataloging-in-Publication Data
Kazi, Seema.
In Kashmir : gender, militarization, and the modern nation-state / Seema Kazi ;
   p. cm.
Includes bibliographical references.
ISBN 978-0-89608-792-7 (alk. paper)
1. Women and war—India—Jammu and Kashmir. 2. Militarism—India—Jammu and Kashmir. 3. War and society—India—Jammu and Kashmir. 4. Jammu and Kashmir (India)—Social conditions. I. Title.
JZ6405.W66K39 2010
954.05—dc22
                          2010019783

South End Press gratefully acknowledges the major institutional support of Medgar Evers College of the City University of New York for providing a physical and intellectual home for the world of independent publishing.

South End Press
Medgar Evers College
1650 Bedford Avenue, Brooklyn, NY 11225
www.southendpress.org

Contents

FOR KASHMIR

I've fallen beast-like in a snare:
Light, people, freedom, somewhere bide:
But at my back I hear the chase
And there is no escape outside.

Darkest wood and lakeside shore,
Gaunt trunk of a levelled tree,
My way is cut off on all sides:
Let what may, come; all's one to me.

Is there some ill I have committed?
Am I a murderer, miscreant?
For I have made the whole world weep
Over the beauty of my land.

But even at the very grave
I trust the time shall come to be
When over malice, over wrong,
The good will win its victory

Boris Pasternak 1959

Acknowledgements

This book is the product of PhD studies at the Gender Institute, London School of Economics. I have benefited enormously from the friendship and advice of many people during the course of this research. I would particularly like to thank Mary Kaldor and Anne Phillips at the LSE for their support and criticism, which was always couched in very generous terms. My deepest thanks and gratitude to the women I interviewed in Srinagar—most of whom cannot be named: thank you for trusting me without knowing me. Grateful thanks also to Professor Bashir Ahmed Dabla and Dr. Hameeda Bano at the University of Kashmir; Parvez Imroz, Khurram Parvez, Parveena Ahanger, Vijayan M.J., Dr. Nusrat Andrabi, Imtiaz Ahmed Khan, Yasmeen Raja, Sohail Ahmed, Showkat Kathjoo, Feizal Mir, Isaq Nehvi, Veena and Sunita, the Principal and teachers at Government College for Women, Srinagar, Yasin Malik, Showkat Ahmed Dar and Tahir Ahmed Mir—all of whom gave generously of their time and knowledge. Thanks also to Assabah Khan for her hospitality in Srinagar.

A number of friends reposed great trust in my ability to undertake this research, and I wish to thank Thanh-Dam Truong, Welmoed Koekebakker, Rawwida Baksh, Riet Turksma and Mark Behr for doing so. Warm and grateful thanks to Marjan Lucas for her friendship and support over the years. Thanks also to Ritu Menon for her valuable criticism and for not letting me get away with much! Special and very warm thanks to Cynthia Cockburn for her friendship, generosity—and the room at Bartholomew Road where much of this was written.

Introduction

This monograph focuses on the militarisation of a secessionist movement involving Kashmiri militants, and Indian military and paramilitary forces (hereafter referred to as the military), in the state of Jammu and Kashmir (hereafter referred to as Kashmir). Between 80,000 to 1,00,000 people have been killed in Kashmir since the beginning of the crisis in 1989–90. In 2008 the conflict entered its eighteenth year, with little hope of cessation in the violence or human rights abuse that characterise militarisation in the Valley. The term militarisation here connotes the crisis *of* the militarised state *and*, more importantly, the growing influence of the military *within* the state, with profound implications for state and citizens.

The end of World War II and the decline of colonial power led to the emergence of a number of new states in the global South, based on the model of the European nation-state. This model was centred on the concept of state security from external threats that were presumed to be predominantly *military* in nature. The idea of military security, in turn, was based on a realist interpretation of world politics, premised on the assumption that states exist in an 'anarchic' world that demands the possession and consolidation of military power in order to resist or deter attacks from rival states. "Such logic dictates that each nation develop, maintain and exercise coercive . . . power. . . . The capacity to coerce, kill and destroy becomes an important source of power, and thus the pre-eminent safeguard for national security" (Azar and Moon 1988, 4).

A number of states in the global South, including India, replicated the idea of military security to reinforce militarisation at a global level. Militarisation for external defence, as Keith Krause notes is "*systemic*, in the sense that it reinforces militarisation at an international level where both Northern and Southern states participate in [a] 'global military order'" (1996, 174, emphasis added). Critiques of militarisation—particularly during the Cold War decades—focused on its (external) systemic dimensions to highlight the dangers of states' attempt to seek 'security' through military means, and the political and economic integration of new nation-states in the global South within a western-dominated global military-industrial order. While the demise of the Cold War signalled the end of a super-power rivalry defined primarily in military and nuclear terms, its implications for the global South were not so profound; Paul Bracken notes that "the Cold War shaped Europe much more than it did Asia" (Bracken 1999, xv). As Europe, the arena of so many wars, became more secure and cut back on its armed forces, a range of states in Asia—China, India, North Korea, Pakistan—embarked on military and nuclear programmes of their own.

In contrast to western nation-states, military consolidation in the global South was not driven as much by identifiable external (military) threats to the state as by diverse non-military/political factors. While a modern, professional military was a symbol of state sovereignty in the immediate post-colonial period, this symbolism was subsequently overtaken by the emergence of bombs and missiles as the new markers of modernity and nationhood. For instance, in Asia, the Chinese testing of nuclear weapons in 1964 was matched by India in 1974. Further, the pursuit of weapons of mass destruction by states such as India derived from a convergence between nationalism and newly destructive technologies where "mass politicisation of military competition . . . creates an overwhelming impulse to catch up, even if there is no catching up to do . . . Nationalism, [in the Asian context] has made a second nuclear age" (Bracken 1999, 90).

Among the modern institutions adopted by newly-independent states in the global South was a professional military meant to defend the state against external threat. However, the role of the military in a great number of these states is not restricted to that of external defence; rather, it is increasingly used to neutralise *domestic* political challenges to the state. While the nature of these challenges is diverse and historically contingent, what is of interest here is their *negotiation* through military rather than institutional means—a trend that propels the military into an increasingly *political* role *within* states in the global South. States' use of the military for domestic repression is synonymous with large-scale violence against civilians, the destruction of civil society, and profound social transformations. In contrast to conventional, classic war where the military was subject to the laws of war designed to minimise direct violence against civilians, militarisation in the domestic context is neither subject to, nor circumscribed by, international law.

Militarisation's domestic variant includes not only direct violence against civilians by the military, but also patterns of gendered abuse such as rape—both of which constitute part of the *methodology* of war. Direct violence (by the military) against citizens opposed to the state—including arbitrary detention, extrajudicial killings, torture, rape and sexual abuse—"profoundly affects the social, economic, and political status, roles and responsibilities of women and alters their relations with men during and after conflict. . ." (Kumar 2001, 7). For precisely this reason, militarisation in the domestic context exerts a long-term social influence on the societies within which it unfolds.

The acquisition of arms and weapons by states across the world, including in the global South, is an important and compelling area of analysis. The focus on militarisation's systemic (global) dimensions, however, is often achieved at the cost of the national/state level of analysis. This point is particularly significant vis-à-vis the global South where a pattern of extraordinary military consolidation—ostensibly for 'national' defence—together with the increasing political influence (or dominance) of the military *within* is not so much a response to an imminent *military* threat to the state as it is driven by *domestic* political considerations. Indeed, ever since their emergence, states in the global South have witnessed wars that relate to state-formation and nation-building rather than to external threat.[1]

These wars involve the military yet represent a departure from the norms, rules and conduct of conventional warfare. In contrast to the conventional inter-state wars of the nineteenth and early twentieth centuries, intra-state conflicts now constitute the predominant form of war.[2] Donald Snow notes:

One of the most dramatic ways in which the post-Cold War
world differs from the Cold War international system is the pattern
of violence that has been developing. Warfare in its most
traditional sense has virtually disappeared from the scene . . .. A
different, darker pattern of violence has begun to emerge . . ..
These wars . . . seem . . . less principled in political terms, less
focused on the attainment of some political ideal (1996, 1).

They constitute what this study refers to as the *domestic* crisis of
militarisation *within* states in the global South that has explicitly
political (non-military) origins. Militarisation, as Roland
Simbulan notes:

. . . is the process of using the military . . . to suppress the
people's just demands for a humane society. It logically connotes
human rights violations by the physical presence or even
saturation of soldiers . . . a situation which, to the general
perception, implies and results in coercion . . . The main pretext
of militarisation is the achievement or maintenance of 'political
stability,' national security,' or other similar goals, but whose
real purpose is the maintenance of the regime in power (1988,
38).

The term militarisation is used across the disciplines of
International Relations and Political Theory; whereas the former
connotes the external military behaviour of states, the latter is
employed in relation to the (domestic) institutional dimensions
of state violence. Both dimensions are assumed to be mutually
exclusive. This study does not conform to this categorisation.
The argument made here is that the military consolidation of
states in the global South, including India, *and* the growing
political influence of the military within them are interlinked
processes. Accordingly, this research situates militarisation *of* and
within the state within a *single* frame of analysis.

The case of India in this regard is particularly interesting.
India's initial rejection of the normative icons of militarisation
(i.e., nuclear weapons) was influenced by the twin themes of
Nehruvian internationalism and Gandhian non-violence.
Paradoxically, a state that committed itself to the principles of
peace and disarmament subsequently embraced the weapons of

mass destruction it had initially rejected. This transformation, I argue, is the outcome of constructions and imaginings of the 'nation' and 'national power' that have a historical presence in Indian society.

Further, the idea of a (militarily) powerful 'nation' in the Indian context is underpinned by the construct of a centralised, *unitary* state and a "fictive homogeneity . . . predicated on the belief that each unit of territory is ideally occupied by a singular conception of the national citizen" (Krishna 1999, 231). This construct of state and nation is, in effect, a replication of the European model of the nation-state that is at odds with India's ethnic and cultural diversity. For precisely this reason, "the quest to 'secure' the nation is premised on practices that generate the multiple insecurities that unravel the nation even as it is being made" (Krishna 1999, 209).

Kashmir exemplifies the intersection between militarisation for external defence and the use of the military for domestic repression, an intersection that has transformed the Indian state into a source of deep insecurity for its citizens and converted the Indian military into an illegitimate agent of repression. Both, in turn, seriously undermine the democratic credentials of the state. In contrast to conventional approaches, this study explores militarisation in, and over, Kashmir as a complex, multi-dimensional, intersecting process: as a military impasse between the states of India and Pakistan with nuclear overtones; as a war between Indian soldiers and Kashmiri militants; a war between Indian soldiers and militants supported by the state of Pakistan; and last, but by no means least, as a war waged by the Indian state (i.e., the military) against Kashmir's citizens.

My primary focus here is on Kashmir's citizens and society, and in this respect this study constitutes a departure from conventional analyses. By focusing on Kashmir's civilian dimensions, it spotlights a contemporary context where militarisation *includes,* yet also *transcends,* its military-strategic and/or institutional dimensions. In other words, this research highlights that state military processes in Kashmir are not separate from but embedded *within* Kashmir's social fabric. Militarisation in Kashmir—characterised by military consolidation, nuclear nationalism, the use of the military as an agent of domestic repression, the dissolution of civil-military distinctions, the destruction of civil society, and gender transformations—cannot therefore fit within state or male-centric theoretical perspectives. Indeed, such frameworks "legitimate a way of thinking about violence and conflict that . . . misses the dynamics associated with the actual experience of violence" (Nordstrom and Martin 1992, 4). This is not to deny or understate the importance of Kashmir's institutional/military-strategic dimensions, but to underline their deep and enduring intersection with the lives of Kashmiri citizens.

By placing women's subjective experience of militarisation at the centre of the analytic frame, this study seeks to establish the link between state military processes at a 'national' level and gender transformations at a local/societal level. In contrast to dominant approaches that attempt to fit empirical reality into a particular theoretical framework, this research utilises women's experiences in Kashmir to both inform and expand theoretical perspectives on militarisation.

Representing women: empowering or exclusionary?

This monograph is not a representative study. By focusing on the experiences of a small group of women (and a smaller number of men) in Srinagar, it examines the social and gender dimensions of militarisation in the Kashmir Valley. Apart from being the state capital, Srinagar is an important historical, political, cultural and educational centre and is home to press and media offices, major political parties and militant factions, non-government and civil society organisations and the University of Kashmir. The 1989–90 revolt centred in and was influenced by events in Srinagar.

Linda Alcoff maintains that the project of representing 'others' experience or of speaking on their behalf is not a neutral exercise: "There is a strong, albeit contested current . . . which holds that speaking for others—even for other women—is arrogant, vain, unethical and politically illegitimate" (1995, 98). This concern derives from fears of appropriating the voice and content of the speaker—rendering the latter ever more marginal. Against women's diversity and the dangers of appropriating what one seeks to defend, the act of representation is, in short, a politically fraught exercise. Alcoff articulates the dilemma: "We must begin to ask ourselves whether there ever is a legitimate authority, and if so, is it ever valid to speak for others who are unlike us or less privileged than us?" (1995, 99). In the following discussion I engage with the political and epistemological dimensions of representing the experience of a diverse group of (Kashmiri) women.

The intersection between militarisation and women's lives in Kashmir underscores the importance of challenging dominant narratives where the state is the *subject* of knowledge, and where masculine (state *vs* male militants) experience is assumed to be the substantive and valid experience of militarisation. While the conflation of male experience with human experience is justly criticised, the argument around gender cannot claim an 'authentic' women's experience, for it would then conform to the same essentialist argument that constitutes the basis of its critique. What gender does legitimately seek is its validity as a constitutive element of national and international politics.[3] The political and epistemological claim of gender critiques, accordingly, is that social relations of gender are an integral dimension of world politics.

To the extent that (Kashmiri) women are absent in dominant narratives on Kashmir, reclaiming women's experiences is a step towards the larger project of challenging such narratives. Yet, privileged locations, i.e., "systematic divergences in social location between the speaker and those spoken for, [may] have a significant effect on the content of what is said" (Alcoff 1995, 98). Representation may not accurately reflect the opinions or concerns of those spoken for. If representation does not achieve its intended objective, should it be undertaken at all? Should a gender critique resort to what Alcoff calls the "retreat" option, i.e., choosing not to speak for fear of establishing a privileged discursive position in the field and silencing "authenticity"? (1995, 107). Before answering this question, we need to ask whether or not Kashmiri women are the *only* legitimate or valid constituency to represent themselves.

The idea of a "pure," non-ideological "authenticity," Spivak argues, is an essentialist construct. While invested with individual subjectivity, the "subaltern subject is irretrievably heterogeneous" (1988, 284). There is, accordingly, no "authentic" "non-ideological" subordinate/marginal subject and the pure authentic/original voice does not exist (Spivak 1988, 307). The task of a gender critique accordingly, is neither to pursue an illusory "original/authentic" voice nor to supplant or appropriate the subordinate voice; rather, to "listen to" instead of "speaking for" in order to subvert the "authorising power" of dominant, positivist narratives (Alcoff 1995, 110). This may serve as a possible method of knowledge production, which is essentially a *partial* account within a larger collective of meanings, yet a more desirable (and necessary) option than withdrawal. The counter-narrative, in other words, functions as a *means* to dislodge entrenched hierarchies, while the retreat or withdrawal option may only serve to continue the imperialist project.[4] To quote Spivak again: "Representation has not withered away. The female intellectual has a circumscribed task which she must not disown with a flourish" (1988, 308).

Representing Kashmiri women therefore is a *legitimate* exercise as long as it is cognisant of its own partiality within a larger, complex context. As Miriam Cooke notes: "There is no one history, no one story about war, that has greater claim to truth . . . history is made up of multiple stories, many of them herstories, which emanate from and then reconstruct events" (1996, 4). This research highlights "nuclear age wars [where] women—whom the War Story had described as at home and safe because defended by their men at the front—are increasingly acknowledged to be attractive military targets" (1996, 38). In so doing, it inserts women back into the story of militarisation in Kashmir. This act is not a purely 'academic' exercise, but an undertaking invested with political responsibility *and* epistemic validity. The term political responsibility refers to the commitment on the part of the researcher to non-hierarchical, politically grounded and accountable research, while epistemic validity refers to the political project of reclaiming marginal voices. What follows is a brief discussion regarding the significance of both.

Political responsibility derives from an acknowledgement of the partiality of research, together with a commitment to the non-hierarchical, non-normative, counter-narrative. Accordingly, while fully conscious of the power relationship between researcher and the researched, as well as the partiality of research, as long as representation constitutes women's *political* opposition to the dominant, normalising narrative of the "War Story" (Cooke 1996) it is a legitimate (and necessary) basis of action. *Political* opposition or resistance, as Chandra Mohanty asserts: "is encoded in the practices of remembering and writing. . . The very practice of remembering against the grain of 'public' or hegemonic history . . . the struggle to assert knowledge which is outside the parameters of the dominant, suggests a rethinking of sociality itself (1991, 38–39). This scholarship is

> . . . not the mere production of knowledge about a certain subject. It is a directly political and discursive practice in that it is purposeful and ideological. It is best seen as a mode of intervention into particular hegemonic discourses: it is a political praxis which counters and resists the totalising imperative of age-old "legitimate" and "scientific" bodies of knowledge. [It is] a scholarly practice (whether reading, writing, critical or textual) . . . inscribed in relations of power—relations which they counter, resist or perhaps implicitly support. There can, of course, be no apolitical scholarship (Mohanty 1991, 53).

Mohanty's point regarding the ideological stance/motivation of the research/researcher is crucial, for this determines whether knowledge production/research reinforces or dismantles hierarchy and, by extension, whether or not the research is politically legitimate.

The epistemic validity of research, on the other hand, derives from the representation of the category 'women' and, by extension, from the project of reclaiming marginal voices/experiences. One problem associated with representation is the inherent contradiction contained in the term 'women'. Women do not constitute a singular, undifferentiated social group, nor are they bound by homogenous experience. An emphasis on the importance of women's subjective experience of militarisation in Kashmir should therefore be accompanied by the necessary clarification that it is not possible to make generalisations. Women in Kashmir experience conflict 'differently'. While it is essential to acknowledge and accept the diversity of women's experience and the dangers of generalisation, the subjective experience of a small group of Kashmiri women *can* nevertheless be synthesised towards a larger understanding of gender vis-à-vis militarisation in Kashmir. Accordingly, while it is not possible to arrive at any definitive 'conclusion' or 'truth' (reflected in words such as 'impact' or 'effect') regarding a diverse group's experience of militarisation (indeed, such an approach conjures up a static, rather than a dynamic picture, reducing prospects of transformative change), what can be attempted is the "production of women" (Mohanty 1991, 64) in terms of the social relations of gender underpinning militarisation in Kashmir. The particularity of (Kashmiri) women's subjective experience of militarisation illustrates the (re)production of gender relations of power within a situation of military conflict. Although this experience cannot be conflated with that of Kashmiri women in general, it nevertheless illuminates the intrinsic link between state (and inter-state) military processes on the one hand, and gender transformations on the other.

Finally, given the importance of political responsibility and epistemic validity in an academic setting defined by dominant positivist frameworks, it is necessary to prevent the counter-narrative from being submerged within the latter. A difficult yet scrupulous way to do so would be *not* to resort to the conventional disclaimer acknowledging potential drawbacks of one's research, but "to remain open to criticism and attempt actively, attentively, and sensitively to 'hear' the criticism (i.e., understand it). A quick impulse to reject criticism, must make us wary" (Alcoff 1995, 113). Any representation is accountable to limitations and problems and must be open to critique from other "locations". Empirical work must emphasise the production of women as a "partial perspective" derived from, and accountable to, the researcher's specific subjective *location* where "partiality is not universality, but constitutive of a particular knowledge claim" (Haraway 1988, 195). This is not merely a responsibility but a mandatory obligation on the part of the researcher. Discharging this obligation is perhaps the only way to produce historically located, socially inclusive and politically legitimate knowledge constructions of a complex and changing world.

Scope

Chapter 1 focuses on the academic debate regarding militarism where I begin with an analysis of early theories of militarism that did not anticipate—and therefore could not explain—militarism's dynamics during the first half of the twentieth century. The emergence of the post-1945 nation-state system, I maintain, profoundly altered the meaning of militarism. From being perceived as an institutional anomaly and/or a province of capitalism, militarism was transformed into a permanent attribute of the territorial nation-state with war, or the threat of war, being *the* ultimate guarantor of the freedom and autonomy of the state.[5] The consolidation of the destructive capability of individual states, I argue, represents militarism's external (systemic) crisis based on the misleading logic that "if you want peace, then prepare for war" (Walker 1990, 5). The idea of military security for the state formed the backdrop for the emergence of post-colonial nation-states in the global South, replicating the logic and rituals of national defence to reinforce militarism at a global (systemic) level.

Militarism *within* states in the global South is of a rather different order than its external (systemic) dimension. It derives from *political* challenges to the state *within* national borders rather than from *military* threats (by rival states) beyond them. Militarism's domestic variant involves mobilisation of the military against social groups and/or communities opposed to the state— a mobilisation characterised by large-scale violence against citizens. One of the most important characteristics of this crisis is the transformation of the military from a legitimate instrument of external defence into an illegitimate agent of domestic repression. In short, militarism's domestic variant in the global South represents a paradox whereby the nation-state itself has become a significant source of *insecurity* for its citizens.

The external and internal dimensions of militarism in the global South are not necessarily mutually exclusive, but (frequently, if not inevitably) interlinked; they encompass the problem of military defence *of* the nation-state *and* political crises *within* the nation-state that are negotiated through military means. Since both crises have political rather than military origins, their empirical characteristics do not fit within the explanatory framework of early (western) liberal, Marxist or modernist theories (of militarism). Using empirical examples from Latin America, Africa and South Asia, I highlight the profound implications of militarisation's domestic crisis for state and citizen. Focusing on South Asia and India in particular, I demonstrate that militarism in the South Asian context does not derive from conventional notions of external (military) threat to the state but from a specific historical context of arbitrary and contested post-colonial frontiers, and a crisis of legitimacy within state borders. I further illustrate that the use of the military for domestic repression by the state is not a phenomenon confined to the military, but a state-society *process* characterised by the elimination of civil-military distinctions.

The term militarism, I further argue, is too narrow to capture the complexity of this crisis, and therefore make the case for using the term militarisation. There are four important advantages for the use of this term. The first relates to the limited relevance of militarism which connotes *military* dominance over civil authority and/or an undue emphasis on military power in foreign policy. This does not accord with contemporary contexts (such as in India) where formal control of the military rests in civilian hands, even as the military is used as an instrument of domestic repression. In other words, although militarism connotes military dominance *over* (domestic) civil authority and an emphasis on military force by states in international relations (symbolised by the military consolidation of states) it does not address the domestic (instrumental) role of the military *within* states.

Second, the term militarism does not address the socio-political dimensions of the crisis that flow from such instrumental use of the military. This crisis *involves*, but is not confined to, the military. It encompasses an assortment of military and paramilitary forces, insurgent groups, secret armies, rival militias and intelligence outfits where civilians, rather than being protected are, instead, specific *targets* of violence. In this context, violence against women is not an *outcome* but a *constituent* of military conflict—a means to inflict defeat and humiliation on the 'enemy' through the appropriation of cultural meanings of gender. Further, militarism does not take into account a contemporary context in which the military functions not only as an illegitimate instrument of state power, but as a violator of the rule of law, the rules of war and citizens' democratic and human rights.

Third, militarism does not address the *ideological* dimensions underpinning the domestic use of military. This may not be a universal characteristic, yet as the very different examples of Latin America and South Asia illustrate, domestic repression by the military has been justified in 'national' terms. This dimension has special salience vis-à-vis India where constructions of 'the nation' and 'national interest' serve as an alibi for militarily-backed political repression.

Finally, I argue that the crisis of militarism in the global South is not gender-neutral. Conventional militarism involved professional militaries whose conduct was subject to the laws of war that categorised women as non-combatants which, as historical evidence suggests, were almost always breached. Women's sexual slavery enforced by the Japanese army during World War II is a notable example,[6] while the wars in former Yugoslavia, Rwanda or Iraq are contemporary instances of the same. Although women have been, and are, used and abused by the military in conventional war, the military remains a legitimate (and accountable) agent of the state, subject to the Geneva Convention.[7] The contemporary (domestic) crisis of militarism within the nation-state, however, transforms the military into an illegitimate (and unaccountable) agent of the state not only *not* bound by the rules of war or the Geneva Convention, but in fact empowered to violate both with impunity. Rape and sexual abuse of women by the military is as much part of the crisis of militarism as the arbitrary and unlawful killing of civilians.

Given these complexities, I argue that the term militarisation is a more appropriate analytical concept. I discuss the advantages afforded by a concept that transcends normative disciplinary divisions in order to analyse the relationship between the state, the military and society within a *single* (national) historical context. The understanding of militarisation as a multi-dimensional *historical process* bridges the disciplinary distinction between International Relations and Political Theory (based on the academic distinction between inter and intra-state military conflict) to place both within a *general* historical frame that captures the *converging* crises of, and within, the militarised state where the military is used for external defence *and* as an instrument of domestic repression. With regard to the latter, militarisation refers to those aspects of civilian life that result from direct military intervention in people's lives and behaviour,[8] including institutional measures such as special legislation or de facto impunity accorded to military forces that undermine the rule of law and citizen's democratic rights.

Further, the understanding of militarisation as a process located *within* rather than beyond society corresponds with a contemporary context where extra-judicial killings, unlawful detention, torture, rape and sexual abuse are integral to the process of militarisation. Indeed, it is in this context that gender critiques are crucial, in that they highlight not just the social fabric of militarisation and but the ways in which this fabric is imprinted with meanings and constructions of gender.

Finally, the concept of militarisation as an *ideological* process is especially relevant in the case of India, where nationalism functions as a powerful legitimising ground for state military and nuclear consolidation without, *and* use of the military for domestic repression within.

I develop a working definition of militarisation for this study which I define as the growing influence and institutionalisation of military power (albeit not military control of the state) in domestic and foreign policy that involves institutional, ideological and social transformations.

Chapter 2 focuses on the relationship between militarisation and the Indian state. Situating this relationship within a *general* historical frame, I highlight the paradox between the Indian state's moral commitment to disarmament and its pragmatic desire for international recognition and status. The initial pursuit of nuclear weapons by the Indian state was not, as IR theory would have us believe, based on realpolitik notions of state security, rather it was shaped by ideas of modernity, post-colonial identity and scientific achievement. Nuclear weapons, I argue, were part of a 'national' narrative premised on the idea of India as an "independent, great state ... morally superior to its colonisers and the dominant states of the international system" (Perkovich 2000, 448). In short, nuclear weapons symbolised *Indian* identity, achievement and power; they were a measure of what modern India could accomplish.

In a (Cold War) context where state power was defined in primarily military terms—to which India was no exception—military defeat at the hands of China in 1962 dealt a blow to the Indian state's self-perception of power and status in the international realm. The perception of India as a militarily 'weak' state precipitated an extraordinary post-1962 military build-up; the consolidation of military 'power' propelled India into the front ranks of (militarily) 'powerful' states and resolved her (initial) contradiction between the moral and pragmatic. The possession of formidable military 'power,' I argue, fails to insulate the Indian state from a greater and perhaps more perilous paradox: the crisis of legitimacy *within* national borders. Fortified by military (and nuclear) power, the Indian state is nevertheless beset with a domestic crisis of legitimacy that assumed full-blown proportions at a moment when it seemed militarily invincible.

While this crisis is manifest in a diverse range of struggles and movements, my focus is limited to wars or 'insurgencies' across the northern periphery of the Indian state where the Indian military functions as an instrument of political power and domestic repression. I situate India's domestic crisis of militarisation within the larger, multi-dimensional crisis of the Indian state in order to illustrate the link between a crisis of state legitimacy within, and the consolidation and assertion of state military (and nuclear) 'power' without. In particular, I demonstrate how the eroding legitimacy of the Indian state, together with a lack of democratic accountability, generated a crisis of extraordinary proportions that was sought to be masked by its (the state's) self-projection as a *unitary* and militarily 'powerful' state in the realist tradition. The nuclearisation and reinvention of India in exclusively Hindu terms is, I argue, a response of the Indian *state*,[9] to what in great measure is its own, largely self-generated crisis. In short, my argument is that militarisation of, and within, the Indian state have *common* political origins.

The ideological dimensions of this crisis originate from a 'national' imaginaire that places a range of social and/or cultural groups/communities beyond the pale of 'the nation', and *objectifies* state violence on a grand scale—a violence academically referred to as the nation-state building enterprise. The project of (unitary) nation-state building and its underlying national(ist) imaginaire lies at the heart of India's domestic crisis of militarisation. The use of the military in civil governance and as an instrument of repression in Assam, India's north-eastern region, and Kashmir exemplify this crisis.[10]

Chapter 3 focuses on militarisation in Kashmir. The intersection between the Indian state's attempt to maintain the political status quo *over* Kashmir (vis-à-vis Pakistan) by using over half a million soldiers, an assortment of high-tech weaponry and nuclear weapons, and its simultaneous use of the military for repression *within* Kashmir are discussed. While I hold the Indian state primarily responsible for militarisation in Kashmir, I also acknowledge Pakistan's (secondary) role and influence in the state.

I then highlight the *ideological* underpinnings of the crisis, where a state of virtual military rule within Kashmir is legitimised by an across-the-board political consensus that constructs a civil struggle for justice in parochial 'national' terms—a representation that deflects the issue of state accountability even as it legitimises militarisation in and over Kashmir.

Kashmir's citizens, I argue, pay the highest and most grievous price for the intersecting streams of violence unleashed by militarisation. Using interviews conducted in Srinagar, I highlight how the Indian state's attempt at external 'defence' (of Kashmir) and internal political consolidation through military means in Kashmir are built upon foundations of collective violence, terror and pain. Militarisation in and over Kashmir tears into Kashmir's social fabric to generate individual and collective trauma, social dislocation, cultural destruction, socio-economic devastation, ethnic fragmentation and the destruction of Kashmir's civil society. Kashmir's landscape of missing or 'disappeared' young men, extra-judicial killings, widows and half-widows, orphans, ubiquitous graveyards and collective fear, grief and trauma underscore the paradox of a *democracy* that *invests* the military with the power to derogate citizens' non-derogable rights, even as it simultaneously *insulates* the military from public scrutiny and accountability. Kashmir, in other words, symbolises the enduring contradiction between the Indian state's claim to democracy and legitimacy, and its undemocratic and illegitimate violation of the rule of law.

Chapter 4 focuses on militarisation's gender dimensions in the Valley. This chapter puts forward two arguments. The first relates to mainstream IR or political analyses based on a (male) state-as-actor paradigm—Kashmir being no exception to this trend. My argument here does not suggest changing IR and/or political theory, but addressing an important absence across both disciplines. A gender analysis of militarisation in Kashmir, I maintain, is not so much about 'adding' women as it is about challenging the public-private dichotomies that construct militarisation as an essentially male domain. The nature of contemporary military conflict underscores the importance of gender as an *integral* rather than a 'separate' or subsidiary category of analysis. In short, my argument is that social relations of gender are a *constituent* rather than a consequence of militarisation in Kashmir.

My second argument relates to women's (subjective) *political* experience of militarisation. This experience is mediated by social constructions of gender though it comes with the necessary caveat that it may also be influenced by other factors such as class or location. Thus, militarisation in Kashmir is a *social* process, informed and acted upon by meanings of gender in ways that reproduce and/or reinforce social hierarchy.

The struggle for *azadi* centres on women's conventional role as mothers, wives and sisters. I demonstrate how these roles have become politicised in the face of a gendered onslaught by the Indian state against Kashmiri men. I then highlight the essential paradox between women's public support for, and significant role in, the struggle for *azadi* on the one hand, and their political marginalisation on the other. This contradiction is shaped by a conservative and patriarchal social context as well as the instrumental relationship between Kashmiri women and the Kashmiri militant leadership.

Elaborating on the implications of this contradiction, I discuss how militarisation produces a landscape of widows and half-widows whose conventional economic dependence on men is exacerbated by the temporary, if not permanent, absence of the latter. Widowhood heightens economic insecurity, emotional stress and sexual vulnerability and impacts women's right to property and custody of children, even as it simultaneously subjects them to greater social surveillance and policing. Not uncommonly, it also subjects them to sexual abuse by the military. Such abuse in Kashmir is at least tolerated if not actually condoned by the establishment. Such rape represents the appropriation of cultural constructions of 'honour' in order to inflict collective defeat on the 'enemy.'

In what I call the 'cultural politics of militarisation', I argue that women pay an essentially *political* price for a military occupation centred on the humiliation and emasculation of Kashmiri men. Militarisation in Kashmir has generated a masculinist social environment that, in turn, subjects women to greater social policing and control and regressive versions of 'Islamic' identity. This trend must not be taken as incontrovertible evidence of the 'fundamentalist' character of Kashmir's political struggle. Rather, it should be viewed in the larger context of the denial of democracy and democratic rights in Kashmir, and the usurpation of the rule of law by the military that has facilitated a parallel appropriation of secular space by Islamists. In short, my argument is that Kashmir's 'fundamentalist' politics are fuelled and sustained by a policy of militarisation that undermines the rule of law and citizens' democratic and human rights.

In sum, I argue that Kashmir's gender dimensions illustrate how militarisation in Kashmir is a process mediated through constructions of gender in ways that reproduce and/or reinforce social hierarchy. I end by highlighting the corruption of the struggle for *azadi* that has deviated from the dreams and longings of many Kashmiris who took part in it. These longings are a symbolic defeat for the Indian state and its policy of militarisation, even as they underline the urgent necessity of ending Kashmir's unconscionable human tragedy. The impasse in and over Kashmir offers an opportunity to the Indian state to extricate itself from its self-created abyss of violence.

By way of conclusion, in Chapter 5, I underline the limits and dangers of military 'power' that has transformed India into a source of insecurity for Indian and South Asian citizens *and* converted the Indian military into an illegitimate instrument of domestic repression. A decentralised, democratic Indian state, premised on a plural concept of nation and identity can restore to Kashmir's people the dignity and justice for which they pay so dear a price. A restored Kashmir offers the Indian state an opportunity to build a constructive, non-military relationship with Pakistan that, in turn, may eliminate the principal source of insecurity and fear for Indian and South Asian citizens.

Notes

1 Luc Van De Goor, Kumar Rupesinghe and Paul Sciarone (eds.), *Between Development and Destruction: An Enquiry into the Causes of Conflict in Post-Colonial States* (London; New York: Macmillan 1996), p. 1.

2 Dietrich Jung, Klause Schlichte and Jens Siegelberg, 'Ongoing Wars and their Explanation' in Goor et al., *Between Development and Destruction*, p. 57.

3 Rebecca Grant and Kathleen Newland, 'Introduction' in R. Grant and K. Newland (eds.), *Gender and International Relations* (Milton Keynes: Open Press, 1991), p. 5.

4 Gayatri Chakravorty Spivak, 'Can the Subaltern Speak?' in Cary Nelson and Lawrence Grossberg (eds.), *Marxism and the Interpretation of Culture* (Basingstoke: Macmillan Education, 1988), p. 298.

5 R.B.J. Walker, 'Security, Sovereignty, and the Challenge of World Politics', *Alternatives* 15 (1): 3–27(1990), p. 4.

6 "Between 1931–1945, the Japanese 'conscripted' at least 200,000 girls and women from Korea, China, Taiwan, Indonesia and the Philippines as sex slaves or 'comfort women'. Japanese authorities refused to acknowledge that its military ran the programme until 1993." Rhonda Hammer, 'Militarism and Family Terrorism: A Critical Feminist Perspective', in *The Review of Education, Pedagogy and Cultural Studies* (2000), Vol. 25, p. 240.

7 The laws of war are subject to the 1949 Geneva Convention "relating to the . . . protection of civilians in times of war". David Sills (ed), *International Encyclopaedia of the Social Sciences*, Vol. 10 (London: Collier Macmillan 1968), p. 319.

8 Such as arbitrary arrest, detention, rape, extra-judicial killing, torture, disappearances, etc. See Jim Zwick, 'Militarism and Repression in the Phillippines' in Michael Stohl and George A. Lopez (eds.), *The State as Terrorist* (Westport, Conn.: Greenwood Press 1984), p. 124.

9 Sumantra Bose, 'Hindu Nationalism and the Crisis of the Indian State' in Saugata Bose and Ayesha Jalal (eds.), *Nationalism, Democracy and Development: State and Politics in India* (New Delhi: Oxford University Press, 1998), p. 158.

10 In contrast to military deployment in Kashmir and the north–eastern states, Punjab witnessed excessive reliance on the police as an instrument of repression.

1 Militarism and Militarisation

> Traditional warfare has today been superceded by conflicts of unspeakable violence conducted by regular armies. . . . As a result, violations of humanitarian law are increasingly frequent and serious.
>
> *International Committee of the Red Cross* 1995, 4

> We wish to stress once again that women's rights are human rights, that human rights are above national interests, and that the state must not kill its citizens.
>
> *Belgrade Women's Lobby*, 1993).[1]

Militarism in the modern world

The term militarism is used with reference to a range of developments including interstate military conflict, the transnational arms race, the military-industrial complex, military juntas, militant nationalism, and so on. This rather broad category shares a single attribute that links them to each other, namely, their relationship with the military.[2] Two clarifications are in order here. First, the term military in this study refers to state military forces that are used for the purpose of external territorial defence. Second, the term militarism is used not in its legal sense, i.e., the presence of a national army or military establishment but rather, in its sociological sense, namely, the use of the military *within* states as a means to achieve *political* objectives.[3] In other words, the "mere existence of a military does not imply a militarist state" (Chenoy 2002, 6); It is when the military assumes extra-legal powers and functions as an instrument of political repression that militarism assumes a meaning beyond the military. In this context militarism "pertains to values, attitudes and practices which connote a bias or *preference* for military means where they are *unnecessary* from the standpoint of territorial defence" (Wolpin 1986, 2; emphasis in the original).

The debate on militarism during the early twentieth century was based on the Liberal and Marxist positions. According to the former, militarism was a political and constitutional problem, a remnant of a pre-capitalist, pre-industrial age where political dominance of the military over civilian institutions constituted a deviation from representative government based on a civil-military distinction. The establishment of constitutional government accordingly, was deemed an appropriate remedy for militarism. Civilian rule, liberals argued, would not only remove the undue influence of the military in civil affairs but also generate industrial production and economic prosperity that would, in turn, render military power superfluous. Industrial capitalism and parliamentary democracy, in other words, were perceived to be the perfect antidote to militarism.[4] One of the earliest and most influential proponents of the liberal argument was Alfred Vagts; civilian control of the military and maintenance of the civil-military distinction, according to him, was the best possible safeguard against militarism. The true counterpart of militarism, was not pacificism but civilianism.[5]

Marxist analyses, on the other hand, emphasised militarism's economic dimensions, i.e., class relations within a particular mode of production. Karl Leibknecht's formulation is succinct:

> A history of militarism in the deepest sense discloses the very essence of human development and its motive forces . . . [it] is . . . the history of the political, social, economic and, in general, the cultural relations of tensions between states and nations, as well as the history of class struggles within individual states and national units (1973, 17).

Volker Berghahn quotes Rosa Luxemburg who extended the Marxist argument to analyse militarism not just in relation to capitalism and class relations, but as an instrument of colonialism and imperialism.[6] Despite their contrasting arguments, both Marxists and Liberals viewed militarism in terms of the undue emphasis on military power by states and regimes. For Marxists, it was an instrument of capitalist interests and an impediment to working-class opposition to war; for Liberals, on the other hand, it was a relic of autocratic/monarchic political orders and the dominance of the military within them. For proponents of both positions, however, militarism was a passing anomaly that would be overcome with the passage of time. The debate, accordingly, was "not merely when and under what circumstances militarism could be seen to exist, but also when and under what circumstances it would disappear" (Berghahn 1981, 27).

Notwithstanding this, the experience of war in Europe exposed the limitations of their respective arguments. As Berghahn notes, this was primarily because "neither the Liberals nor the Marxists had fully anticipated the impact of modern warfare upon the material life and psychology of the participating nations" (1981, 27). Germany's defeat and the dismantling of its military power—considered by Liberals to be *the* source of militarism—did not extinguish the latter. On the contrary, post-war Germany witnessed a growing consensus regarding the role and position of the military in German politics and society, justifying it as a political necessity and "a principle of German life and culture" (Berghahn 1981, 32). For Marxists, the post-war dilemma was equally acute. Working class solidarity and the labour movement had not prevented Europe's descent into war, and lay completely collapsed during it. Emotions of patriotism and nationalism had, in the end, proved stronger than class loyalty or solidarity.[7]

A major problem with the Liberal argument was that its explanation for militarism was confined to the arena of *formal* politics. Liberals overlooked the fact that militarism did not necessarily have purely institutional origins; indeed, post-war analyses revealed how inter-war socio-economic dislocation in Germany and Japan precipitated "repression at home and expansionist wars abroad," both of which "laid the basis for German and Japanese militarism" (Berghahn 1981, 68). These analyses situated militarism within its specific *historical* context: they were unpopular because they challenged the notion that Nazi Germany and Imperial Japan were militarist in ways that others were not. As Berghahn notes: "The attempt to place militarism within a European context was unpopular with Allied historians who stressed the uniqueness of German militarism"

(1981, 52). To this extent, the Liberal position 'externalised' militarism and represented it as a characteristic of 'other' nations or anomalous political formations—Bonapartist France, Nazi Germany, Imperial Japan and subsequently, totalitarian Soviet Union.

The Marxist position, too, was not without flaws. Even as Marxist analyses explained militarism in historical terms, the classical Marxist argument emphasising militarism's class dimensions faltered as it obscured its own contradictions by removing socialist countries from its frame of analysis. As Kjell Skjelsbaek wrote:

> A weakness in the Marxist approach is found in its disregard for important group or class criteria other than the relationship to the means of production. . . . The conflicts which nevertheless exist within and between these countries are therefore either denied, or blamed on imperialist subversion, and in any case, poorly understood (1980, 86).

Finally, both Liberal and Marxist arguments made an explicit distinction between militarism and its *social* context. This distinction, or rather the civil-military divide as it subsequently came to be known, was inconsistent with the historical experience of modern Europe, whose nation-states were forged not just through inter-state military conflict but also through mass nationalist mobilisation and the formation of hostile national identities. The civil-military distinction obscured the fact that the 'national' armies that fought at the front during World War II were, at the same time, symbolic repositories of the prejudice and hostility of nations and citizens. It ignored the blurring of combat zones (during aerial bombardment) that dissolved the difference between soldiers and civilians. Nor did it take into account "the censorship, the criminalisation of opponents of the war, the internment of enemy civilians or the state-sponsored patriotic mobilisation that were all part of the process of militarism" (Geyer 1989, 74). In other words, Europe's experience of war was embedded *in* its social fabric. Militarism, thus, was not merely about the *political* eminence of militarist or fascist orders that waged war; nor was it *only* a process of capitalist accumulation based on exploitative class relations. Rather, as Michael Geyer notes, it embodied the mobilisation of resources and people based on the idea of defending a perceived collectivity. "As a result, what we got were not calculated military confrontations for specific gains, but wars over 'identity'; that is, wars in which societies defined themselves in opposition to a mortal 'enemy'" (1989, 99).

Geyer's argument highlights the civil-military distinction that served to obscure the *social* foundations of European militarism—a perception that perpetuated the notion of militarism as an 'external' anomaly. This perception was further reinforced in post-war Europe; war and aggression "civilianised Western states" and spelt the end of regimes identified with militarism, as civilian rule became established as one of the cornerstones of the modern European state (Tilly 1985, 75–76). The emergence of representative government, together with the absence of war within and between European states, served to validate the Liberal argument in which civilian rule was perceived to be *the* safeguard against militarism. Seen from this perspective, "the Western case was clear-cut: it was wrong to talk of militarism when there existed legitimate governments" and "strong civilian institutions that guaranteed civilian control of political decision-making, including military affairs. In short Western parliamentary democracies could not be called militarist" (Berghahn 1981, 85).

While this seemed to be a convincing argument, closer scrutiny does not bear out its assumption. The post-1945 period did not spell the *end* of militarism, it reflected a *shift* in its meaning and dynamics. The *meaning* of militarism was still linked to military power but, in a post-war period, where the nation-state was no longer being extended, the new militarism came to centre on its *defence*.[8] This shift was not necessarily an inherent virtue of *civilian* rule; rather, the stabilisation of the European state-system *required* an end to (inter-state) wars of territorial expansion. The demise of the latter *altered* both the nature and course of militarism, symbolised by the transformation of War Departments into what were subsequently termed Departments of Defence.[9]

Post-war militarism transformed into an attribute of the nation-state to function as a civil-military consensus for the purpose of 'national defence' that, in effect, was synonymous with the preparation for war.[10] The establishment of civilian rule in western nation-states, thus, did not *eliminate* militarism, it *masked* its transformation from an age of open aggression and glorification of war to an era of muted preparation for the latter that was characterised by a military-industrial collaboration or what came to be known as the military-industrial complex (MIC).[11] The structure and workings of the MIC epitomised the elimination of the civil-military distinction.

The MIC was not restricted to the United States or (some) western European states. Organising for war came to be a central economic and industrial feature of the Soviet Union, that one writer aptly described as "militarised socialism" (Mann 1987, 36). For the Soviet Union, the race towards the production and accumulation of the weapons of war "served to endorse Western . . . criteria of what constitutes military power and, by the late 1970s, to establish the Soviet Union as the second superpower on the basis of those criteria" (Kaldor 1982, 100).

Militarism's military-economic dimensions were linked to its political-ideological orientation. Just as the alleged Soviet 'threat' served as an ideological justification for the MIC in the United States, the Soviet military-industrial complex was, in turn, legitimised by the latter. Both were

> not in conflict but were *complementary*, tied together by the same historical experience. Both needed the other. Both required a high level of civil-military collaboration, military spending and a permanent external threat. The existence of each provided a legitimation for the other (Kaldor 1990, 33, emphasis in the original).

The global military order forged by the United States and the Soviet Union symbolised a complex, interconnected web between government, economy, industry, technology and, by extension, society.[12] Militarism in the western hemisphere, however, was not uniform; western European states such as Switzerland and Austria, or countries like Japan, Canada or New Zealand spent much less on defence than the 'superpowers'. The point here, however, relates to the emergence of a new militarism that was "not up-front, but more subtle and diverse" (Mann 1987, 36) characterised by a civil-military nexus that "concealed its purposes and obscured its consequences" (Gillis 1989, 7). Michael Mann captures the irony: "We have planning for war that would be utterly devastating, yet that planning has broad *popular* support" (1987, 40, emphasis added).

As the dynamics of militarism moved beyond the military, explanations for the new militarism did not quite fit existing Liberal or Marxist frameworks. The proposition that militarism was attributable to a particular class, economic or political system was historically invalid; nor could the new militarism be characterised as the 'other' or a remnant of the 'past.' Indeed, both assumptions centred on the "artificial separation between social and political history" and "obscured deeper *social processes* that transcend national political boundaries" (Gillis 1989, 2, emphasis added). If anything, such assumptions only "serve to shift the blame onto others and divert attention from society's own condition" (1989, 3) This is as true of the contemporary world as it was six decades ago.

To sum up, militarism in the modern (twentieth century) western world was a dynamic process shaped by its own particular historical context that, in turn, influenced the political, economic and social life of its constituent nation-states. Militarism began with the political dominance of imperial orders and militarist regimes that fuelled the great wars in Europe. These wars were not confined to the military but encompassed a wider arena of social and ideological mobilisation. The forces unleashed by western militarism could not, however, be contained within Europe, for European militarism "fed on itself, ultimately destroying those national units that had given it birth, in order to create an entirely new international order dominated by the superpowers" (Gillis, 1989, 8). This new international order had profound implications for militarism in the global South.

Militarism in the global South

The post-1945 period coincided with the emergence and consolidation of a number of post-colonial states in the global South, many of whom replicated the structures of their former colonial masters—namely, constitutional government, civilian institutions, a civil bureaucracy and a subordinated military. In the immediate absence of theoretical and empirical studies on militarism in the region, analyses of militarism here during the 1960s–70s centred on the experience of state-making in Europe. Accordingly, it was analysed with reference to the political dominance of the military in formal politics. The old Liberal argument regarding constitutional government and the civil-military distinction was reiterated to explain the *coups d'état* and military dictatorships in Asia, Africa and Latin America. Among its earliest and most notable proponents was Vagts who attributed post-1945 "Eastern militarism" [sic] to "the failure or patent weakness of democratic-parliamentary governance in most countries between Turkey and China" (1959, 490).

The problem with the extension of the Liberal argument to the global South is that it was based on a (western) model of the state "where there was far less distance between state organisation on the one hand, and society and citizens on the other" (Buzan 1988, 16). In the absence of inter-state wars—other than the larger East-West (Cold War) conflict—military power in (western) states in the immediate post-1945 period came to centre on the physical protection of the state. This concept of military defence did not, however, quite correspond with the empirical realities of states in the global South—including South Asia—where the creation of new, often artificial, post-colonial 'national' frontiers and/or the lack of internal political cohesion within the latter, meant that the sense of insecurity from which these states suffered emanated much more from *within* than without. In other words, although states in the global South emulated the formal (western) structures of governance and the attendant concept of (external) territorial defence, their internal empirical reality remained inconsistent with the latter. For precisely this reason, the establishment of *civilian* rule in states across the global South did not spell the *end* of the political dominance of the military; on the contrary, it shot into prominence in a number of new states and, by 1981, dominated 54 of the world's 141 independent states.[13]

A second problem with the Liberal argument vis-à-vis the global South is that it was ahistorical. Since Liberals viewed militarism in institutional, not historical terms, they failed to take into account *internal* state processes that precipitated the emergence of not just the proverbial military junta, but also the frequent resort to military rule by civilian regimes. Further, the uncritical acceptance of civilian government by Liberals as *the* indisputable safeguard against militarism was based on the notion of state legitimacy—a notion that has historically been keenly contested by citizens in states across the global South. In sum, *because* the Liberal argument did not address the *historical* context of militarism in these countries, its explanation for it remained limited.

Proponents of the modernist school, on the other hand, proffered an alternative explanation which mirrored the emerging debate on 'modernisation', whereby newly independent states in the South were assumed to follow the political and economic trajectory of the West, i.e., industrial capitalism and liberal democracy. To this extent, the modernist argument was no different from the Liberal perspective; where they differed was in their respective views of the military establishment. In contrast to traditional Liberal hostility towards the military, modernists considered it an instrument of political stability and a 'progressive' force in the implementation of national, social and economic transformation (Pauker 1958, 342; Pye 1962, 80).

The modernist position was politically conservative. It endorsed greater military aid and closer military ties between the global South and western industrial powers, together with the implementation of a neo-liberal economic policy. According to Lucien Pye, (an advocate of the modernist school), the military is "one of the more modernised of the authoritative agencies of government in transitional societies" that can "play key roles in the process by which traditional ways give way to more westernised ideas and practices" (1962, 80). Much like its Liberal counterpart, the modernist position too, was ahistorical. For this reason, empirical evidence was not in consonance with its central theoretical premise regarding the military as an agent of social transformation. Enforced political stability by it did not necessarily translate into economic or social transformation. On the contrary, the record of governance by military regimes across the global South has generally been poor.[14]

The third position in the debate is the Marxist critique of militarism which argued that militarism in the global South was an outcome of historical and institutional particularities, part of a global system of militarism symbolised by the MIC.[15] The Marxist 'world system' approach viewed it as a capitalist superstructure embodying a hierarchy between a 'core' of western industrialised states and a range of poorer ones at the 'periphery', whose lack of industrial capacity served to integrate them within a global (capitalist) military order. The result of this integration, Marxists argued, was the establishment of a relationship of economic dependency between 'core' and 'periphery', and a flow of weapons towards the latter. Militarism, in other words, was a system of western military-industrial production that simultaneously functioned as an exploitative international economy order to create "enclaves" or "subsidiaries of the military-industrial complex all over the world" (Kaldor 1982, 139).

Among all the approaches, Marxist critiques alone offered a historically grounded analysis of militarism as a (global) system of military-industrial production. Notwithstanding this however, they still focused more on militarism's economic and political dimensions at an *international* level rather than on the relationship between militarism and state processes *within* national boundaries. In other words, their "almost exclusive concentration on the systemic level of analysis" was "at the expense of the unit level" (Ayoob 1995, 2).[16]

The relationship between militarism and (domestic) state processes has special significance in the global South, where a crisis of state legitimacy rooted in the state's failure to effect social and distributive justice is exacerbated by forces of modernisation that reinforce social, ethnic, linguistic, cultural and religious divisions.[17] This crisis involves the use of the military against political opponents of the state—an aspect that is relatively unexamined in Liberal and Marxist analyses. Francis Deng describes the *political* origins of the crisis of militarism within states in the global South where "'normal politics' has broken down [and] the real nature of politics is a war between society (or a faction of the society) and government, which continues even when a new group of society becomes the government" (1996, 227). These wars have taken millions of lives and generated humanitarian crises of extraordinary proportions. This (domestic) variant of militarism mandates closer analysis in a context where the use of the military as a "reservoir of political power" (Krause 1996, 185) has important implications for states and citizens as well as the relationship between them.

In sum, militarism in the global South embodies external and internal dimensions. It must therefore be examined at least as much in terms of the (domestic) *political* crisis of the state that is negotiated through *military* means, as in the external defence of the state from *military* threats. Both dimensions, I argue, are interlinked.

Inside/outside the nation-state in the global South

The creation of nation-states in the global South reinforced a state-centric international military order characterised by the military consolidation of individual states. Their integration into the international state-system binds them to a system whose underlying logic is that "one state's security is another state's insecurity. . . . The consequence is a competition between states that [takes] the form of arms races" (Oberg 1980, 69–70). This logic translated into a progressive consolidation of the (external) military capacity of states across Asia, Africa and Latin America[18] and in this respect, militarism in the global South mirrors the characteristics of *global* militarism.[19] At the same time, however, militarism's *domestic* crisis in the global South is rooted in internal state processes that unfold *within* the latter. Ronald McLaurin sums up its essence:

> Throughout the Third World the fragility of institutions, the shallowness of political legitimacy, the divisions of society, the disjunctions between real political culture and the new political institutions, and the inability of these institutions to meet popular aspirations and expectations . . . creates a state of constant political crisis . . . [where] the government . . . use[s] violence to suppress such a challenge (1988, 267).

This crisis challenges one of the fundamental attributes of the nation-state: its claim to legitimacy and, by extension, its monopoly over violence; it also contains an essential paradox in that the resort to violence against citizens by the state serves to further erode state legitimacy.

The use of the military as an instrument of domestic

repression in states across the global South is not disconnected from its external military/security dimensions. The *external* military consolidation of states here, is contingent upon the *internal* restructuring of national armies according to the political norms, organisational patterns and weaponry of (western) powers.[20] While the former integrates states in the global South within a western military-industrial order, the latter is oriented towards dealing with the discontents of this integration.[21] To quote Mary Kaldor:

> The primary function of the industrial army is not so much combat as political intervention . . . The major weapons may have prestige significance and they may be used in external war . . . but, first and foremost, they orientate the soldier toward a particular political tendency (1978, 70).

Accordingly, the world military order—based on heavy military spending and consolidation—not only reinforces the economic hierarchy between the global North and South and/or the global military system, but has *political* implications for citizens in the global South.[22]

A militarism that embodies use of the military against citizens and the denial of citizens' civil and political liberties represents what Michael Randle calls militarism's instrumental dimension:

> The instrumental level refers not only to the self-evident fact that the military in many countries [is] a major arm of repression[23] used directly to keep the population in subjection and carry out repressive practices, but also to the way liberties are threatened or infringed upon in the process of doing so (1980, 2).

What mandates attention here is not just the *institutional* abuse of the military by the state but also the *conduct and nature* of violence that closely approximates Kaldor's concept of 'new wars' that she defines as "a mixture of war, human rights abuse and the privatisation of violence" (2001, 5).[24] Militarism's domestic dimension is characterised by the elimination of conventional military-civil, combatant-non-combatant, inside-outside, public-private and external-internal distinctions. In other words, militarism within states reflects a pattern of violence based on complete ignorance of, if not utter disdain for, the laws of war.[25]

Accordingly, militarism in the global South is not "confined to the acquisition of dangerous and sophisticated weapons," it is simultaneously "associated with . . . the political and social structure . . . a trend towards authoritarian regimes relying on military (and paramilitary) force as an instrument of governance" (Luckham 1979, 232). In this crisis, the military functions as an illegitimate instrument of governance and domestic repression, an abuse of its legitimate role of external defence. In Anthony Giddens' words:

> The issues raised by the existence of the modern military . . . concern not just the distinction between civil and military regimes, but *the use of force in the process of governing*. . . . There is no shortage of states in which civil liberties have been curtailed . . . opponents of the regime repressed . . . be they under civilian governments or under the military (1985, 251–252, emphasis in the original).

To conclude, militarism in the global South connotes the mobilisation of state military power against external *and* internal threats to the state. Thus, while it is helpful to separate militarism's internal and external factors, "we must always remember that [they] normally work together and *reinforce each other,*" and that "it is the very mixing of these factors that underlies the . . . [crisis] . . . of militarism" (Klare 1980, 41, emphasis in the original). A framework that attempts to explain militarism in the global South without considering its internal dimension is, therefore, limited in its explanatory potential. Thus, while militarism's domestic dimension is context-specific and historically contingent it is also, simultaneously, integrated within and influenced by the dominant values of a world military order.[26] For precisely this reason, while the former remains the principal focus of this research, it is placed in constant reference to the latter.

A 'state' of militarism

Latin America in the 1980s exemplifies the intersection between militarism's internal and external dimensions; indeed, they have a far more institutionalised history than states in other regions of the global South.[27] Victor Alba notes that the Latin American "militarist tradition . . . has turned armies into instruments of political manoeuvre and has encouraged military men . . . to believe that their proper role is one of politics and power" (1962, 178). Against a notable absence of external threats to the state, arms and military transfers in the region were used primarily for internal repression.[28] The consolidation of the external military capacity of the state concentrated political power in the hands of the military, to breed a vicious cycle of authoritarian and repressive military regimes.[29] The situation, as Richard Falk clarifies, is

> . . . fundamentally shaped by a crisis in capital formation . . . generated by a series of factors. Perhaps the most significant of these is the inability of modern political elites to maintain stability without redistributive and welfare programmes. . . . As a result discontent, instability and economic chaos emerge, creating a context that invites a takeover by those social forces (the military and its allies) willing and able to impose 'discipline' on the polity (1977, 220).

As state *military* power transforms into a locus of *state* power, the military assumes "a counter-insurgency outlook towards their own population" (Falk 1980, 209). The ensuing crisis unfolds as an assault on citizens' political and human rights and exemplifies a 'state' of 'total' war where:

> there are no clear battle lines . . . no large concentration of arms and men, no final battle to signal victory. Waged against ideological frontiers this 'total' war threaten[s] the most elemental spheres of daily life: the family, the school and the workplace. . . . Civil society itself [is] threatened. . . . The modalities of a free and open society could have no place in this war. . . . Parliaments would have to be dissolved and judiciaries disabled; political and union activity suppressed; the media censored; and universities purged. Civil guarantees including the right to a fair trial [have] to be suspended. . . . War could not abide by the paralysing mechanism of democratic society. . . . A 'state of war' involve[ing] armed attack against the physical integrity of the citizen makes a legitimate tactic of war out of what in civil society would be considered an illegitimate derogation of human rights (Egan 1988, 189, 196).

A range of states in Africa experienced a crisis of militarism during the latter half of the twentieth century. Wars in states such as Angola and Mozambique which were legacies of the South African apartheid regime were replaced, among others, by wars in Rwanda, Somalia and Sierra Leone that derived from a crisis of state legitimacy or from the demise of the state itself. In Ethiopia, for instance, internal fragmentation and a lack of political legitimacy generated a series of violent internal wars during the 1970s and 1980s. Between 1974–1984 annual military spending in Ethiopia increased by 420 per cent to half a billion dollars.[30] Like Latin America, militarism in Africa is characterised not so much by external (military) threat to the state as by (ethnic, tribal, or religious) challenges to state legitimacy and the rise of groups and factions that are organised to provide protection where the state cannot.[31] The discontents associated with the absence of a "framework of consensus within the nation-state" (Deng 1996, 226) are negotiated through military means and correspond with high military spending and self-perpetuating cycles of authoritarianism and repression.[32] While the empirical context of Africa is very different from that of South Asia, the lack of a democratic consensus within the nation-state in South Asia, including India, has generated domestic challenges to the state that are addressed through military means.

State against nation

Militarism in the South Asian region[33] is, in a way, the opposite of Latin America and Africa. Unlike the latter where the military usurped civil authority, here the crisis is characterised by the misuse of the military by *civilian* regimes.[34] With the exception of Pakistan where there is far greater institutionalisation of the military, civilian regimes in India, Sri Lanka, Bangladesh (and Pakistan) share a record of using the military as an instrument of domestic repression. Before elaborating on militarism's domestic dimensions in South Asia however, it is useful to situate it within its historical context.

The external crisis of militarism in South Asia[35] derives from the militarised and nuclearised rivalry between its two largest states, India and Pakistan, and is linked to the process of decolonisation and the creation of post-colonial 'national' frontiers that do not correspond with 'the nation' within. A bitter and violent political division between India and Pakistan in 1947 assumed military dimensions and generated an 'insecurity' that originates, in part, from the division of a sub-national community (i.e., the Kashmiris) between the two 'sovereign' states. An essentially *political* impasse *assumed* military (and nuclear) dimensions to precipitate an unprecedented arms race in the region. As Mahmud Ali notes:

> In the first four decades of their independence, South Asian political leaders devoted much of their diplomatic efforts towards the acquisition of a military capability while seeking to neutralise the effects of such action on others. A 'my pre-emptive capability before yours' rationale appeared to drive the dynamic of regional interactions (1993, 5).

The crisis *of* the militarised state in South Asia parallels the crisis of militarism *within* its borders. The latter derives from what is referred to as the discrepancy between state and nation in the South Asian context. "The idea of the nation-state," as Barry Buzan notes, "was a western one and . . . western states themselves played such a large role in transplanting their political self-image all around the planet" (1988, 16). Post-colonial states were "created in the western image but did not have nations to fit them. The political legacy of most Third World governments was therefore a state without a nation or a state with many nations" (Buzan 1988, 26).

Subsequent attempts by the state to forge a homogenous 'nation' from component groups in South Asia became fraught with violence not because of cultural and ethnic diversity but because of a 'national' imaginaire premised on the concept of a European nation-state that views the state and nation in singular terms. However, in contrast to the European nation-state,[36] the modern state in South Asia contains within it a number of sub-nationalities. As a result of this disjuncture, the state has sought to "discipline and punish anyone wavering on the issue of singular allegiance to the twin monoliths of state and nation" (Jalal 1995, 247). The state's failure to accommodate sub-national aspirations paved the way for a crisis that pits state against citizen, and is reinforced by the centralisation of power in ways that deepen the divide between state and nation (citizens). Centralisation of the state generates fears of assimilation and marginalisation among minorities in South Asia, and assumes the shape of ethnic rebellion. Over the years these rebellions have been viewed with increasing suspicion and hostility and are perceived as a threat to the very existence of the state.

While a discussion on the diverse and complex conflicts in South Asia is neither possible nor feasible, a few examples serve to illustrate my point. In India, the people of Nagaland, Mizoram, Manipur, Assam and Kashmir have resisted coercive integration within the Indian Union and made a strong case for separate statehood.[37] In Sri Lanka, Sinhala hegemony precipitated a political conflict with the island's Tamil minority.[38] Feelings of discrimination and alienation among Pakistan's Baluch minority have generated demands for 'independence' from what, in the Baluch view, is an authoritarian and increasingly repressive (Pakistani) state.[39] In Bangladesh, the hegemony and control of the Bengali 'nation' over the non-Bengali population of the state dispossessed tribal communities of the land that constitutes the basis of their economic, social and cultural lives—a discord that involves organised violence against non-Bengali tribal citizens.[40] In short, the record of the South Asian post-colonial state in accommodating the aspirations of its culturally diverse citizenry is poor. This failure is compounded by states' attempts to counter political grievance through military means. Ali sums it up as follows:

> As the post-colonial state accentuated rather than bridged the class/caste, gender and ethnic divide, and as the appeal of inclusionary nationalism waned, resistance to what was now perceived as an enforced identity was treated as a threat to the status quo and met with all the resources at the disposal of the state (1993, 19).

While the empirical contexts of Latin America, Africa or South Asia are not similar, they nevertheless reflect two generic similarities. First, all three contexts are (differentially) integrated within a 'world military order' where there has been an extraordinary diversion of economic resources towards military consolidation for the purpose of external, territorial defence. Second, militarism's domestic dimension (particularly in South Asia) is defined by challenges to state authority and legitimacy, symbolised by powerful dissident (or secessionist) movements where the state resorts to its only other base of authority—coercion. Since this challenge has popular (i.e., civilian) roots, the state's counter-offensive is not limited to the political (or military) challenge mounted by dissident groups but its social base, i.e., citizens as well. The ensuing crisis is characterised by a form of warfare that "avoids large-scale direct clashes with main units of a conventionally organised government force, which generally would be organised along classic European lines and have superior firepower" (Snow 1996, 65). Instead, it targets and engages with small, isolated government (military) units where the form of warfare is not synonymous with the norms of conventional war, but approximates a form of political violence characterised by:

> (*i*) a blurring of the distinctions between war (usually defined as violence between states or organised political groups for political motives);
> (*ii*) organised crime (violence undertaken by privately organised groups for private purposes); and
> (*iii*) large-scale violations of human rights (violence undertaken by states or politically organised groups against individuals) (Kaldor 2001, 2).

Thus, I underline three important theoretical implications of the discussion so far. First, the assumption that militarism necessarily derives from an *external* threat to the state, and that this threat is essentially *military* in nature is only partially valid. Indeed, domestic rather than external challenges present a far greater threat to the state, and cut across military dominated *and* civilian dominated polities.[41] Militarism in the global South, in other words, is thus not necessarily a characteristic of *military* regimes; it can and does co-exist with representative democracy. Second, the external military consolidation of the state intersects with the internal consolidation of state power through military means.[42] This intersection involves the military but also encompasses institutional and societal transformations, with important implications for citizens' political and human rights. Third, no single theory can accommodate militarism's empirical diversity in the global South.[43] Whereas Latin America and Africa represent the extra-legal appropriation of civil power by the military, South Asia symbolises the civilian endorsement of military rule[44] that contradicts the liberal view of parliamentary democracy being inimical to militarism. Indeed, the empirical context of democracies in India, Sri Lanka and Bangladesh, for instance, includes domestic spaces where the use of the military for civil governance and the denial of citizens' rights has legislative (i.e., civilian) sanction.

The theoretical limitation in accommodating militarism's complexity underscores the point that the domestic crisis of militarism in the global South is shaped at least as much by the *political* history of the nation-state, as by the military within it. For this reason, this crisis cannot be explained *only* in institutional (Liberal) or economic (Marxist, structuralist) terms. For, "from the traditional preoccupation with the expansionist and bellicose aspects of militarism", concern has turned inwards "to the *internal* space," and to "the systemic disruption caused by militarism" through "governmental rigidities, repressive measures and the seizure of civil competencies by the military" (Thee 1980, 17). The term militarisation encapsulates this convergence.

Militarisation

While militarism and militarisation shared a conceptual relationship over a period time, militarism is the older and more conventional concept, that generally refers to military-based values and ideals,[45] without addressing its social dimensions. Indeed this connection is not possible given that the concept of militarism is premised on a civil-military[46] distinction, with a deeply popularised image of a powerful military set against civil society.[47] But the contemporary context is characterised by a *dissolution* of civil-military distinctions in the production, preparation and execution of war. The erosion of the boundary between civil society and military organisation is a central attribute of the modern state and a defining feature of modern politics. It is therefore inappropriate to continue to use the term militarism in the era of the nation-state, where civilian governments and professional militaries are no longer institutionally separate but collaborate jointly in the pursuit of war.[48]

By contrast, the concept of militarisation as a *socially* centred, multi-dimensional *process* "allows us to confront history in totality and to override the conventional distinctions between political, economic, cultural and social history that currently dominate the field" (Gillis 1989, 3) and highlights the "*interconnections*"[49] that are part of its overall dynamics. War, the ideology of war, or the economic, political or social mobilisation for war, are *all* integral aspects of the *overall* process of militarisation. Militarisation, thus, is not a *temporary* (institutional) aberration, but a *continuous* process that flourishes in peace-time as well as during war. As Cynthia Enloe notes, "what is distinctive about the era in which we are currently living is that militarisation is no longer conceived of as a wartime, short-term anomaly; it is the new normality. The present post-war era is militarised peace-time" (1983, 190).

The concept of militarisation reconfigures the meaning of war/military conflict to illustrate it as not merely a function confined to the *military*, but a 'national' or even 'international' undertaking that operates in breach of rather than in conformity with the civil-military distinction. Current wars in Iraq and Afghanistan by a coalition of civilian regimes, or legislatively sanctioned wars in Sri Lanka, Chechnya or Kashmir, where they function as a source and symbol of 'national' identity or 'sovereignty,' reflect this trend. In an age where war can secure civilian approval, and nationalism can endorse collective violence, the claim that (civil) society is *always* a victim of warring states, military elites, or an ever-expanding military complex seems tenuous; this is not to deny the institutional dimensions of war/ military conflict or indeed its socio-economic implications, but to emphasise its *societal* foundations. Finally, unlike militarism, militarisation is not an ideal category, which also means that there can be no single or precise definition for the term. This limitation however is offset by the advantage of understanding it as "the habitualisation of war—that is, a condition in which the preparation and use of violence [are] no longer seen as exceptional or as deviations from the norms of civil society, but [have] bec[o]me their embodiment" (Geyer 1989, 101).

The concept of militarisation as a *state-society* process is particularly useful given the *nature* of contemporary crises where war/military conflict is characterised by an *elimination* of the distinction between war and human rights abuse, with high civilian casualties.[50] Indeed, as Nordstrom and Martin assert, it is:

> . . . not only naïve to assume that conflict takes place within an arena demarcated by the formal institutions designated as responsible for waging and controlling aggression, it is dangerous. On average, 90 per cent of all war-related deaths now occur among civilian populations. . . . Focusing solely on traditional analyses of war may prove a mistake in trying to understand the patterns of non-conventional war and domination and repression that characterise political violence in the world today (1992, 14).

By bridging what John Gillis appropriately terms "the artificial distinction between political and social history" (of the nation-state) it is possible to "place the question of militarisation at the centre of *general* historical interest" (1989, 2, emphasis added).

Militarisation and the nation-state

The concept of militarisation as *historical* process is particularly useful in examining the relationship between the nation-state,[51] the military and society in the global South. This relationship is mediated by two factors. The first relates to militarisation's systemic (external) dimension, i.e., consolidating the military capacity of the state—militarisation for external defence is assumed to be a guarantor of state security in an 'anarchic' world.[52] This (realist) view of the state and the international state-system is based on the logic that the survival of the state depends on the maximisation of military power. By characterising the state-system as anarchic and according primacy to the idea of the state's military security, realism justifies militarisation *of* the state as both necessary and inevitable. While this is not the place to analyse it, I briefly mention three aspects that are relevant to this discussion.

First, realism's legitimation of the instrumental morality of the state *reproduces* the conditions of 'insecurity' that it seeks to eliminate. A model of state security premised on military power increases *insecurity* for *other* states—a competitive cycle that can only be resolved through war. Second, its emphasis on state security is at the cost of human security for citizens on the ground.[53] There cannot be a more compelling case against the dangers of realist perspectives than the nuclearisation of India and Pakistan over Kashmir—ostensibly for self-defence—yet failing to acknowledge that the targets the rulers have in mind for these weapons are, in the end, none other than their own people.[54] Finally, realism's discourse of (external) threat is based on the assumption that "the state in some sense embodies the collective identity and will of 'the people'" (Steans 1998, 62)—an assumption that is inconsistent with the crisis of legitimacy that pits the state (military) against citizens (nation).

Normative political analyses, on the other hand, view the mobilisation of military power to negotiate domestic challenges to the state as a measure of state legitimacy. This argument takes the European experience of state-making as its benchmark to insist that the coercive function of the state is a necessary prerequisite for "the twin processes of state-building and nation-building" (Ayoob 1994, 25). Much like the concept of the military security of the state, the argument for state-sanctioned organised violence is fixated on ends rather than means, and ignores the implications of coercive state-making and nation-building (hereafter referred to as nation-state building) for citizens and society. Before summing up, I elaborate three points regarding the project of nation-state building that have a crucial bearing on militarisation within the nation-state in South Asia.

There exists deep disenchantment with the project of nation-state building in South Asia, including India, with little possibility of this crisis being resolved militarily. The resort to organised violence by the state against citizens reinforces collective grievance and prompts greater repression, generating the very conditions it seeks to eliminate: an enduring fissure between state and nation in the form of alienated and embittered citizens and/or communities. For precisely this reason, it is difficult to defend, much less advocate, militarisation as a necessary or inevitable price of nation-state building. Second, the project of nation-state building by military means is not a political abstraction but has important human rights and social implications. Militarisation associated with nation-state building is synonymous not only with the physical dimensions of political repression but also its *social* implications that contribute to and/or reinforce existing structural inequalities within society. In effect, the project of nation-state building is not merely a political process, it encompasses *social*[55] transformations as well. Finally, militarisation contains an ideological element, i.e., the mobilisation of nationalism for political purposes. This mobilisation corresponds closely to the "instrumentalist" use of nationalism, that must be understood as a reaction to the growing impotence and declining legitimacy of the state and the struggle on its part to neutralise this challenge.[56] In this context, nationalism does not function as an inclusive, progressive imaginary, but as a means to retain and consolidate political power through military means.

In sum, although the external and internal military behaviour of states is not necessarily mutually exclusive, the division between both is reified by a disciplinary (and disciplining) distinction which suggests that "what goes on between states is in principle quite different from what goes on within states" (Walker 1993, 63). Contrary to what normative IR and political theory would have us believe, however, military defence *of* the state, as mentioned already, is as much a source of human insecurity as the nation-state *itself*. Nor, as the aforementioned examples of Latin America, Africa and South Asia illustrate, are they mutually exclusive processes. Militarisation *of* the state, as we have seen, is not separate from militarisation *in* the state; both function as an interconnected and intersecting arena where the military, the state and society constitute interpenetrating fields of violence.[57] For this very reason, the relationship between militarisation and the nation-state must be situated within a *single* historical and analytic frame.

Militarisation encompasses the arena of institutional violence *and* its social context. In this study, I use the term to connote the institutional and social dimensions of militarisation *and* its normative (external) dimension. I define it as the privileging of the military in domestic *and* foreign policy, where it connotes a progressive increase in the military capacity of the state, *and* the use of domestic [military] force by the state to secure the acquiescence of social groups.[58] By understating militarisation's economic dimensions, I do not imply its insignificance. However, given that the case against disproportionate allocation of economic resources towards military consolidation is generally accepted, this dimension is highlighted selectively. For the purposes of this study then, militarisation obtains when:

> (*i*) there is a marked increase in the consolidation of the destructive capacity of the state;
> (*ii*) the state uses organised violence against citizens as a means to negotiate domestic challenges; and
> (*iii*) the state resorts to nationalist manipulation in order to legitimise military intervention in civil affairs.

This definition is in keeping with a contemporary (domestic) context where militarisation is normalised by narrow and exclusivist constructs of 'the nation' that resonate at the local (societal) level in socially specific ways. By addressing the social dimensions of political violence, militarisation dismantles the public-private dichotomies of war: it is precisely in this context that gender functions as a particularly crucial category of analysis.

War, gender and the state

The relationship between war and the state in the global South is generally addressed by two separate disciplines: International Relations theory views war as a function *of* the state; "Men, states and wars," accordingly, are "the basis of theory, not women" (Grant and Newland 1991, 21). Political analyses on the other hand, explain war *within* state boundaries in institutional terms, or as the inevitable outcome of the project of nation-state building. Gender is assumed to be about interpersonal relations between men and women, as belonging to the family or household and therefore "antithetical to the 'real' business of politics" (Tickner 1997, 614). The absence of gender as a category of analysis across both disciplines is informed by the singular assumption that matters of defence/security and/or political violence are 'male' arenas, dominated by men.

Gender critiques contest this paradigm[59] at several levels. First, they highlight the link between gender and the *discourse* of war. On the face of it, there seems little in IR (realist) theory that provides an entry point for gender "grounded as it is in an epistemology that takes social relations as its central category of analysis" (Tickner 1997, 616). Yet, by highlighting how the military behaviour of states is constructed *through* gender, gender analyses contest the notion of war as a gender-neutral domain. In an incisive analysis of the centrality of gender to the discourse of (nuclear) war (in the United States), Carol Cohn illustrates how gender functions as

> a symbolic system . . . that not only shapes how we experience and understand ourselves as men and women, but that also interweaves with other discourses and shapes *them*—and therefore shapes other aspects of our world—such as how nuclear weapons are thought about and deployed (1993, 228).

Cohn's essential point is not that nuclear discourse is masculine, rather that gender discourse is interwoven *through* nuclear discourse in ways that distort public debate regarding war (1993, 228, emphasis added).[60]

The example of South Asia is no less instructive. Gender is integral to a 'security' discourse where nuclear weapons are symbols of 'national' security *and* patriarchal constructs of the nation-state. As Runa Das notes: "Indian nuclearisation has been justified not just to protect (Hindu) India, but also (the Hindu) woman who constitutes an important segment of the Hindu culture as *snehamoyee patni/mata* (nurturing wives and mothers)" (2003, 81).[61] Rubina Saigol quotes former Foreign Minister of Pakistan, Sardar Assef Ali, who declared: "To us, the nuclear programme is similar to the honour of our mothers and sisters, and we are committed to defending it at all costs" (2000, 109). The construction of women as repositories of national honour is the gendered sub-text underlying militarisation in South Asia, in much the same way as patriarchal visions of the nation-state justify military aggression as a legitimate 'defence' of the 'nation'. Both examples illustrate how the discourse of war is constructed and legitimised *through* meanings of gender in ways that pre-empt democratic debate[62] and, as the examples of India and Pakistan indicate, uphold social hierarchy. While this particular aspect is not the focus of this study, it nonetheless illustrates the theoretical convergence between the discourse of war and constructions of gender.

A second point of entry for theorising the relationship between war and gender is the cultural argument that sees war as a function of male masculinity. Men, in other words, are responsible for war and violence while women are its victims. The analogy between war and masculinity is a powerful one with considerable contemporary resonance. The intersection between both reveals that "in a range of cultures, being a 'proper' man is inseparable from the capacity to wield weapons" (Jacobs et al 2000a, 11). In her research on the convergence between war and masculinity, Cynthia Cockburn quotes Rada, a woman from Bosnia who said that "masculine culture and patriarchal inheritance . . . the too-valued manly traits of pride, bravado, superiority . . . were deeply implicated in the war" (1998, 221). A similar analogy is made by men in Colombia where "ex-combatants revealed [that] the gun had become so much part of male identity that it was almost a part of their bod[ies]" (Pearce 2006, 50).

Notwithstanding the important intersection between constructions of masculinity and war, it would nevertheless be a mistake to reduce the latter to an innate (and unchangeable) manifestation of the former. The assumption of universal male aggression and female victimhood is ahistorical as it essentialises a historical context where women are both victims *and* collaborators in the politics and ideology of war. Just as there are women and men in peace movements, so women have been part of war and national liberation struggles whether or not they participate in combat. Historically, both men and women have supported war and war-efforts; by casting women as "the first victims" of "a patriarchal state of war," this argument ends with questionable conclusions regarding women as a morally superior and innately 'peaceful' constituency. To quote Micaela Di Leonardo:

> Our first, radical . . . response that rival state military behaviour is simply masculine rivalry writ large—the 'boys with toys' is too

limiting. . . . This frame does not tell us much about war except that it is male, and wrong (1985; 607, 615). [What we] need to . . . consider [are] the possible links between nation-state behaviour and gender contradictions. [Gender] theorists must . . . develop complex theories of the state . . . because gender is at the centre of . . . the militarisation process (1985, 615).

The intersection between war, gender and the state as Liz Kelly maintains, "has become increasingly the concern of women from the global South where their states are explicitly militarised. Indeed, how gender is deployed in the development and changing forms of militarisation has become an important arena of investigation" (2000, 49). Kelly underlines what, in effect, is a third point of entry for gender theory, based on the concept of war as a gendered dynamic.[63] Social history contests normative constructions of war/military conflict as an essentially male arena by highlighting the gendered fabric of war. There exists compelling historical evidence regarding the relationship between war and gender across diverse historical contexts. Enforced sexual slavery by the Japanese army during World War II, the widespread rape of Bangladeshi women by Pakistani soldiers during the 1971 civil war, or more recently, patterns of gendered violence played out in such diverse locales as Bosnia.[64] Rwanda[65] and post-war Iraq[66] highlight this intersection and defy conventional notions of war based on a civil-military distinction and the protection of women and civilians. These wars are part of a general pattern where "women continue to face abuses associated with armed conflict and civil unrest. Rape and sexual assault, in particular, [are] employed to achieve specific military or *political* objectives" (Women's Human Rights Watch 2002, 9, emphasis added).

These characteristics correspond with a contemporary context where war/military conflict mostly occur in the global South. Between 1990 and 1999, there were 118 military conflicts in the region during the course of which approximately six million civilians were killed.[67] They derived from political crises within the state and involved the deployment of the military against civilian populations to perpetuate a vicious cycle of state repression and societal violence. The characteristics of *this* crisis, as Miriam Cooke notes, "approximate less and less the glorious War Story

with which many of us were raised" (1996, 297); indeed, they
reflect a darker reality with no clear battle-front or enemy, with
war being waged in spaces conventionally designated as 'outside'
the combat/war-zone, against civilians—legally bound to be
protected by the military—who are explicit *targets* of violence.
In short, these wars "deny two critical boundaries: home versus
front and civilian versus combatant" (Cooke 1996, 296). It is in
this context that gender critiques illustrate how even as "women
have been officially separated" from collective violence "in the
era of modern nation-state" they are, nonetheless, "essential to
it" (Elshtain and Tobias 1990, ix).

Gender, militarisation and the state

In her essay on gendered violence in the war in former Yugoslavia,
Vesna Kesič writes:

> Many characteristics of the wars that appeared in sequence from
> 1991 to 1999 bear the characteristics of 'dirty wars'. The term
> originates in Latin America and implies the emergence of physical
> and psychological terrorism unleashed against the civilian
> population [characterised by] flows of refugees . . . extra-judicial
> killings, threats to civilian populations, disappearances, the
> appearance of paramilitary groups and armed civilians. . . . War
> conventions and customs of war [are] not respected (2000, 24).

While the concept of militarisation examines political violence in
terms of the intersection between its institutional and civilian
dimensions, gender critiques of militarisation take the analysis
further to illustrate how violence by the state combines with
"social-patriarchal violence" to shape "gender-specific forms of
. . . violence" (Kesic 2000, 26).

State-making is not just a political process linked to the
centralisation of political authority, but also a *social* process
marked by the institutionalisation of gender relations.[68] The
coercive apparatus of the state accordingly, is "part of a wider
structure of gender relations that embody violence or other means
of control". In other words, the state is a structure of power and
an "organiser of the power relations of gender" (Connell 1990,
520). An emphasis regarding the significance of the state must,

as Connell goes on to note, come with the necessary caveat that "state action cannot be reduced to an innate 'masculinity'". Rather, the relationship between gender and the state lies in "the perception that patriarchy is embedded in *procedure*, in the state's ways of functioning . . . [where] sexual politics [is located] in the realm of social action" (Connell, 1990, 517, emphasis in the original).

Gender critiques challenge the epistemological basis of state and male-centric approaches that overlook militarisation's gender dimensions. Their basic argument is that women's invisibility and absence are *not* an *empirical* oversight but an *epistemological* claim, based on a public-private dichotomy and the denial of gender relations as a structural constituent of militarisation. By removing women from the canvas of war, normative analyses reinforce the public-private and civil-military spatial dichotomies that simply do not exist. Using the public-private dichotomy as a point of departure, gender analyses reconstruct and (re)present the meaning of militarisation "as a space that is restricted neither to men nor to women but [includes] . . . the presence of both. . . ." Women have always been *in* war (Cooke and Rustomji-Kearns 1994a, 1–2, emphasis added); their experience of militarisation highlights not just the dissolution of the combatant-non-combatant dichotomy, but the crisis of the state that deploys the military against 'non-combatants' whom the state and the military are legally and morally bound to protect.

Further, in contrast to normative androcentric narratives, the War Story for women is not synonymous with heroic 'combat;' rather, it is "a story of chaos, not revolution, of daily surviving, not of relentless hatred and fighting" (Cooke 1996, 4). This story dismantles the public-private dichotomy of normative narratives to emphasise the importance of challenging gender stereotypes and "the dichotomous social production and reproduction of male and female identities and behaviours . . . [that] symbolise the ideological construction of military conflict rather than its subjective experience" (Cooke 1996, 14). It therefore follows that women's absence is not an 'anomaly' or empirical oversight that needs to be redressed; what it really amounts to is a denial of women's *political* experience (of militarisation) *as women*. Gender critiques expand the meaning and construction of militarisation to highlight how violence by the state is not only deeply anchored in society but combines with "the everyday violence of patriarchy" (Kesič 2000, 26) to generate and/or reinforce patriarchal social relations.

Gender critiques also highlight gender-specific *forms* of violence experienced by women. Sexual violence/abuse is the most extreme and frequent form of direct violence against women, that is also simultaneously employed as a means to terrorise and humiliate political opponents of the state through the sexual subjugation of women. In contexts such as South Asia where the notion of 'honour' has strong cultural resonance, its appropriation by the military deprives women of protection by the state *and* the community that, in turn, renders them ever more vulnerable to predatory violence by men. Rape by the military exemplifies not just the sexualised contours of militarisation but also the illegitimacy of a state that uses sexual violence against female citizens.

Furthermore, gender analyses illustrate how militarisation's sequential effects are disproportionately borne by women. Deprived of traditional protection from men *and* support from the state, the loss (or disappearance) of male kin is not only a source of personal trauma for individual women and their families, it can be catastrophic for poor women for whom traditional economic dependence degenerates into destitution. Empirical studies illustrate the gender implications of the destruction of human capital[69] where female education and health are seriously affected because teaching and nursing are generally female-dominated professions.[70] Moreover, the collapse of primary health services leads to an appalling rise in maternal and child mortality and morbidity.[71] In general, the violence associated with militarisation's political dimensions has grave negative gender implications for women.

Finally, gender critiques reveal how forms of 'public' or institutional violence reinforce 'private' gender power relations. Violence and the abuse of male citizens (including illegal detention, torture, disappearance, extra-judicial killing) associated with militarisation undermines notions of masculinity centred on dominant power relations and the logic of male protection of women. Frustrated, often humiliated, by the failure to 'protect,' and unable to resist a powerful state/military, a besieged masculinity seeks redemption by exerting greater control over women. As the state's assault against the male population fosters what Patricia Albanese calls the "militarisation of everyday life," (2001, 1017), "male power grow[s] at the expense of female power" (2001, 1018).

Gender critiques enhance our understanding of militarisation to demonstrate the manner in which gendered inequalities uphold and sustain militarisation's social fabric. Rape and sexual abuse of women, the denial of women's political rights or the policing of women's behaviour and mobility, illustrate how militarisation both shapes, and is shaped by, constructions of gender. By highlighting these dimensions, gender critiques validate the claim that state and inter-state military processes are not gender-neutral but have important implications for women's position in society. In short, they argue that gender relations are an integral *constituent*, rather than an external *consequence* of war. The analytic significance of gender analyses lies in illustrating how the social subordination of women is integral to the *process* of militarisation.[72] The essential point here is *not* that state-centric (IR and political) analyses are superfluous; gender analyses do not advocate re-theorising IR or political theory; rather, they are critical of reductive and positivist frameworks that do not take into account militarisation's gender dimensions.

Even as gender critiques emphasise the enduring intersection between state military processes and society, this argument comes with the necessary caveat that gender is not a template that can be readily applied to produce a gender perspective on militarisation, nor does it suggest any "grand conspiracy theory" (Zalewski 1995, 341, 351). Essentially, they highlight the social complexities of militarisation; with reference to this study, a gender analysis underlines the *illegitimacy* of militarisation and, by extension, the illegitimacy of a state where "just warriors are not fighting to protect women somewhere else, but are targeting them at home and physically" (Cooke 1996, 296).

Notes

1. Opening Statement of the Autonomous Women's Centre Against Sexual Violence. Lepa Mladjenovic and Donna M. Hughes, 'Feminist Resistance to War and Violence in Serbia' in Marguerite R. Waller and Jennifer Rycenga (eds.), *Frontline Feminisms: Women, War and Resistance* (New York: Garland Publishing Inc. 2000), p. 267.

2. Kjell Skjelsbaek, 'Militarism, Its Dimensions and Corollaries: An Attempt at Conceptual Clarification' in Asbjorn Eide and Marek Thee (eds.), *Problems of Contemporary Militarism* (London: Croom-Helm, 1980), p. 78.

3. Ibid. p. 81.

4. Volker R. Berghahn, *Militarism: The History of an International Debate 1861–1979* (Warwickshire: Berg Publishers 1981), p. 18.

5. Alfred Vagts, *A History of Militarism* (New York: Free Press, 1959), p. 17.

6. Berghahn, *Militarism*, op. cit., pp. 24–25. Militarism according to Luxemburg was "a province of capitalism" where its economic function within a capitalist system was to "implement a foreign and colonial policy in order to appropriate the means of production of non-capitalist countries." Rosa Luxemburg, *The Accumulation of Capital* (Berlin 1913) cited in Berghahn, pp. 24–25.

7. Geoffrey Best, 'The Militarisation of European Society 1870–1914' in John R. Gillis (ed.), *The Militarisation of the Western World* (New Brunswick: Rutgers University Press, 1989), p. 25.

8. The nation "was no longer being extended, but it need[ed] defending". Michael Mann, 'The Roots and Contradictions of Modern Militarism' in *The New Left Review*, Vol. I/162, 1987, p. 48.

9. Barry Buzan, *People, States, Fear: The National Security Problem in International Relations* (Sussex: Wheatsheaf Books 1988), p. 15.

10. B. Abrahamsson, *Military Professionalisation and Political Power* (Beverley Hills: Sage Publications, 1972), p. 63. This trend "was a period in which military preparedness was viewed as the supreme national concern". Michael Klare, 'East-West versus North-South: Dominant and Subordinate Themes in U.S. Military Strategy since 1945' in Gillis (ed.) *The Militarisation of the Western World*, p. 142.

11. This link was "not merely an idea" but characterised by "the weapon system" that "implied the existence of an entire supporting cast—scientists to invent the weapons, workers to build them, soldiers to use them and technicians to repair them". Mary Kaldor, *The Baroque Arsenal* (London: Andre Deutsch, 1982), p. 12.

12. See Gillis 'Introduction', in Gillis (ed.), op. cit., p. 9 and Marek Thee, 'Militarism and Militarisation in Contemporary International Relations' in Eide and Thee (eds.), *Problems of Contemporary Militarism*, p. 22. The civilian base of militarism reflected a shift in the relationship between the military, the state and society where the confluence between them constituted the basis of this shift. "Military research and development absorb an estimated 20–25 per cent of all the world's manpower and material resources.

.. Around the globe, about 500,000 highly skilled scientists and engineers devote their talents to organising for violence". John Gillis, 'Introduction,' in Gillis (ed.), op. cit., p. 9. See also Thee, 'Militarism and Militarisation', p. 22.

13 Charles Tilly, 'War and the Power of Warmakers in Europe and Elsewhere, 1600–1980' in Peter Wallenstein, Johan Galtung and Carlos Portales (eds.), *Global Militarisation* (Boulder: Westview Press, 1985), p. 76.

14 See Nicole Ball, 'Third World Militaries and Politics' in Mac Graham, R. Jolly and C. Smith (eds.), *Disarmament and World Development* (Oxford: Pergamon Press, 1985), p. 17; Kirk Bowman, *Militarisation, Democracy and Development: Perils of Praetorianism in Latin America* (Pennsylvania: Pennsylvania State University Press, 2002), p. 4 and p. 253, Eric Nordlinger, 'Soldiers in Mufti: The Impact of Military Rule Upon Economic and Social Change in the Non-Western States', *The American Political Science Review* 64 (4): 1131–1148 (1970), p. 1148.

15 Ulrike Albrecht and Mary Kaldor (1979a), 'Introduction' in U. Albrecht and M. Kaldor (eds.), *The World Military Order: The Impact of Military Technology on the Third World* (London: Macmillan, 1979), pp. 1–15; Robin Luckham, 'Militarism: Force, Class and International Conflict' in Albrecht and Kaldor (eds.), *The World Military Order*, pp. 232–234; Thee, 'Militarism and Militarisation', pp. 21–22.

16 Even neo-Marxist analyses, particularly of the dependent development sub-school, insist that the salience of militarism derives from specific economic actors and not from state political elites. Mohammed Ayoob, *The Third World Security Predicament: State-Making, Regional Conflict and the International System* (Boulder: Lynne Rienner, 1995), p. 2.

17 Edward E. Azar and Chungin Moon, 'Rethinking Third World National Security' in E. Azar and C. Moon (eds.) *National Security in the Third World* (Aldershot: Edward Elgar Publishing Limited, 1988), p. 2.

18 "Both Marxist and non-Marxist analysts agreed that more than economic advantage was at stake when arms were being exported to developing countries". Berghahn, *Militarism*, p. 90.

19 Several states in the global South became producers. They include South Africa, Israel, Argentina, Brazil and India. Mary Kaldor, *The Baroque Arsenal*, p. 140. "The arms transfer system had transformed into a commodity market much like any other, without the political or moral opprobrium applied to such sales during the height of the Cold War." David J. Louscher and James Sperling, 'Arms Transfers and the Structure of International Power', in Norman A. Graham (ed.), *Seeking Security and Development: The Impact of Military Spending and Arms Transfers* (Boulder and London: Lynne Rienner, 1994), pp. 59–60.

20 Miles Wolpin, *Militarisation, Internal Repression and Social Welfare in the Third World* (London: Croom-Helm, 1986), p. 13.

21 Kaldor, *The Baroque Arsenal*, p. 162.

22 Albrecht and Kaldor (1979), *The World Military Order*, p. 14.

[23] I use Randle's definition of the term repression to refer to: "(i) the use of government sanctions to deny basic human freedoms, such as the right to live; to have access to the basic necessities of life; to hold, discuss and propagate opinions; and to associate with others to achieve social, economic and political objectives; and (ii) the use of inhuman sanctions such as torture for any objective whatsoever". Michael Randle, *Militarism and Repression* (Boston, Mass.: International Seminars On Training For Nonviolent Action, 1980), p. 4. "Domestic repression in the form of surveillance, arbitrary arrest and torture is widespread in the Third World, and the instruments of repression are supplied by advanced industrial countries." Kaldor, *The Baroque Arsenal*, p. 154.

[24] Against the erosion of political legitimacy and a simultaneous rise in criminality, corruption and inefficency, violence is increasingly privatised as a result of organised crime and the emergence of paramilitary groups. Mary Kaldor, *New and Old Wars: Organised Violence in a Global Era* (Cambridge: Polity, 2001), p. 5.

[25] See Kaldor, *New and Old Wars*, pp. 8 and 17–18; Donald Snow, *Uncivil Wars: International Security and the New Internal Conflicts* (Boulder: Lynne Rienner, 1996), pp. 110–111. "The law of war comprises that branch of international law which governs the rights and obligations of belligerents. Its basic objective is to protect combatants and non-combatants from unnecessary suffering and to safeguard the fundamental human rights of victims of war, such as prisoners of war, the wounded and the sick, and civilians, including the inhabitants of occupied territory." Sills, *International Encyclopaedia*, p. 317.

[26] See Albrecht and Kaldor, *The World Military Order*, p. 15.

[27] For a fuller discussion regarding democracy and militarisation see Bowman, *Militarisation, Democracy and Development*, pp. 69–141 and 183–207.

[28] Among the notable features of militarism in Latin America was "the absence of credible threats of war from neighbours". Ibid, p. 34.

[29] Among others, Guatemala 1954, Brazil and the Dominican Republic 1965, Chile 1973, Argentina, 1974, El Salvador 1979. See Bowman, *Militarisation, Democracy and Development*, pp. 207–234. See also Azar and Moon (1988a), 'Towards an Alternative Conceptualisation' in Azar and Moon (eds.), *National Security in the Third World*, p. 293.

[30] Marcus Cheatham, 'War, Military Spending and Food Security in Africa' in Graham (ed.), *Seeking Security and Development*, pp. 230–236.

[31] See Rene Lemarchand, 'The Dynamics of Factionalism in Contemporary Africa' in Zaki Ergas (ed.), *The African State in Transition* (London: Macmillan, 1987), pp. 149–165.

[32] To pay for the military, African governments have distorted their agricultural and foreign exchange policies that in the long term have depressed food production and slowed down economic growth. The lack of economic and social justice generated challenges to the state by various separatist and irredentist groups. Marcus Cheatham, 'War, Military Spending and Food Security', pp. 229–232.

[33] South Asia incorporates the countries of the South Asian Association for Regional Cooperation (SAARC). Its members are Bangladesh, Bhutan, India, Maldives, Nepal, Pakistan and Sri Lanka. In this discussion I use the term South Asia primarily with reference to India and Pakistan.

[34] South Asia is one of the world's most multi-ethnic regions. Out of 18 conflicts, within the span of five decades, India witnessed ten (Khalistan, Kashmir, Meitei, Mizo, Naga, Assamese, Dravidistan, Gorkha, Tripura, Bodo), followed by five in Pakistan (East Pakistan, Sindh, Mohajir, Baluch, Pakhtun), and one each in Sri Lanka (Eelam), Bangladesh (Chittagong Hill Tracts), and Bhutan (Lhotshampa). See P. Sahadevan, 'Ethnic Conflict and Militarism in South Asia'. Kroc Occasional Paper No. 16:OP: 4 (Notre Dame: Joan B Kroc Institute For International Peace Studies, 1999), pp. 5–7.

[35] The continuing arms race between India and Pakistan in the South Asian region tends to overshadow militarism in other states of the region. The military has been used as a means for internal counter-insurgency in Sri Lanka, Bangladesh and Bhutan though these states' (external) military consolidation does not match that of India or Pakistan.

[36] The emulation and adoption of the western state-system has caused serious problems and conflicts in the global South. "In the Third World, the form of the modern state was adopted without necessarily the concomitant emergence of a dominant nationality in each society." Yoshikazu Sakamoto (1988a), 'Conditions for Peace in the Asia-Pacific Region,' in Yoshikazu Sakamoto (ed.), *Asia: Militarisation and Regional Conflict* (Tokyo and London: Zed Books, 1988), p. 237.

[37] For a fuller discussion regarding this point see P. Sahadevan, 'Ethnic Conflict and Militarism', op. cit.

[38] For a cogent analysis of constructions of nationhood and ethnic rebellion see Sankaran Krishna, *Postcolonial Insecurities: India, Sri Lanka and the Question of Nationhood* (Minneapolis: University of Minnesota Press 1999), especially pp. 59–60, 66–77.

[39] For a fuller discussion regarding the Baluch rebellion see Iftekhar H. Malik, 'The Politics of Ethnic Conflict in Sindh: Nation, Region and Community in Pakistan' in Subrata K. Mitra and R. Alison Lewis (eds.), *Subnational Movements in South Asia* (Boulder: Westview Press, 1996), pp. 68–74.

[40] See Amena Mohsin, 'Gendered Nation, Gendered Peace'. Paper Presented at WISCOMP Summer Symposium on Human Security in the New Millennium, New Delhi 21–26 August, 2000, p. 11.

[41] Mohammed Ayoob, 'Security in the Third World: Searching for the Core Variable' in Graham (ed.), *Seeking Security*, p. 26; Mohammed Ayoob, *The Third World Security Predicament*, p. 7.

[42] See Eide and Thee, 'Introduction', p. 10; Thee, 'Militarism and Militarisation', p. 41; Wolpin, op. cit., p. 13.

[43] Militarism "is multi-dimensional and varied, with different manifestations in various circumstances, dependent on the historical background, national traditions, class structure, social conditions, economic strength, and so on". Thee, 'Militarism and Militarisation', pp. 15–35.

[44] Militarism, in this instance originates within civilian government, rather than from the military. Regehr, 'What is Militarism?', p. 132.

[45] See Patrick Regan, *Organising Societies for War: The Process and Consequences of Societal Militarisation* (Westport, Connecticut: Praeger, 1994), p. 5; Geyer, 'The Militarisation of Europe' p. 79; Gillis (1989a) 'Introduction' in Gillis, op. cit., p. 1.

[46] "With the collapse of the boundaries between civil society and the military, there was no longer a place for . . . the transfer of military values into civil society; for civil society has reconstituted itself on the basis of violence, that is, in the pursuit of war. In this it differs profoundly from nineteenth-century militarism. . ." Micheal Geyer, 'The Militarisation of Europe 1914–1945', in Gillis (ed.), op. cit., p. 80.

[47] Ibid. p. 67.

[48] For a fuller exposition of this argument, see Ibid. especially pp. 70–75.

[49] Ibid., p. 5.

[50] "At the turn of the century, the ratio of military to civilian casualties in wars was 8:1. Today, this has been almost exactly reversed; in new wars of the 1990s, the ratio of military to civilian casualties is approximately 1:8." Kaldor, *New and Old Wars*, p. 8.

[51] "The nation-state . . . is a set of institutional forms of governance maintaining an administrative monopoly over a territory with demarcated boundaries, its rule being sanctioned by law and direct control of the means of internal and external violence." Anthony Giddens, *The Nation-State and Violence: A Critique of Historical Materialism Vol. 2* (London: Polity, 1987), p. 171.

[52] For instance, see Robert J Art, 'The Fungibility of Force,' in Robert J Art and Kenneth N Waltz (eds), *The Use of Force: Military Power and International Relations* (Lanham, Md: Rowman and Littlefield, 2004a), pp. 3–22.

[53] The poverty of this logic was reflected in a statement by George Fernandes, former Indian Defence Minister: "India can survive a nuclear attack but Pakistan cannot. In other words, however many millions of Indians and Pakistanis may be slaughtered in a nuclear exchange, the great Indian nation shall survive." Paul R Brass, 'Nirvana is Tomorrow,' *Outlook* (August 21, 2006), p. 60.

[54] Amitava Ghosh, *Countdown* (New Delhi: Ravi Dayal, 1998), p. 106.

[55] See Jim Zwick, 'Militarism and Repression in the Phillippines' in Michael Stohl and George. A. Lopez (eds.), *The State as Terrorist: The Dynamics of Governmental Violence and Repression* (Westport, Connecticut: Greenwood Press, 1984), p. 124.

[56] Kaldor, *New and Old Wars*, p. 35.

[57] Kay B. Warren, 'Death Squads and Wider Complicities' in Jeffrey A. Sluka (ed.), *Death Squad: The Anthropology of State Terror, The Ethnography of Political Violence* (Philadelphia: University of Pennsylvania Press, 2000), p. 229.

[58] Tanter employs a similar definition. See Richard Tanter, 'Trends in Asia', *Alternatives* 10 (1): 161–191 (1984), p. 163.

[59] Steans quotes Kuhn's definition of a paradigm that refers to a shared understanding and way of approaching problems, accepted by scholars and used to explain ways of "knowing the world". "Paradigms do not describe the world, they construct it." Jill Steans, *Gender and International Relations: An Introduction* (Cambridge: Polity Press, 1998), p. 41.

[60] "In an 'objective,' 'universal' discourse that valorises the 'masculine' and de-authorises the 'feminine', it is only the 'feminine' emotions that are noticed and labelled as emotions, and thus in need of banning from the analytic process. 'Masculine' emotions—such as feelings of aggression, competition, macho pride and swagger, or the sense of identity resting on carefully defended borders—are not easily identified as emotions, and are instead invisibly folded into 'self-evident,' so-called realist paradigms and analyses. It is both the interweaving of gender discourse in national security thinking *and* the blindness to its presence and impact that have deleterious effects." Carol Cohn, 'War, Wimps and Women: Talking Gender and Thinking War' in Miriam Cooke and Angela Woollacott (eds.), *Gendering War Talk* (Princeton: Princeton University Press, 1993, emphasis in the original), p. 242. See also Cohn, 'Clean Bombs and Clean Language' in Jean Bethke Elshtain and Sheila Tobias (eds.) *Women, Militarism & War: Essays in History, Politics and Social Theory* (Rowman and Littlefield 1990), pp. 33–44.

[61] "It enables the Hindu Right to discursively utilise the image of Hindu women as an authentic tradition of India, to establish Islam as an outsider/ threat to India, and bestow upon the Indian state, as a patriarchal institution, the task of protecting the rights and status of women in India." Runa Das, 'Engendering Post-Colonial Nuclear Policies through the Lens of Hindutva: Rethinking the Security Paradigm of India,' *Comparative Studies of South Asia, Africa and the Middle East*, Vol. XXII No. 1&2, 2002, p. 82.

[62] Bal Thackeray's declaration, "We have to prove we are not eunuchs" in the wake of India's nuclear tests, symbolised the masculinisation of nuclear discourse. See Srirupa Roy, 'Nuclear Frames: Official Nationalism, the Nuclear Bomb and the Anti-Nuclear Movement in India' in M.V. Ramana and C. Rammanohar Reddy (eds.), *Prisoners of the Nuclear Dream* (Hyderabad: Orient Longman, 2003), p. 350. In 1998, Benazir Bhutto challenged Prime Minister Nawaz Sharif to respond in kind to India's nuclear tests by taking off her bangles and throwing them into the crowd, suggesting that he was not man enough for the job. Pervez Hoodbhoy quoted in 'Bhutto Launches Election Campaign, *St. Petersburg Times* (Florida), on-line edition (December 2, 2007). http://www.sptimes.com/ 2007/12/02/news_pf/Worldandnation/Bhutto_launches_elect.shtml Accessed May 3, 2008.

By devaluing bangles and, by extension, denigrating women, Bhutto subverted democratic debate regarding nuclear weapons, reducing it to an issue of competing masculinities. Much in the same vein, Pakistan's President General Pervez Musharraf declared: "We in Pakistan have not worn bangles . . . and we can fight India on our own without any assistance from any other country." Quoted in 'Keeping the Kashmir Cauldron Boiling', *The Tribune* (Chandigarh), October 24, 2001.

[63] In this discussion I do not distinguish between inter and intra-state war. This is not to deny the difference between both in terms of definition, but to emphasise the dissolution of civil-military distinctions in contemporary warfare.

[64] According to estimates, between 20,000 and 60,000 women were raped in former Yugoslavia. Anuradha Chenoy, *Militarism and Women in South Asia* (New Delhi: Kali for Women, 2002), p. 28. In Kosovo there was repeated incidence of homosexual rape in special rape camps. Grateful thanks to Mary Kaldor for bringing my attention to this point.

[65] An estimated 60,000 women were raped in Rwanda. Chenoy, *Militarism and Women in South Asia*, p. 28.

[66] "Three years after the US-led invasion of Iraq, women's secular freedoms . . . have been snatched away. . ." Terri Judd, 'For the Women in Iraq, the War is just Beginning', *The Independent* (London), June 8, 2006.

[67] Inger Skjelsbaek and Dan Smith, 'Introduction', in Inger Skjelsbaek and Dan Smith (eds.), *Gender, Peace and Conflict* (London: Sage, 2001), p. 3.

[68] V. Spike Peterson, *Gendered States: Feminist (Re)Visions of International Relations Theory* (Boulder: Lynne Rienner, 1992), p. 3.

[69] "Human capital includes investments in education, health and the nutrition of individuals. . . When violent conflict reduces access to, or the quality of, education and health services, there are important gender-related implications." Caroline O.N. Moser (2001), 'Gendered Continuum of Violence and Conflict' in Caroline O.N. Moser and Fiona C. Clarke (eds.) *Victims, Perpetrators or Actors? Gender, Armed Conflict and Political Violence* (New Delhi: Kali For Women, 2001), p. 42.

[70] Moser, 'Gendered Continuum', p. 43.

[71] Cynthia Cockburn, *The Space Between Us: Negotiating Gender and National Identities in Conflict* (London: Zed Books, 2001), p. 21.

[72] Chenoy, *Militarism and Women*, op. cit., pp. 17–19; Jennifer Turpin and Lois A. Lorentzen (1996), 'Introduction: The Gendered New World Order' in J.E. Turpin and L.A. Lorentzen (eds.), *The Gendered New World Order: Militarism, Development and the Environment* (New York & London: Routledge, 1996a), p. 2.

2 Militarisation and the Indian State

> In the mass of Asia, in Asia ravaged by war, we have the one country that has been seeking to apply the principles of democracy. I have always felt that political India might be the light of Asia.
>
> *Clement Attlee* 1946[1]

Independent India's status in the modern world derived from her position as a post-colonial, democratic state committed to the principles of peace and disarmament. The Indian state's rejection of the weapons of war symbolised its commitment to a new international order where state power was not defined in purely military terms. Towards the end of the century, however, India was again the focus of world attention—this time in breach of, rather than in keeping with, her pledge to the world. From being a leading proponent of a new, non-military international order, India transformed herself into a nuclear state and, in just over five decades, came to be perceived as a threat to the South Asian region and the world at large.

It is argued that one of modern India's achievements is to have remained a democracy in a region where military intervention is the rule rather than the exception. India's success in forestalling military take-overs is notable, although her inheritance of a geographically vast territory and culturally diverse society renders the possibility of military rule improbable, if not altogether impossible. At the same time, however, the *practice* of formal democracy in India—expressed in the holding of national and state (regional) elections—*coexists* with frequent and widespread use of the military for domestic repression. The contradiction between civilian control of the military on the one hand, and the military's intrusive influence in citizens' lives on the other is a striking paradox of modern India, albeit a little examined one. Direct intervention by the military[2] in state and local matters has increased steadily with a concomitant disruption in civil governance and the denial of citizens' rights and liberties. According to Stephen Cohen, in 1984, there were approximately 40 million Indians living under military rule, if not military law, making India one of the world's largest military-dominated states, while it was simultaneously the world's largest democracy.[3] This chapter addresses both contradictions.

My main argument draws upon three points elaborated in the previous chapter. The first concerns analysing the relationship between militarisation and the Indian state within a *single* historical frame, allowing for an examination of this relationship in its *totality*. The second point concerns militarisation *of* the Indian state, where a *historical* frame of analysis reveals that its acquisition of the instruments of 'security' is not an *exclusive* function of external defence, but informed by ideas of 'national' identity and 'power'. The third point relates to the disjuncture between state and nation that has particular salience vis-à-vis India's domestic crisis of militarisation, that is the outcome of a centralised and militarised state's attempt to forge a singular 'nation' out of its culturally and ethnically diverse citizenry. The essential argument linking all three points is that militarisation *of* and *within* the Indian state is the story of producing 'the nation' and 'national' identity.

In order to substantiate this argument, this discussion is divided into three parts. The first focuses on India's state-led nuclear programme, where I demonstrate that the initial drift (1947–1962) of the state towards nuclear weapons was *not*, as normative (IR) discourse would have it, driven by specific *military* concerns but by an attempt to recast a socially diverse and fragmented 'nation' around the project of secular modernity and national (scientific) achievement.[4] The second part discusses the post-1962 period of aggressive military consolidation by the Indian state, shaped at least as much by its *domestic* constraints and ambitions as by its requirements of external defence. I highlight the paradox of the Indian state's emergence as a front-rank military 'power' during the 1980s and 1990s and its deepening crisis of legitimacy within. I subsequently focus on one crucial dimension of this crisis, i.e., a state of militarisation that pits state against nation (citizens). In the third section, I draw links between India's domestic and external crises of militarisation by providing a background to the *general* crisis of state legitimacy, arguing that it is *this* crisis rather than any explicit military threat that precipitated India's 1998 nuclear tests (Pokharan II). In short, my argument is that the assertion of military (and nuclear) 'power' without has the *same political origins* as the project of nation-state building through military means, within. Kashmir symbolises the interface between both. The inscription of the 'national' idea through military means *in* Kashmir intersects with the attempt to secure 'the nation' (Kashmir's territory) by nuclear means *without*.

A requiem for non-violence (1947–1962)

> Whatever might happen, whatever the circumstances, we shall never use atomic energy for evil purposes.
>
> *Jawaharlal Nehru*[5]

> *Raj Chengappa*: You, more than anyone else, had the unique choice of building vehicles of peace at the space department or making weapons of war in defence. Why did you choose the latter when you know that it is capable of so much destruction and bloodshed?

> *Dr. A.P.J. Kalam*: I had no qualms. By building such an arsenal I actually ensure peace for my country. Now no nation dare attack us. These are truly weapons of peace.[6]

The words of India's first Prime Minister symbolise the legacy of Nehruvian internationalism[7] and Gandhian non-violence, in which India took the lead in calling for the suspension of nuclear testing, the ending of the arms race, and the abolition of nuclear weapons. Aabha Dixit quotes Nehru's speech to the United Nations General Assembly on November 3, 1948: "I am not afraid of the bigness of great powers, and their armies and fleets and their atom bombs. . . . We stood as an unarmed people against a great country and a powerful empire" (1996, 54). India's criticism and renunciation of the nuclear option was based on a rejection of the weapons of war, guided by the belief that such weapons could not ensure 'security', a position informed by Gandhi's rejection of the bomb. He said: "The moral to be legitimately drawn from the supreme tragedy of the bomb is that it will not be destroyed by counter-bombs even as violence cannot be met by counter-violence" (Dixit 1996, 54). In taking this position, "India was different, and this difference reflected well on humanity's capacity for moral reasoning, for resistance to temptation, for moderation and forbearance" (Perkovich 2002, 55).

The public disavowal of nuclear weapons by the Indian state, however, was paradoxical. A closer examination reveals an enduring tension between the state's *moral* position against nuclear weapons and its pragmatic *desire* for international recognition and power by acquiring the weapons of war. The rejection of nuclear weapons by the Indian state thus sat uneasily with its realpolitik desire and ambition. George Perkovich notes the ambiguity in Prime Minister Nehru's statement in the Constituent Assembly in 1948:

> Indeed, I think we must develop it (atomic energy) for peaceful purposes . . .. Of course, if we are compelled *as a nation* to use it for other purposes, possibly no pious sentiments of any of us will stop *the nation* from using it that way (2000, 20, emphasis added).

It is not my contention that this course was predetermined or preordained. Indeed, the confluence between the Indian state and nuclear weapons has multiple histories and is as much a consequence of historical conjuncture as of state design.[8] The argument here is that the *motivation* to acquire nuclear weapons—particularly the ambition that set India on course to her "tryst with nuclear destiny"[9]—was unrelated to military or security concerns. Rather, the Indian state's pursuit of nuclear weapons was informed by ideas of post-colonial identity and international status. Indeed, as diverse commentators[10] have noted, nuclear weapons were part of the modernist narrative of India based on the perceived analogy between science and post-colonial modernity, an analogy that subscribed to the idea that colonialism had retarded Indian industrial and scientific potential and obstructed her tryst with modernity. Science (read modernity), or rather the lack of it, was an explanation for colonialism. Perkovich quotes Nehru's statement in the Indian Constituent Assembly:

> Consider the past few hundred years of history, the world developed a new source of power, that is steam—the steam engine and the like—and the industrial age came in. India with all her virtues did not develop that source of power. *It became a backward country in that sense; it became a slave country because of that. . ..* Now we are facing the atomic age; we are on the verge of it. And this is obviously something infinitely more powerful than either steam or electricity . . .. The point I should like the House to consider is this, that if we are to remain abreast in the world *as a nation* which keeps ahead of things, we must develop this atomic energy (2000, 20, emphases added).

Science, represented by the ability of Indian scientists to master nuclear technology, would not only symbolise 'modern' India but also place it at the forefront of scientific ability and achievement. In this post-colonial nuclear cosmology, nuclear weapons were icons of modernity and their appropriation by the Indian state was an affirmation of 'modern', post-colonial nationhood. "As India gropes its way towards modern nationhood which implies a modern state *and* a modern society, the bomb . . . become[s] a proud and seductive symbol of national achievement" (Sahni 1996, 88, emphasis in the original).

The attempt to (re)mould 'national' identity around science and modernity was fraught with contradictions. A notable anomaly was that of a *formally* democratic state with an institutional legacy that functioned through coercion and dominance.[11] Further, even as nuclear weapons *appeared* to be symbols of 'modernity,' their appropriation within a 'national' narrative was an *imitation* of a western-dominated militarised order that the Indian state had, in principle, repudiated. Apart from these contradictions, the ambiguity that characterised India's nuclear programme during the Nehruvian era rendered the state's insistence on the difference between 'peaceful' and military uses of nuclear energy increasingly untenable. This contradiction was manifest in The Atomic Energy Act (1962) that withheld and denied information regarding

India's nuclear weapons programme to her citizens, parliament and press.[12]

The year, 1962, that accorded legal sanction for blanket secrecy on India's nuclear project witnessed a border dispute with China that ended in disastrous defeat for India.[13] Military defeat and nuclear tests by the Chinese state in 1964 dealt a blow to Indian elites' sense of India's status and significance in the world, and deepened their anxieties about India being overtaken by a militarily superior China. The 1962 defeat was also a blow to the Nehruvian legacy that was overtaken by the voices of realism which had hitherto remained muted.[14] State endorsement of the consolidation of military power in the post-1962 period was now legitimised and driven by the notion of the alleged external 'threat' to the state. Retrospectively, 1962 was a watershed in terms of its implications for Indian self-perceptions of 'national power'. From that year onwards, a strong sense of realism pervaded the polity. Military power was projected to be *the* new basis of India's relationship not only with China but with the rest of the world as well. Cohen notes the new realism:

> If military weakness was the source of extreme shame, then India would pursue a policy of overwhelming military strength, turning to several outside sources for assistance. Defence studies burgeoned, *realpolitik* became the guiding star, and the military was elevated to a place of honour, despite its defeat in 1962 (1976, 212).

Post-1962 military consolidation dissolved the tension between India as a non-violent force in the world and India's new self-image as a military power. The former was replaced by a worldview that constructed 'power' in narrow, military terms and sought to advance the idea of a 'powerful' Indian state on the basis of this perception.[15] While this perception is not representative of the country as such, it does nevertheless reflect approval for the Indian version of the Monroe doctrine[16] across dominant sections of Indian public opinion, based on a construct of 'national' power in military terms and the exercise of centrally-backed coercive power as the optimal means to negotiate relations between states, *and* domestic challenges *within* them. Endorsement for the Monroe doctrine is not limited to the polity but resonates across politically influential sections of Indian civil society where Indian military dominance is legitimised on the basis of inflated perceptions regarding India's role and status in the world. "News media, the academic community, urban middle classes [a]re all, to varying degrees, complicitous with an exaggerated sense of India's 'legitimate' role in the region" (Krishna 2001, 54). By 1990, India was among the world's most 'powerful' states in military terms. Paradoxically, however, the construct of 'national' power in military terms submerged within it a domestic context pitting state (the military) against 'nation' (citizens).

A 'state' of militarisation

Domestic challenges to state power during the 1970s and 1980s symbolised what, in effect, was the unfolding crisis of legitimacy of the Indian state. While a discussion on the origins and trajectory of this crisis is beyond the scope of this study, suffice it to state that the post-independence nationalist-secular consensus that had defined the Indian political mainstream during the Nehru era, no longer commanded a reliable majority and was replaced by regional, social and sectarian divisions in a complex and diverse body politic.[17] The attempt to unite India around secularism, modernity and progress had begun to unravel, and one of its immediate casualties was an overall decline in the *legitimacy* of the political system—reflected in the widening chasm between state power and state authority. "The state still wielded enormous *power*, but its commensurate *authority* was on the decline" (Kothari 1989, 93, emphasis in the original). As a result of this discrepancy, the authority of the Indian state increasingly rested on the non-elected institutions of the state, especially the military. It was in this context that the *domestic* variant of the Monroe doctrine—characterised by increased willingness on the part of the state to negotiate *political* challenges through *military* means—was put into effect. The trend of military intervention in the political system stemmed from an erosion in legitimacy and a simultaneous increase in 'aid-to-civil' operations, where the declining authority of the state was sought to be retrieved through military means—a policy that translated into virtual military rule[18] across several states.

Among the manifestations of the unfolding crisis was a range of secessionist movements across the northern periphery of the Indian state. In each of these contexts, a failure in democratic governance was exacerbated by military intervention as a means to counter the collective discontents of centrally-backed authoritarianism. The frequency and scale of political consolidation through military means propelled the military into an increasingly political role within the state. Against the extraordinary preparations for (external) defence the military was, paradoxically, increasingly drawn into domestic war within. As Gautam Navlakha notes,

> India's armed forces remain the busiest 'peacetime' army fighting internal wars . . . More than one-third of the army is engaged in counter-insurgency . . . if paramilitary forces are added to this, no less than 50 per cent of the security force is deployed against . . . people (2000, 1713).

The displacement of civil authority by military authority blurs the important distinction between the role of the military and norms of civil governance, and raises disturbing questions regarding the relationship between citizens and the state. A few examples serve to illustrate.

A movement for Assamese sub-nationalism during the 1980s precipitated military intervention during which thousands of civilians were killed. In 1990, the Indian army launched Operation Bajrang in Assam that continued until 1992, during which the military conducted massive search-and-arrest operations in thousands of villages in Assam.[19] In Nagaland, a culturally and ethnically distinct region, popular aspirations for autonomy and adequate safeguards against central dominance by New Delhi could not be realised. Nagaland was absorbed into the Indian Union in 1947, reflecting the Indian state's intention to treat it as an area under central jurisdiction. The assertion of central authority in a region that had long enjoyed de facto independence fostered feelings of Naga nationalism and generated a popularly backed insurgency against the state. The state on its part "adopted a policy of suppression by military means, which at times involved an entire Indian army division and various other paramilitary . . .

forces [and] the complete suspension of civil liberties" (Brass 1994, 202).

Between 1967–1977, the north-eastern state of Mizoram witnessed mass discontent in the wake of a famine. Public anger directed at what an independent report called the "callous indifference" and "brutal neglect" of state authorities towards the death of thousands of Mizo citizens, evoked feelings of estrangement and resentment and paved the way towards demands for secession (People's Union for Democratic Rights 1986, 579). The state's refusal to negotiate with the Mizo leadership and its resort to political brinkmanship during the crisis, served to consolidate state power at a moment when it was vigorously challenged. The political costs of this consolidation for Mizoram's citizens, however, were extraordinarily painful.[20]

During the 1980s in Punjab, over 16,000 were killed in a long drawn-out and extremely violent crisis—a considerable proportion of whom were Sikh youth.[21] This crisis originated from a disregard for constitutional propriety by an intrusive, centralised political order, provoking the demand for Sikh separatism. Sikh rebellion and the demand for Khalistan by Sikh extremists was, in turn, exploited by the incumbent (Congress) regime to legitimise intervention by the police in Punjab, together with the imposition of a range of repressive legislative measures. According to Paul Brass, a state of "total war which did not spare the family members of combatants was being waged in the late 1980s and early 1990s . . . in which the death toll continued each year to range in the thousands" (1994, 199).[22]

The range of rebellions against the Indian state in the 1990s—from Punjab in the north to Assam, Manipur, Mizoram, Nagaland, Meghalaya and Tripura in the north-east—were a graphic illustration of how "the vulgar display of the state's armed capacity bec[a]me a normal part of governance, coexisting with elections and other rituals of democracy" (Baruah 1999, xiv). Entire infantry brigades and battalions of the Indian army were deployed to quell these rebellions.[23] Although each rebellion is defined by its respective political context, it would be a mistake to reduce *all* rebellions to the alleged 'separatist' or secessionist tendencies of the concerned ethnic group. Ethnic rebellion in

India is not the cause but a *consequence* of centralised tyranny that, in turn, generates ethnic revolt. Its *origins*, in other words, lie in a centralised and militarised political order which seeks to retrieve its diminishing authority through military means. As Keppley Mahmood notes:

> . . . Punjab, Kashmir, Assam . . . and every place else in India are part of a *single political order*. It speaks to the great success of those who dominate [this] order that rebellions against it are couched in particularistic terms that can quite effectively be dealt with from the centre on a case by case basis. A more insidious form of success is the fact that the academic vision of India has been refracted into similarly particularistic visions, which is asking why Sikhs are rebelling, why Kashmiris are rebelling, why tribals are rebelling, and so on. It seems to put the burden of explanation on the rebels rather than *the order* against which they all chafe (2000, 86, emphasis added).

The centralisation of political power backed by coercive force meant that while the state retained the 'power' to crush regional opposition, its legitimacy and credibility as a democracy was severely undermined.

Noting the extraordinary levels of state violence and political repression just three decades into independence, writer Ved Mehta reflected: "How could the suspension of all civil liberties and human rights ever be justified in a *democratic* society?" (1978, 111, emphasis added). His words reflect the paradox of 'democracy' where citizens' democratic rights are subject to unilateral suspension by a state more concerned with maintaining its ever tenuous hold over centralised power than with protecting the substantive rights of citizenship. Echoing similar concerns a decade later, Rajni Kothari concluded: "It is an illusion to think that [the Indian state] is any longer a democracy . . . it is based on a centralised and increasingly brutal state apparatus backed by . . . sophisticated military hardware" (1989, 296).

The crisis of legitimacy that generated regional opposition and state violence against citizens was sought to be concealed and suppressed by instrumental constructions of 'the nation'. Against mounting challenges to central authority, successive regimes attempted to augment their diminishing power and legitimacy by representing regional opposition movements as 'threats' to 'the nation'.

Between democracy and nation

> Democracy is not more important than the nation. There is no choice between democracy and the nation.
>
> *Indira Gandhi*, 1977[24]

During the 1980s, the theme of 'threat' to the nation legitimised the consolidation of state power through military means. Political challenges in Punjab, Assam and India's north-eastern region were blamed on the disloyal and reactionary tendencies of 'other' ethnic/religious groups. The instrumental use of the ethnic/religious card by the state to promote the idea of an endangered 'nation' coincided with a coercive assertion of central authority—particularly in states where the challenge to state legitimacy was vigorous. Congress regimes (1966–1977 and 1980–1984) typified this trend. Regional (state) demands for a re-negotiation of centre-state relations were not directly engaged with; instead, secular demands for greater autonomy or decentralisation were painted in religious colours as a strategy to neutralise challenges towards an increasingly centralised and authoritarian political dispensation.[25]

The (mis)representation of secular demands as a conspiracy against 'the nation' yielded significant political dividends. For instance, in the 1983 elections to Kashmir's state assembly, where the Congress faced the rival National Conference, a predominantly but not exclusively Muslim political party, Mrs. Gandhi won the elections on an explicitly parochial campaign in which the Conference was accused of harbouring "anti-national" and "pro-Pakistani inclinations".[26] During the same period, the long-standing secular demand for the inclusion of Chandigarh in the state of Punjab and a greater share of the river waters for the state were given a religious colour, culminating in prolonged state-societal violence and an ill-fated military assault on the Golden Temple in Amritsar in 1984. Soon after, "Mrs Gandhi . . . said openly and directly that Hindu *dharma* was under attack . . . She made an impassioned appeal to save the Hindu *sanskriti* from the attack that was coming from the Sikhs, the Muslims and the others" (Kothari 1989, 247).

By reducing the discontents of centralised hegemony to the alleged subversive tendency of the ethnic 'other', the narrative of 'the nation' rationalised militarily-backed nation-building and the disciplining of 'errant' ethnicities. The legitimation for militarisation thus achieved was politically expedient but dangerously counter-productive in the context of multi-ethnic India, where authoritarian constructs of 'the nation' mirrored a state bent upon the marginalisation of minorities. The frequency of ethnic rebellion mandates closer scrutiny of a dominant, centralised political order whose representation of the crisis in 'national' terms masks its own complicity in generating the very rebellions it then seeks to contain. The *cause* of ethnic rebellion, to quote Keppley Mahmood again, does *not* lie in any 'inherent' attribute of ethnic groups as such, but in a *central* order and its compulsion for power:

> The fact that such rebellion is occurring in all the peripheral and non-Hindu areas of the Indian nation implies . . . that the causes of such rebellion are not to be sought in the internal attributes of the peripheral groups themselves. What we are seeing is a concert of reactions against the centre, whose own characteristics are to be seen as the prime mover (1989, 336).

Regional challenges to the state were also blamed on 'external threats' and the ubiquitous 'foreign hand'—a charge that further legitimised the consolidation of central authority through military means. For instance, in 1991, in the wake of mass rebellion in Kashmir at the subversion of democracy in the state by the Congress, a senior member of the Communist Party of India (Marxist)—usually a staunch critic of the former—attributed Kashmir's revolt to "imperialism, especially United States imperialism" [that was] "bent upon destabilising the country and is working for its balkanisation".[27] The increased influence of the military in domestic politics paralleled the consolidation of a foreign policy based on the primacy of military power vis-à-vis South Asia (Pakistan and China) as well as the United States and the Soviet Union.[28] The representation of 'the nation' as threatened without and besieged within legitimised militarisation *of* and *within* the state. Stephen Cohen notes:

> There is no doubt that she (Mrs.Gandhi) believes that internal
> and external enemies require continued vigilance, militancy and
> preparedness. In the face of such enemies . . . poverty and civil
> liberties are expendable and in fact might obstruct progress . . .
> Although India lacks a garrison state's discipline or resources,
> Mrs. Gandhi is attempting to use internal and external threats
> and enemies to mobilise those resources and that discipline (1976,
> 211).[29]

The transformation of the military into a locus of state power is
explained in terms of institutional weakness or decay that allowed
successive regimes to escape democratic accountability. Atul Kohli
believes that during the 1970s and 1980s some of India's
established institutions were battered, especially by leaders in
power.[30] The decline of institutional integrity that facilitated non-
institutional methods of political consolidation, however, is a
consequence of centralised power politics. In other words, it is the
centralised, centrist imaginaire and its underlying concept of a
singular, homogenous nation that has undermined institutional
integrity and distorted the institutional framework of mediation
between state and society in India. This hierarchy of power
discredits and de-legitimises regional/ethnic resistance through
a legitimising narrative of 'the nation'. Zoya Hasan notes the
link between *unitary* constructs of the Indian state and its
compulsions for centralised power: "the *centralising* tendency of
the Indian state *requires* a [homogenising] ideology of [national]
unity" (1991, 152, emphasis added). Accordingly, while
militarisation in Assam, Nagaland or Mizoram *embody*
institutional failure, this failure is not the cause but a *consequence*
of a centralised state and its attendant hegemony of 'national
unity.' The political and ideological hierarchy that undermines
institutional integrity in the name of 'national unity' is, in other
words, the same hierarchy that disciplines citizens for resisting
centralised hegemony. In this context, invocations of 'the nation'
or 'national unity' serve as a convenient and effective alibi for
militarisation. Underlining the significance between ideology and
(state) power Spike Peterson notes:

> Legitimation processes become key to maintaining (reproducing)
> state power—and are therefore pivotal to our understanding of
> that power . . .. Ideologies assume centrality on our analyses not
> because they are more potent than physical coercion but because
> they secure the reproduction of . . . hierarchy with less resort to
> (but no less reliance upon) physical coercion (1992, 39).

The "monological imagination" (Krishna 1999, 242) underpinning the centralised state which demands that citizens subordinate all other loyalties and interests to those of the state is, in the case of India, deeply problematic. Not only is the assumed congruence between state and nation ahistorical and inconsistent with India's empirical reality, the idea of a 'unitary' Indian nation is in perpetual conflict with India's ethnic, linguistic, cultural and religious diversity. The state's domestic crisis of militarisation derives from an ideological fixation around the production of a unitary state and a single 'national' identity, where every social and political movement for greater state or regional autonomy and alternative identity is perceived as "being anti-national and potentially secessionist, hence deserving of a hard-line response" (Krishna 1999, 233–4).

The misfit between state and nation is an empirical feature of the post-colonial nation-state in South Asia[31] where states have had to produce nations and citizens. The division of sub-national communities between 'sovereign' states—most notably the Kashmiris between India and Pakistan—meant that the narrative of the 'nation' could never correspond with, or be contained within, the territorial limits of the state. The disjuncture between state and nation explains the empirical absence of internal political cohesion so crucial to the European/Westphalian[32] concept of the nation-state.

Normative International Relations theory does not address militarisation within the state—embedded as it is within the concept of the sovereign state. It is in the realm of (normative) political theory that this violence is recognised—not so much because of its political implications for citizens, as for threatening the cardinal principle (of legitimacy) of the nation-state itself. For challenging and resisting its attempt to produce a unitary state and a homogenous 'nation,' the Indian state disciplines citizens and communities for nurturing dreams, imaginings and longings that are not in keeping with its desired prototype of the loyal citizen-subject.[33] Sadly, this is also the reason why "thousands have been killed for being on the wrong side of the borderlines; for suggesting that they wish their own imagined realms; for dreaming alternative futures" (Krishna 1992, 859).

This violence is academically legitimised as the project of nation-state building whereby states in the global South are supposedly struggling to translate their "juridical statehood" into "empirical statehood".[34] According to Mohammed Ayoob, an influential proponent of this worldview, militarily-backed nation-state building is an essential and integral part of producing 'the nation':

> Third World state elites' commitment to Westphalian values derive from . . . a lack of adequate stateness, defined as demonstrated centralised control over territory and population, monopoly over the means of violence within the state's boundaries, and the capacity to significantly permeate the society encompassed by the state (1995, 27).

In order to achieve this objective—of "adequate stateness"—Ayoob recommends a concerted effort "by states to reach [this] goal within the shortest time possible or risk international ridicule and permanent peripherality within the system of states" (1996, 72). Yet, as we have just seen, the replication of a Westphalian imaginaire in the context of India endorses a highly centralised, hierarchical and rigid concept of state and nation and a conservative politics that denies or seeks to erase alternative forms of identity. Its stark prescription for creating the 'modern state' objectifies the incredible levels of violence contained in the nation-state building exercise in what Ayoob calls the Third World:

> To replicate the process by which modern national states are created, Third World state-makers need . . . a relatively *free hand* to persuade and coerce the disparate populations under their nominal rule to accept the legitimacy of state boundaries and institutions, to accept the right of the state to extract resources from them, and to let the state regulate important aspects of their lives (1995, 29, emphasis added).

With reference to India, Ayoob endorses coercive nation-state building in Punjab, Kashmir and the North-eastern region as a necessary and legitimate means to consolidate state authority in regions where it is vigorously challenged.[35] The unitary state that is assumed to be realised through the nation-state building enterprise legitimises state violence on a grand scale even as it diminishes the possibility for alternatives. To highlight the link between the domestic crisis of militarisation and the nation-state building enterprise is to underscore the compelling need for re-imagining a state that is not hostile to, but accommodative of, alternative forms of community and identity. Nowhere is this more relevant than in India where, as Sankaran Krishna succinctly puts it:

> The project of constructing a unified state has reached its *reductio ad absurdum* in the subcontinent. The final verdict of state elites has come down to this proposition: we will maintain the integrity of the nation-state even if we have to kill large numbers of people within its borders to do so (1992, 862).

The violence unleashed by the state-nation making enterprise in India cannot be contained, reconciled or healed within a unitary and exclusivist rendering of the nation-state in the European tradition. Indeed, the attempt to do so has generated a crisis of militarisation within and, as I proceed to illustrate in the case of Kashmir, reinforced militarisation of the Indian state without. By invoking the idea of a pan-Indian identity and de-legitimising sub-national aspiration as antagonist, and therefore 'anti-national', a centralised state *legitimises* the consolidation of political power through an extraordinarily violent nation-state building exercise.

A policy of militarisation legitimised through nationalist manipulation successfully deflects the principle of state accountability. As Mansfield and Snyder note: "The exclusion of opponents from political participation on the grounds that they are the 'enemies of the nation' is the means by which state elites escape democratic accountability even as they consolidate political power" (2002, 301). State invocations of alleged 'threats' to 'the nation' or 'national unity' undermine the federal basis of democracy in India and legitimise the implementation of a range of repressive, anti-democratic legislation including the right to *habeas corpus*. Kashmir, as we shall see, is a telling example of the instrumental use of the 'ethnicity as danger' theme with grave implications for citizens' rights and liberties. Desai noted this disturbing trend of *legislatively sanctioned* subversion of democracy which he characterises as "Government Lawlessness" (1986, ix).

Paradoxically, the project of militarily-backed nation-state building hastens precisely the very outcome it wishes to avoid: disunity and/or the demand for secession. Militarisation across India's northern periphery (including Kashmir) is a tragic testimony to the centralised, majoritarian impulse of the Indian state that eventually produced what it feared most. Secession, in other words, is *"a direct consequence* of the very imagination that animates the unitary, nationalist impulse of the Indian state" (Krishna 1999, 242, emphasis added). For this reason, Ayoob's prescription for crafting a unitary state in the European tradition is deeply flawed, even as he misses the irony in his stated analogy between the 'democratic' claims of the Indian state and its undemocratic legacy of nation-state building.[36]

The Indian state's possession of a formidable military capacity upon which rests its claims to international 'power' did not correspond with its *domestic* base of power, which has been progressively eroded. The state's claims to being militarily 'powerful' on the one hand, and its declining (domestic) legitimacy on the other, is not merely an interesting paradox; it is a reflection of how its *domestic* crisis of militarisation has transformed the Indian military into an instrument of repression within, and precipitated extraordinary military consolidation, without. The military (and nuclear) consolidation of the Indian state during the 1990s must therefore be perceived not *only* as an expression of the Indian version of the Monroe doctrine, but also understood in terms of the (unsuccessful) attempt by a centralised, coercive state to balance its ambitions of (international) 'power' with its multiple domestic constraints. This balancing act precipitated the consolidation of political power through military means in the domestic realm and the projection of military (and nuclear) 'power' in the external/ international realm. More specifically, it highlighted the discrepancy between the Indian state's claim to political legitimacy and, by extension 'national' identity in the domestic realm, and its assertion of 'national' 'power' in the international arena—a contradiction that deepened during the 1990s.

The 1990s: the 'state' of 'the nation'

By 1990, India was the third largest arms recipient in the world after Iraq and Saudi Arabia.[37] Possession of the world's fourth largest military propelled her into the front ranks of world military powers. This formidable military capability, including an undeclared nuclear capability and a developing missile programme defined her emergence as a pre-eminent military 'power'.[38] But the dynamics of global power and what determined it were beginning to shift. Perkovich quotes Prime Minister Narasimha Rao in 1991, who said that "economic development and integration into the global economy were more important than nuclear weaponry in strengthening India . . .. 'If we cannot make our economic sinews strong,' Rao said, India would have no 'political clout and no one is going to take it seriously'" (2002, 39).

In the same year, the Indian state embarked on a far-reaching programme of economic reforms mirroring the realisation that political power and status in the world was a function of economic, not military, power. With economic strength being the new marker of global standing, the Indian state faced the challenge of fulfilling certain *domestic* objectives that were a precondition for wielding 'power' in the international system.[39] In order to gauge progress towards this end we need to turn our gaze within 'the nation,' so to speak, and undertake a brief overview of the balance-sheet of state achievements by 1990. It is useful to split this evaluation into three broad categories: (*i*) the practice of democracy, (*ii*) the removal of social inequality, and (*iii*) economic progress.[40] What follows is a brief overview of each.

According to Paul Brass, the project of nation-building that is crucial to the Indian state's notion of power and 'national greatness' centres on two principal dimensions, namely, the ability to overcome perceived challenges to national unity and Hindu-Muslim relations.[41]

While India remains a democratic state with regular and reasonably fair elections, its record in democratic *governance* is not as impressive. Despite elections, for instance, Punjab came under President's (central) Rule in 1990. In the same year, the Governor of Assam dismissed the state government and placed Assam under direct rule from Delhi backed by the military, together with a simultaneous suspension of civil liberties. This was followed by military intervention in Kashmir with similar curbs on basic freedoms. This centrally-backed intervention may have been justified as a measure of state 'authority', but it eroded the *democratic* basis of governance and, by extension, a crucial foundation of state legitimacy. The militarisation of regional dissident movements and the concomitant denial of democratic rights to citizens epitomised the enduring contradiction of "the modernising, developmental mission of an elite which was not notably democratic in its own attitude and actions, and which had a history of negating expressions of popular will" (Corbridge and Harriss 2000, xviii).

While the proximate causes for multiple regional rebellions in India—namely, the Nagas, Mizos, Sikhs, Assamese, Kashmiris, Bodos, Tripuris and Meiteis—vary, they nonetheless derive from the particular *form* the nation-state assumed during the post-colonial period. The consolidation of a centrist, unitary centre erased hopes for political autonomy for ethnic groups that had historically enjoyed de facto autonomy, and generated resentment against the integration of these ethnic territories into the Indian Union. The centralisation of power and the distortion of centre-state relations reinforced the resentment. Militarisation in Nagaland, Mizoram and Assam is an outcome of both these factors. Another source of ethnic grievance lies in the process of territorial nation-state formation, where existing feelings of marginalisation among smaller ethnic minorities against a dominant, coercive centre were exacerbated by fears of assimilation by surrounding ethnic groups. The Bodo agitation in Assam, and Meiei resistance in Manipur belong to this category.[42] The centralisation of power underpinned by increasingly parochial constructs of 'the nation' precipitated the rise of ethnic revolts couched in the language of nationalism. The demand for Khalistan in Punjab and the mobilisation for independence in Kashmir were outcomes of an all-powerful, unitary centre and hierarchical constructs of 'the nation' that corroded the federal basis of centre-state relations, and fuelled Sikh and Kashmiri grievance. The crisis was exacerbated by unwillingness on the part of the state to negotiate democratic power-sharing arrangements with its regional constituents, intensifying regional frustrations and "undermining the very basis of national unity that centralisation [was] meant to achieve" (Bardhan 1989, 82).

The use of the military as a proxy for civil governance and as an instrument of repression during the 1990s was part of a wider failure of the state in resolving political challenges through legal means. It resulted in the rise of extremist groups whose access to arms and targeting of state forces undermined state authority further and in turn, rationalised ever higher levels of state violence. The escalating violence provided a opportunity for the state to resort to retributive killings, euphemistically termed 'encounters,' and its cultivation of 'renegades' who were responsible for murdering members of militant groups and major opposition leaders.[43] In this self-perpetuating cycle of violence and counter-violence, the investment of legislatively sanctioned extra-legal powers in the military reflects a singular lack of commitment on the part of the state to democratic politics, and its endorsement of a policy that appeared to justify unlawful detention, torture, murder and rape of citizens. Centrally-backed military coercion placed significant sections of 'the nation' in direct opposition to the state and became the reason that prevented the state from forging a nation. If such a policy was meant to 'integrate' 'the nation' and create a citizenry whose primary loyalty lay with the state, it succeeded in achieving exactly the opposite effect.

The second dimension of 'national' power and 'greatness' namely, Hindu-Muslim relations, was an important marker of the Indian state's claims to secular democracy. Independent India has witnessed regular, if not frequent, occurrences of Hindu-Muslim violence whose victims are mainly Muslim citizens.[44] The state's record in protecting the life and liberty of Muslims during such violence is unfortunate. While it is important to emphasise the divergent origins of such violence, the point here relates to the responsibility of the *state* and its agencies in protecting citizens' rights—one of the basic underlying principles of a secular democracy. During the 1960s and 1970s, a number of reports by duly instituted state commissions of inquiry testify to the consent,

if not active collaboration, of law enforcement agencies, especially
the police, in abetting or directly inflicting violence against Muslim
citizens.[45] This trend continued into the 1980s, during which
time the situation was exacerbated by the rise of the Hindu
nationalist Bharatiya Janata Party (BJP) and allied parties,
coinciding with a spate of anti-Muslim violence across India;[46]
the worst of this was in the state of Bihar where at least 2,000,
mostly poor, Muslims were killed and dozens of predominantly
Muslim villages razed to the ground.[47] Hindu nationalism and
its ideology of 'one nation, one people, one culture', posed a
direct threat to the state's secular identity and to India's cultural
and religious plurality. In its quest to capture state power, Hindu
nationalism replaced the old plural concept of Indian identity
with a singular, explicitly anti-Muslim, concept of Indianness—
a mobilisation that fuelled large-scale violence against Muslim
citizens, particularly in north India which, by the end of the
1980s, was increasingly backed by supporters of 'Hindu' India.
Used initially vis-à-vis the Sikh 'other' during the 1980s, Hindu
nationalism increasingly assumed anti-Muslim overtones,
climaxing in the 1992 demolition of the Babri Masjid and
widespread violence against Muslims across the country, raising
serious concerns regarding Hindu-Muslim relations.

Whereas the Congress' cultivation of a unitary centre and
resort to implicit Hindu majoritarianism were used to neutralise
dissent and consolidate central power, explicit Hindu
majoritarianism drew the state ever deeper into centrist mode.
Its conflation of Indian identity with 'Hindu' identity—based
on ever more exclusive and hierarchical concepts of 'the nation'—
offered little hope for resolving regional conflict, except through
coercive force. Its implications for Muslim citizens were
particularly grim: the explicit anti-Muslim thrust of Hindu
nationalism was not merely an expression of cultural prejudice
against co-citizens but the central plank of a political mobilisation
that was crafted into a potent ideology during the 1990s.

On the other hand, the state's record in effecting distributive
justice and, by extension, reducing social inequality was
disappointing. The contradiction between a formal democratic
structure and an inegalitarian social context was reflected in
widening social disparities. Far from being eradicated, persistent

inequality across class[48], caste[49], gender[50], region[51] and religion[52] characterised much of the social landscape of India. Almost half of the population lived in absolute poverty,[53] with significant sections of Indian citizens deprived of basic healthcare, sanitation and safe drinking water.[54] Educational progress in India was markedly uneven with universal literacy remaining a distant goal.[55]

On the economic front, the state's ambition to establish itself as a global economic power did not meet with spectacular success. Notwithstanding the emergence of India as an attractive market for investment, economic growth with reference to conventional economic parameters did not register significant improvement.[56] Despite a liberalised economy, India remained a profoundly unequal society—a major reason for her economic under-performance. The state's failure to invest in its citizens meant that its ambition to establish itself as an economic power and overtake China in economic performance could not be fulfilled.[57] In short, the economic path to global powerdom was too distant to be realised.

This then, very briefly, is the context against which the state's claim to legitimacy and national 'power' needs to be assessed. From unresolved structural problems (caste, class, ethnic fragmentation, centralisation of power, economic stagnation, militarisation) to conflicting ideas regarding 'national' identity, the crisis of legitimacy had intensified. Enduring divisions across caste and class, the replacement of civil governance by the police in Punjab and the military in the north-eastern region, together with a full-blown economic recession and a fiscal crisis that peaked during the early 1990s, deepened anxieties among influential social groups and urban middle classes regarding the 'state of the nation'. The concern of this constituency was that

> the regime, while ceaselessly asserting the 'oneness' of the Indian 'nation' and the inviolability of the Indian state, was actually, through its policies, gradually bringing about the disintegration of that nation and the collapse of that state (Bose 1998, 130),

a perception that facilitated the consolidation of Hindu nationalism, whose political appeal was further reinforced by two key conjunctural developments during 1990. While it is not possible to discuss both at length I digress, very briefly, to explain their significance, vis-à-vis this discussion.

The first development relates to the decision by the state to implement the recommendations of the Mandal Commission (a government instituted body) to reserve a proportion of central government jobs for members belonging to intermediate castes— a decision that prompted violent agitation and riots by upper caste groups across north India. The relevance of the anti-Mandal stir derived from the *political* import of an agitation that not only placed the politically divisive issue of caste at the forefront of national politics but, more fundamentally, "cleaved the monolithic façade of (mythical) Hindu unity right down the middle" (Bose 1998, 147). In this respect, the anti-Mandal agitation threatened to seriously undermine the growing momentum of Hindu nationalism and its underlying idea of 'national' (read Hindu) unity.

The second development was the 1990 mass rebellion in Kashmir—an uprising that challenged state authority and legitimacy in much the same way as it had been challenged in Punjab, Assam and the North-east. The *timing* of this particular rebellion however, was crucial, for Kashmir served as a convenient foil *against* the potentially threatening issue of caste that effectively dismantled the idea of 'national (Hindu) unity.' Kashmir's revolt, and the support it subsequently received from certain quarters of the Pakistani establishment, vindicated the growing (Hindu) nationalist consensus which represented the rebellion as a Pakistan-led, pan-Islamic conspiracy to splinter the Indian nation. Kashmir's uprising pushed the contentious issue of caste into the background, even as it offered significant respite to an increasingly challenged central order which resurrected the image of the 'threat' to 'the nation'—this time by the Kashmiri 'other' in league with none other than the 'enemy' across the border. An extraordinarily violent nation-state building exercise was the central response to what, in effect, was its *own* failure in administering secular and democratic governance in Kashmir. Like Punjab, Assam and the North-east, Kashmir, too, slipped under the shadow of militarily-backed central rule.

To sum up, the Indian state's *domestic* political and economic constraints during the 1990s were major impediments towards realising its ambitions of global 'power' and status. A fractured social context could hardly connote 'the nation' or 'national' power; if anything, it underlined the difficulty of amalgamating India's cultural and ethnic plurality into unitary nationhood. This limitation was further exacerbated by the disinclination on the part of the state towards decentralisation, democratisation and accountability that, in fact, was the only way to consolidate its eroding legitimacy. Militarisation symbolised increasing opposition to state (regional) policy that centred on coercive force rather than democratic consensus.

A fractured and inegalitarian society, a discredited polity and a crisis-ridden economy could hardly be reconciled with claims to international 'power.' One option that remained open however, was the military, or rather, the nuclear option. Against the multiple crises at hand, the bomb offered a window of opportunity for a hard-pressed and increasingly challenged central order to mask its multiple failures through assertions of military/nuclear 'power'. The bomb could drive home the message of India as a 'powerful' nation and a major international 'power' in the nuclear big league. The motivation for the bomb, in other words, derived from domestic compulsions and imaginings of national and international 'power' rather than from an imminent military threat to the state.[58]

There remained, however, the crucial question of reconciling nuclear powerdom with Indian identity. How could the idea of nuclear India in the 1990s be reconciled with a definition of Indian identity in a political context that was radically different from the time when the analogy between both symbolised post-colonial secular modernity? By militarising the imagery of 'Hindu' India, Hindu nationalism sought to consolidate political power at the centre *and* re-position India in the wider space of international relations.[59]

Militarised (nuclear) nationalism: inside/outside the nation-state

With the concept of 'national sovereignty' under considerable siege in a globally restructured world, the nation-state is weakened by powerful global forces and no longer remains the principal locus of identity or loyalty. Changes wrought by the erosion of 'national' power have generated and fostered a range of 'new' nationalisms which, as Kaldor notes

> can be viewed as a reaction to the growing impotence and declining legitimacy of the established political classes. From this perspective, it [nationalism] is a politics fostered from above which plays to and inculcates popular prejudice. It is a form of political mobilisation, a survival tactic, for politicians. . . (2001, 78).

India, as we shall see, was no exception to this trend.

The 1990 anti-reservation stir exacerbated anxieties among influential social groups and the urban middle classes as the issue of caste threatened notions of 'national' unity. The revolt in Kashmir served to reinforce the idea that the 'unity of the nation' could no longer be entrusted to regimes that were not only incapable of resolving the multiple crises at hand but had, in fact, exacerbated them. In this context, the invocation and promise towards forging a united, 'powerful' Indian nation had considerable resonance—especially among those disillusioned and anxious social groups who were critical of what in their eyes was a weak and feeble state. The multiple crises of state legitimacy, the ceding of ideological and political space by the Congress, and the emergence of politically assertive social groups that increased elite insecurity,[60] generated a political climate in which the ideology of Hindu nationalism gained ground.

These crises that originated in the 1960s and continued into the 1990s, implicated successive regimes. Indeed, no regime can be absolved of its cultivation of a centralised and rigid centre, the propagation of the idea of a monolithic 'nation' and nationalism, and the violation of the principles of federalism and democratic accountability, all of which seriously undermined the overall integrity of the state. India's domestic crisis of militarisation, backed by parliamentary and judicial approval, is but one example of the crisis. In their quest to maintain an increasingly challenged political status quo centrist regimes, both in and out of power, misused and consequently severely damaged the autonomy and integrity of state institutions (in the specific case of militarisation—the autonomy of the state legislature, the independence and integrity of the state judiciary, police and bureaucracy, and the role and integrity of the military were severely undermined). The crisis at hand therefore, is attributable not just to undemocratic and centrist regimes—both past and present—but to the *entire* state. The rise of majoritarian Hindu nationalism, accordingly, is not a sudden or transient anomaly; nor can it be ascribed *solely* to the political eminence of the Bharatiya Janata Party. Rather, its ascent must be understood as a response of the *Indian state* [61] to what in great measure is its own, self-generated crisis.

Nonetheless, the implications of Hindu nationalism are grave. Its reinvention of India as a culturally unified, quintessentially 'Hindu' nation represented a departure from civic nationalism based on the secular state. The privileging of Hindu identity was centred on a narrow, parochial construct of the nation, whereby 'other' non-Hindu identities needed to assimilate themselves to Hinduness before being accorded legitimacy or respect. In this cosmology of nation and nationalism, India was both culturally *and* territorially Hindu. The demolition of the Babri Masjid in Ayodhya by the BJP-Vishwa Hindu Parishad (VHP) combine was an assertion of the idea of India as an essentially Hindu space, and a forceful challenge to the idea of secular India. By the late 1990s, the project of reinventing India as a quintessentially 'Hindu' nation was in advanced gear.

By recasting India as militarily strong, moreover, the Indian state sought to reposition India in the wider sphere of international relations. State discourse in the wake of the 1998 nuclear tests centred on 'national strength' and 'power'. Prime Minister Atal Behari Vajpayee declared: "India is now a nuclear weapons state . . .. The tests . . . have given India *shakti* (power), they have given strength, they have given India self-confidence" (Ram 1999, 2). Sadly, support for nuclear nationalism was not restricted to supporters of Hindu nationalism or members of the Bharatiya Janata Party and its allies, but reverberated *across* the entire Indian political spectrum, including the BJP's most trenchant critics.[62] The former Prime Minister, I.K.Gujral, who had argued for peace and friendship between India and Pakistan joined the 'national' chorus: "I heartily felicitate the scientists in charge of our nuclear facility on this historic occasion. It is a matter of national pride." More ironic, perhaps, was the joint declaration by the Communist Party of India (M) and the Communist Party of India (CPI) which declared:

> Our two parties have been appreciating the contribution of Indian scientists in the development of nuclear research . . . which has led to India developing its independent nuclear capability *without any relaxation in our defence preparedness.* . . (Ananth 2003, 327–32, emphasis added).

The remarkable *consensus* for nuclear weapons across the Indian polity reflects a disturbing endorsement of not only the very weapons India had once rejected as immoral and dangerous, but of a conservative and congealed politics of national 'power' that had so much to do with the crisis within. Other officially stated motivations for the 1998 nuclear tests related to a discriminatory non-proliferation treaty and India's ambitions for membership to the United Nations Security Council; but essentially, as Shiv Viswanathan notes, the (new) international message reflected a newfound and misplaced conceit regarding 'national' military power: "We have the fourth largest army in the world . . . Beware. We are one of the six in the nuclear club" (2001, 179).

The image of a 'powerful' nuclear-tipped Hindu nation— premised on 'Hindu' identity and an essentialised Hindu past, reduced India's cultural and religious diversity to a single dichotomy: the distinction between Indians and non-Indians. Dr. A.P.J. Abdul Kalam's statement in the wake of the 1998 nuclear tests highlighted the parochial heart of nuclearised Hindu nationalism:

> A nuclear armed India will be free of foreign invasions which have remoulded the ancient Hindu civilisation . . . For 2,500 years India has never invaded anybody. But others have come here, so many others have come (Ram 1999, 65).

The message of militarised Hindu nationalism, however, was not confined to the international arena; it encompassed the domestic realm where it assumed a particularly sinister edge. The construct of a culturally unified and militarily strong 'Hindu' nation essentialised the antagonism between India and Pakistan and, by extension, the Indian Muslim community. By defining Indian identity exclusively in *opposition* to Pakistan and, by extension, Indian Muslims, nuclear nationalism (re)cast Muslim citizens as the 'other'/enemy, beyond the pale of 'the nation'. [63]

Perhaps the most insidious aspect of the Hindu nuclear nationalist imaginary was the analogy it drew between nuclear weapons and Indian nationalism. By projecting the nuclear tests as a show of independence and defiance against western power and prospective US sanctions, Hindu nationalism used the bomb to appropriate the mantle of Indian nationalism itself. Opponents of the bomb, according to this logic, were not merely anti-BJP but 'anti-national'. Aijaz Ahmed put the new nuclear nationalist offensive in perspective:

> This is a crucial moment in our history. . . . Everyone knows . . . that defiance of imperialism is a basic ingredient in Indian nationalism. For the BJP to graduate from 'Hindu' nationalism to 'Indian' nationalism, and thus to become a nationally hegemonic power, it too must go through this baptism of fire. The real fire it will not go through, but such fires can be simulated by organising mass frenzy . . . These nuclear fireworks help it to cut across the Hindu/secular divide and reach out to claim the mantle of Indian nationalism (2001, 208).

The redefinition of Indian nationalism in militarily aggressive and culturally exclusivist terms ran counter to the secular and democratic traditions of nationalism forged during the struggle against colonialism—a re-invention that revealed the extent to which the old nationalist imaginary had been replaced by parochial jingoism and crude nationalism.

The nuclear dimensions of this redefinition were notable. From being a symbol of secular modernity and national achievement, the bomb was transformed into a symbol of 'national' (read Hindu) power and identity. "The first Indian bomb was designed to reinforce secular nationalism, showing that India was a modern power . . .. It was a statement of what India could do" (Bracken 1999, 92). The second bomb (Pokharan II) no longer symbolised secular modernity. Rather, the *politicisation* of the bomb meant that it was perceived not only as an important symbol of 'national' identity and 'power' but also as a proactive instrument to deter alleged threats to 'the nation'.[64]

The concept of 'threat' in the Hindu nationalist cosmology was both external and internal. Much like its predecessors, the BJP constructed social movements for greater autonomy as (internal) 'threats' to 'the nation'. But it was in Kashmir that the Hindu nationalist construct of the 'threat' to the nation acquired an ominous and dangerous *external* edge. By reducing the *indigenous* roots of Kashmir's rebellion to the territorial conflict with Pakistan, the Indian state embarked on a massive military mobilisation to 'secure' Kashmir's territory. This mobilisation paralleled Kashmir's representation in 'national' terms—informed by the twin themes of 'ethnicity as danger' and the alleged threat posed by Kashmir to 'national' unity—both of which endowed the Indian state's nation-state building exercise *in* Kashmir with special significance. Pakistan's territorial proximity to Kashmir and its support for a section of the separatist movement in the Valley created a situation whereby the attempt to *secure* 'the nation' (Kashmir) without, merged with the attempt to *produce* 'the nation' in Kashmir. Militarisation *in* Kashmir became inextricable from militarisation *over* Kashmir.

By 1998, this convergence had acquired a nuclear edge. As nuclear weapons guarded the *external* borders *of* Kashmir, state (military) power sought to bridge the dichotomy between 'state' and 'nation' *within* Kashmir. Accordingly, even as the Indian Prime Minister justified nuclear weapons in terms of the alleged external threats to the Indian state (primarily China and secondarily, Pakistan), Union Home Minister L.K. Advani declared that: "India's decisive step to become a nuclear weapons state has brought about a qualitatively new stage . . . *particularly in finding a lasting solution to the Kashmir problem*" (Ram 1999, 3, emphasis added). Militarised nuclear nationalism was thus not only a symbol of state 'power' in the international realm but a means to consolidate the domestic political status quo in general, and *within* Kashmir in particular.[65]

In sum then, the militarisation of the Indian state is *not*, as we have seen, an exclusive function of *military* defence rather, it has been shaped and informed by ideas of 'the nation,' 'national' power, and identity. Whereas the Nehruvian privileging of nuclear weapons was largely symbolic (nuclear weapons as symbols of post-colonial identity/modernity), the demise of secular nationalism, the crisis of the centralised state, and the rise of Hindu nationalism reconfigured the secular imaginary and recast 'national' power in primarily military (and nuclear) terms.

The factors that precipitated this recasting are the *same* as those that generate a domestic crisis of militarisation *within* the borders of the Indian state. In short, the political compulsions that seek to define 'power' in military (and nuclear) terms in the international arena are the same that underwrite a crisis of militarisation pitting Indian soldiers against citizens within the state. Kashmir symbolises the intersection between both dimensions. For militarisation *in* Kashmir is inseparable from militarisation *of* the (Indian) state over Kashmir. In the following chapter I highlight the intersection between the exigencies of 'national' defence (*of* Kashmir) and central consolidation through military means *within* Kashmir—an intersection that, as we shall see, is being played out in blood.

Notes

[1] Speech by Clement Attlee, March 15, 1946 cited in Stuart Corbridge and John Harriss, *Reinventing India: Liberalisation, Hindu Nationalism and Popular Democracy* (Cambridge: Polity, 2000), p. 241 n. 1.

[2] See Apurba Kundu, *Militarism in India: The Army and Civil Society in Consensus* (London; New York: I.B. Tauris, 1998), p. 172.

[3] Stephen Cohen, 'The Indian Military and Indian Democracy' in Atul Kohli (ed.), *India's Democracy: An Analysis of Changing State-Society Relations* (Princeton: Princeton University Press, 1990), p. 100.

[4] See Itty Abraham, *The Making of the Indian Atomic Bomb: Science, Secrecy and the Postcolonial State* (Hyderabad: Orient Longman 1999), p. 20; see also Varun Sahni, 'Establishing an Overt Nuclear Weapons Capability' in David Cortright and Amitabh Mattoo (eds.), *India and the Bomb: Public Opinion and Nuclear Options* (Notre Dame: University of Notre Dame Press, 1996), p. 88.

[5] Jawaharlal Nehru cited in Dhirendra Sharma, *India's Nuclear Estate* (New Delhi: Lancers Publishers, 1983), vii.

[6] Dr. A.P.J. Abdul Kalam interviewed by Raj Chengappa in Raj Chengappa, *Weapons of Peace: The Secret Story of India's Quest to be a Nuclear Power* (New Delhi: HarperCollins, 2000), xi.

[7] "Convinced that world peace was essential to Indian development and survival, Nehru refused to become involved in the emerging conflict among

power blocs. This policy became known as 'non-alignment'". See Stanley Kochanek, 'India's Changing Role in the United Nations,' in *Pacific Affairs* (1980), 53(1): 44–68, p. 49.

8   See Abraham, *The Making of the Indian Atomic Bomb*, especially pp. 18, 48.

9   This phrase was originally coined by Dhirendra Sharma. See Sharma, *India's Nuclear Estate*, 1983, p. 22.

10   See George Perkovich *India's Nuclear Bomb: The Impact on Global Proliferation* (New Delhi: Oxford University Press, 2000), p. 6 and p. 448; Aabha Dixit, 'Status Quo: Maintaining Nuclear Ambiguity' in David Cortright and Amitabh Mattoo (eds.), *op. cit.*, p. 54; see also Srirupa Roy, 'Nuclear Frames: Official Nationalism, the Nuclear Bomb and the Anti-Nuclear Movement in India' in M.V. Ramana and C. Rammanohar Reddy (eds.), *Prisoners of the Nuclear Dream* (Hyderabad: Orient Longman, 2003), pp. 336–339.

11   Itty Abraham, op. cit., p. 26. The essence of the contradiction was voiced by Dr. B.R. Ambedkar: "On 26 January 1950 [the founding of the Indian Republic with its new constitution], we are going to enter into a life of contradictions. In politics we will have equality and in social and economic life we will have inequality." Amartya Sen, *The Argumentative Indian: Writings on Indian History, Culture and Identity* (London: Penguin, 2006), p. 36.

12   Sharma, *India's Nuclear Estate*, p. 7.

13   For a critical analysis of the 1962 war see Neville Maxwell, *India's China War* (London: Cape, 1970). See also Maxwell, 'The Threat from China', *International Affairs* (1971), 47(1): 31–44, pp. 37–38.

14   "The defeat at the hands of the Chinese in 1962 strengthened the case of those opposing the Nehruvian model...Realpolitik demanded a thorough review of the country's security policy, including the atom bomb option. The Chinese test at Lop Nor two years later cemented this trend . . . . The argument for weaponisation . . . gained new legitimacy and support." Aabha Dixit, 'Status-Quo', p. 58.

15   During the 1980s, the idea of a *militarily* strong state was advanced by military intervention in northern Sri Lanka (Operations Pawan and Ravana), a game of military brinksmanship with Pakistan (Operation Brasstacks), and military exercises in close proximity to the eastern frontier with China (Operation Checkerboard), igniting fears of a second Sino-Indian military clash. See Bhabani Sen Gupta, 'India in the Twenty-First Century', *International Affairs* 73(2): 297–314, p. 301. The extraordinary military build-up and progress in missile technology paralleled the development of an undisclosed chemical weapons capability that came to light when India had to sign the Chemical Weapons Treaty. Stephen Cohen, *India: Emerging Power* (Washington, D.C.: Brookings Institution Press, 2001), p. 345, n. 59. In 1987, the Indian state purchased weaponry to the tune of $5.2 billion—more than Iran and Iraq combined and twelve times as much as Pakistan. Amit Gupta, 'The Indian Arms Industry: A Lumbering Giant', *Asian Survey* 30 (9): 846–861, p. 711. During the 1985–1995 decade, arms

sales from the Soviet Union to India touched $13 billion, with India emerging as the world's top arms importer. Ibid. p. 856.

[16] According to the 'Indira' version of the doctrine: "India will not tolerate external intervention in a conflict in any South Asian country if that intervention has any implicit or explicit anti-Indian implication. No South Asian government must therefore ask for external military assistance with an anti-Indian bias from any country. If a South Asian country genuinely needs external help to deal with a serious internal conflict situation or with an intolerable threat to a government legitimately established, it should ask for help from a number of neighbouring countries including India. The exclusion of India from such a contingency will be considered to be an anti-Indian move on the part of the government concerned." Bhabani Sen Gupta, 'Regional Security: The Indira Doctrine,' in *India Today* (New Delhi: August 31, 1983). See also Sankaran Krishna, 'Mimetic History: Narrating India Through Foreign Policy' in S.P. Udayakumar (ed.), *Handcuffed to History: Narratives, Pathologies and Violence in South Asia* (Westport, Conn.; London: Praeger, 2001), p. 54; and Anirudha Gupta, 'A Brahmanic Framework of Power in South Asia?', *Economic and Political Weekly of India*, April 7, 1990, p. 704.

[17] Teresita Schaffer and Hemani Saigal-Arora (1999), 'India: A Fragmented Democracy', *The Washington Quarterly* 22 (4): 143–150, p. 143.

[18] In states and regions declared 'Disturbed Areas', the military functions as a proxy for civil governance, with severe restrictions in citizens' rights and liberties. The extraordinary powers accorded to the military in these areas, including immunity from prosecution for the violation of citizens' rights, have legislative sanction. Legislative provisions include The Disturbed Areas Act, The Armed Forces Special Powers Act, The National Security Act, The Jammu and Kashmir Public Safety Act, and the Prevention of Terrorism Ordinance. In each of these contexts, the denial of citizens' basic rights is inimical to the fundamental principles of a democratic state and not very different from the denial of civil liberties under martial law. See also Stephen Cohen, 'The Indian Military and Indian Democracy', in Atul Kohli (ed.), *India's Democracy: An Analysis of Changing State-Society Relations* (Princeton: Princeton University Press, 1990), p. 12 and p. 128 and Kundu, *Militarism in India*, pp. 171–185.

[19] "Villagers have been threatened, harassed, raped, assaulted and killed by soldiers attempting to frighten them into identifying suspected militants . . . Dissent was severely curtailed and . . . human rights activists and journalists arrested for reporting abuses in Assam or for criticising the government's reliance on security legislation. Freed from normal, legal restraints on arrests and detentions and on the use of force, the Indian Army has little reason to fear accountability for its abuses in Assam." *No End in Sight: Human Rights Violations in Assam* (New York: Asia Watch, 1993), p. 1.

[20] "[Mizoram] was saturated with Indian troops . . . . The Indian army's military strategy of economic suppression was meant to further disable the tribal economy. New laws on habitation were passed as a matter of policy. Their

purpose was to cut off the tribal people from their source of food and livelihood, the forest, and to make Mizo people wholly dependent on the government for food and drinking water, for their very survival . . .. Villages were surrounded by the army and quick notice to take bedding was issued. Villages with all their grain stock were then razed to the ground. . . . Grain stocks hidden in the jungle were searched out and destroyed and people going out to work were not allowed to take their meals with them." People's Union for Democratic Rights in A.R. Desai (ed.), *Violation of Democratic Rights in India* (Bombay: Sangam Books, 1986), pp. 579–580.

21 Paul Brass, *The Politics of India Since Independence* (New Delhi: Cambridge University, 1994), p. 200.

22 The political implications of centrally-backed authoritarianism for Punjab's citizens were gruesome. "At one point . . . so many bodies of 'disappeared' Sikhs were being dumped in the state's waterways that the Governor of neighbouring [state] Rajasthan had to issue a complaint that dead bodies from Punjab were clogging up his canals." Cynthia Keppley Mahmood, 'Trials by Fire: Dynamics of Terror in Punjab and Kashmir', in Jeffrey A. Sluka (ed.), *Death Squad: The Anthropology of State Terror* (Philadelphia: University of Pennsylvania Press, 2000), p. 72.

23 See Cohen, *India: Emerging Power*, p. 29; and Cohen, 'The Indian Military', p. 123.

24 Indira Gandhi cited in Ved Mehta, *The New India* (Harmondsworth: Penguin, 1978), p. 90.

25 See G. Balachandran, 'Religion and Nationalism in Modern India', Kaushik Basu and Sanjay Subrahmanyam (eds.), *Unravelling the Nation: Sectarian Conflict and India's Secular Identity* (New Delhi: Penguin, 1996), pp. 116–125.

26 Bose, 'Hindu Nationalism', p. 121.

27 Harkishan Singh Surjeet quoted in 'The Need for a Political Approach in J&K', *The Hindu* (July 26, 1991).

28 Stephen Cohen, 'The Military' in Henry C. Hart (ed.), *Indira Gandhi's India: A Political System Reappraised* (Boulder: Westview Press, 1976), p. 212.

29 "Mrs. Gandhi and her circle often argued that to preserve the Indian state, they as the central government needed overwhelming power. Indeed, during the 'Emergency' of 1975–7, they decreed that democracy and federalism had to be curtailed to save the state." Robin Jeffrey, *What's Happening to India? Punjab, Ethnic Conflict, Mrs. Gandhi's Death and the Test for Federalism* (London: Macmillan, 1986), p. 204.

30 Atul Kohli, 'Can Democracies Accommodate Ethnic Nationalism? The Rise and Decline of Self-Determination Movements in India', in Alaka Basu and Atul Kohli (eds.), *Community Conflicts and the State in India* (New Delhi: Oxford University Press, 1998), p. 16.

31 Other examples are Sindh, Baluchistan and the Northwest Frontier Province in Pakistan; northern and eastern provinces of Sri Lanka and the Chittagong Hill Tracts in Bangladesh. For an analysis of state military intervention vis-

à-vis sub-national movements in South Asia see Sahadevan, 'Ethnic Conflict and Militarism', pp. 2–49.

[32] The concept of the Westphalian state derives from the European Treaty of Westphalia in 1648 that is considered a cornerstone of modern International Relations theory. The Westphalian model emphasises the principle of absolute territorial sovereignty with relations between states determined primarily by the military capacity of individual states.

[33] S.P. Udayakumar (2001), 'Introduction' in Udayakumar (2001a), *Handcuffed to History*, p. 2.

[34] Ayoob defines juridical statehood as "the inalienability of juridical sovereignty . . . conferred by international law and symbolised by membership of the United Nations" and empirical statehood as "a capacity for effective and civil government". See Mohammed Ayoob, 'State-Making, State-Breaking and State Failure', in Goor et al (eds). *Between Development and Destruction*, op. cit., p. 74.

[35] Mohammed Ayoob, *The Third World Security Predicament: State-making, Regional Conflict and the International System* (Boulder: Lynne Rienner, 1995), p. 29.

[36] India is an exception by virtue of being "a democratic political system" where "the important and increasing dominant role of the security apparatus is clearly visible in states such as Punjab and Kashmir, in which the Indian state faces major overt challenges in the state-building and nation-building arenas". Mohammed Ayoob, 'Security in the Third World' in Norman. A. Graham (ed.), *Seeking Security and Development*, op. cit., p. 25.

[37] David J. Louscher and J. Sperling, "Arms Transfers and the Structure of International Power" in Norman A. Graham (ed.), *Seeking Security and Development*, op. cit., p. 69.

[38] Amit Gupta, 'The Indian Arms Industry', p. 856.

[39] George Perkovich, 'Is India a Major Power?' in *The Washington Quarterly* (2003), 27(1): 129–144, p. 47.

[40] This is based upon Amartya Sen's categorisation of India's record since 1947. See Sen, *The Argumentative Indian*, pp. 193–250.

[41] Paul Brass, *The Politics of India*, p. 266.

[42] For a fuller discussion regarding the origins and dynamics of these conflicts, see Sahadevan, 'Ethnic Conflict and Militarism'. See also Chenoy, *Militarism and Women*, op. cit., pp. 122–174.

[43] Patricia Gossman, 'India's Secret Armies' in Bruce B. Campbell and Arthur D. Brenner (eds.), *Death Squads in Global Perspective* (London: Macmillan, 2000), especially pp. 262–270 and pp. 272–279.

[44] "In every riot since Independence, no matter when or where or how the riot takes place, no matter who starts the riots, in the end the victims are mainly Muslims, whether in the number of people killed, wounded, or arrested." Omar Khalidi, *Indian Muslims Since Independence* (New Delhi: Vikas, 1995), pp. 17–18 and pp. 23–35.

[45] This point is highlighted in a report by Sabrang Communications which quotes the Jagmohan Reddy Commission (Ahmedabad riots, 1969); Justice

D.P. Madon Commission (Bhiwandi, Jalgaon and Mahad riots, 1970); Justice Joseph Vithyathil Commission (Tellicherry riots, 1971); Commission of Inquiry into Communal Disturbances (Jamshedpur, 1971); and the Justice B.N. Srikrishna Commission (Mumbai riots, 1992–1993) to underline the complicity of the state administrative machinery during communal violence against Muslims. See *Damning Verdict: Report of the Justice B.N. Srikrishna Commission appointed for inquiry into the riots at Mumbai during December 1992–1993 and the March 12, 1993 bomb blasts* (Mumbai: Sabrang Communications and Publishing Pvt. Ltd., date unspecified), iv–vii.

46 For example, Moradabad, Uttar Pradesh (1980); Nellie, Assam (1983); Hyderabad, Andhra Pradesh (1984); Bhagalpur, Bihar (1989); Ayodhya, Uttar Pradesh (1991); Mumbai, Maharashtra (1992). For an exhaustive list and analysis, see Khalidi, *Indian Muslims*, pp. 11–42.

47 M.J. Akbar, *India: The Siege Within* (Harmondsworth: Penguin, 1985), p. 310; See also Bose, 'Hindu Nationalism', p. 129, n. 75.

48 Bose, 'Hindu Nationalism', p. 125.

49 See for instance, *Broken People: Caste Violence against India's "Untouchables"* (New York: Human Rights Watch, 1999), p. 8.

50 See Jean Drèze and Amartya Sen, *India: Economic Development and Social Opportunity* (Delhi: Oxford University Press, 1996), pp. 140–178.

51 Ibid. pp.195–202.

52 See Abu Saleh Sharif, 'Some Socio-economic and Demographic Aspects of Population According to Religion in India' (Bombay: Centre for the Study of Society and Secularism, 1993).

53 Mahbub ul Haq, *Human Development in South Asia 1997* (Karachi: Oxford University Press, 1997), p. 31.

54 Ibid.

55 Average literacy rates for India at 64 per cent for males and 39 per cent for females were lower than those for sub-Saharan Africa. Ibid, p. 114.

56 According to a 1995 government survey, the annual rates of economic and industrial production were all significantly *lower* than those achieved during the previous decade. See Drèze and Sen, *India: Economic Development*, p. 180.

57 "The four so-called tigers (South Korea, Hong Kong, Singapore, Taiwan) . . . and also post-reform China . . . have all been well ahead of India in many 'social' respects that have made it much easier for them to make use of the economic opportunities offered by the expansion of markets, and they have, in fact, been in that 'better prepared' position even at the inception of their market-based leap forward." Ibid, p. 33.

58 "China was a motivating factor, but less for reasons of national military security than for reasons of national identity . . . and power . . ." George Perkovich, 'What Makes the Indian Bomb Tick?' in D.R. SarDesai and Raju G.C.Thomas (eds.), *Nuclear India in the Twenty-first Century* (New York; Basingstoke: Palgrave, 2002), p. 47. In an elaboration of the non-nuclear origins of the pro-nuclear attitude of Indian elites, Srirupa Roy quotes Achin Vanaik who argues that the "liberalisation of the economy

beginning in the late 1980s resulted in considerable socio-economic upheaval and generated new sets of socio-economic insecurities. In this context, the valorisation of the bomb can be seen as an attempt to resolve (individual and group) insecurity through the acquisition of (international) status". See Roy, 'Nuclear Frames', p. 352, n. 32.

[59] For a fuller discussion see Stuart Corbridge (1999), 'The Militarisation of All Hindudom? The Bharatiya Janata Party, the Bomb and the Political Spaces of Hindu Nationalism' *Economy and Society* 28 (2): 222–255.

[60] M.V. Ramana, 2003, 'La Trahison des Clercs: Scientists and India's Nuclear Bomb', in Ramana and Reddy, *Prisoners of the Nuclear Dream*, p. 215.

[61] Bose, 'Hindu Nationalism', p. 153. For a cogent analysis of the crisis see Ibid. pp. 104–164.

[62] "Every political group wants to be implicated, get a lick of the nuclear ice-cream. The Congress insists it was Rajiv and Indira who made the ice stick. The UF [United Front] insists it is a three-in-one ice-cream. The first layer belongs to Indira, the second to Gujral and the third to the BJP. A truly coalitional ice-cream." Shiv Viswanathan, 'The Patriot Games' in Smitu Kothari and Zia Mian (eds.), *Out of the Nuclear Shadow* (New Delhi: Lokayan and Rainbow Publishers, 2001), pp. 180–181. See also Krishna V. Ananth, 'Politics of the Bomb: Some Observations on the Political Discourse in India in the Context of Pokharan II', in Ramana and Reddy, *Prisoners of the Nuclear Dream*, pp. 327–32.

[63] Pokharan II is part of a political project based on the mobilisation of people "around an aggressive anti-Muslim platform . . . to create a permanent divide between Hindus and Muslims that can justify an authoritarian state". Prakash Karat, 'A Lethal Link', *Frontline*, June 19, 1998.

[64] Cohen, *India: Emerging Power*, p. 176.

[65] "By ordering the nuclear tests and heating up the war in Kashmir, the BJP appealed to India's new, darker form of nationalism to *gain support for its regime*". Bracken, *Fire in the East*, p. 92.

3 Militarisation in Kashmir

Background

Kashmir is known for its singular beauty. As the Himalayas extend over a grand thousand-mile sweep across northern India, "it is in Kashmir alone that, in a special degree, the gentler and wilder aspects of nature are united in harmony" (Ferguson 1961, 9). Kashmir's physical beauty complements its historical and cultural importance as the confluence between the three great religious traditions and cultures of South Asia namely, the Buddhist, the Hindu and the Muslim, that are not consigned to past history; they co-exist till today.

Kashmir is the only place in India in possession of a Sanskrit historical record, Kalhana's *Rajtarangini*, a historical treatise in verse composed during 1148–1150. Its earliest documented history begins from the third century B.C. when Kashmir was part of the great Ashokan[1] empire, with considerable Buddhist influence—a historical legacy that continues in present day Ladakh. Buddhism achieved its zenith under Kanishka, with Kashmir developing close links with Central Asia and China. With the end of Kanishka's reign, approximately six centuries of Buddhist eminence in Kashmir drew to an end, marking the beginning of a period of Hindu influence that was to last for over seven centuries. During this period, irrigation was improved, dams and canals built on Kashmir's main rivers, and large areas of the Valley brought under cultivation. Among the enduring legacies of this period are the spectacular ruins of the famous temple at Martand described by Francis Younghusband:

> But it is at Martand that there is the finest of Kashmiri architecture at its best, built on the most sublime site. . . . On a perfectly

open and even plain, sloping away from a background of snowy
mountains and looking directly out on the entire length of the
Kashmir Valley and the ranges which bound it, stand the ruins of
a temple second only to the Egyptians in massiveness and strength
and to the Greek in elegance (1917, 136).

The lack of internal cohesion and effective administration
foreshadowed the decline of Hinduism in the twelfth century
and the beginning of Muslim influence that was to last until the
early nineteenth century. This period coincided with the arrival
of numerous Muslim preachers into Kashmir from Persia and
Central Asia, consolidating the influence of Islam in the Valley,
whose population became predominantly Muslim with a small
Pandit minority.[2] Notable among Kashmir's medieval rulers was
Sultan Zain-ul-Abidin (1420–1470) whose reign ushered in a
period of religious harmony, intellectual resurgence, rural and
urban consolidation, the promotion of Kashmiri art and culture
and the translation of Sanskrit texts into Persian.[3] Kashmir
retained its independence under a succession of monarchs until
its annexation by Akbar in 1586, marking its end as a kingdom
in its own right.

As Mughal influence in India began to wane during the
eighteenth century, so did its hold over its dominions. Kashmir
lapsed into a period of Afghan rule with Kabul replacing Delhi
as the centre of authority. Seven decades under the Afghans, from
1752 to 1819, were scarred by political violence, cultural
destruction, religious intolerance and non-governance. Unable
to resist an Afghan onslaught characterised by brutality and
coercion, the Kashmiris appealed to Ranjit Singh—ruler of the
north-western kingdom of Punjab—for help. Unfortunately, a
plea for deliverance from one oppressor drew Kashmir into a fateful
and tyrannical bondage with another. Upon annexation, in 1819,
Kashmir constituted part of Ranjit Singh's great Sikh empire in
the Punjab with Lahore as the seat of government. Kashmir under
the Sikhs was an improvement over that under the Afghans, but
the Sikh regime was not overly concerned with governance or
administration; the Sikhs were conquerors, who owed their power
purely to their military prowess and were interested only in
reaping the advantages of their conquest.[4] The advent of the

British and a series of Anglo-Sikh wars in Punjab culminated in the dismemberment of Ranjit Singh's empire. Unable to extract the desired indemnity from Lahore and as reward for colluding with colonial authority, the British transferred the territory of Kashmir to Gulab Singh, the Dogra[5] ruler of Jammu. In 1846, in what came to be known as the infamous Treaty of Amritsar, Kashmir was sold '*forever*' by the British to Gulab Singh for the sum of £500,000.[6] Thus did the Kashmir Valley pass from Sikh into Hindu hands.

Much like his predecessors, Gulab Singh was a skilled soldier, yet he and his Dogra successors lacked the political ability to administer Kashmir. The disastrous economic and social effects of mis-governance were exacerbated by a series of natural disasters. The state suffered a famine in 1877 during which two-thirds of the population is believed to have died of starvation; an official ban on migration prevented people from migrating to places where food was available.[7] This was also, as James Ferguson notes, "a time for the Muslims to suffer. Mosques were closed, the call to prayer forbidden" (1961, 49). No Muslim in the Valley was allowed to carry a firearm and Muslims were not recruited to the army.[8] A grinding tax regime, a corrupt bureaucracy, stifling state monopoly over all commercial enterprise, religious persecution and indifference to human suffering characterised a deeply unpopular Dogra regime in Kashmir at the turn of the century.[9]

Territorially, the Kashmir Valley added to the already existing Dogra dominions of Ladakh, Baltistan (annexed earlier) and Gilgit (retaken in 1860) together with the kingdoms of Hunza and Nagar which received an annual subsidy in return for their recognition of Dogra suzerainty. The jagir or fiefdom of Poonch[10] was a district associated with the Punjab that was eventually brought under Dogra control by 1936. In 1947, all these territories constituted the principal regions of the Princely State[11] of Jammu and Kashmir under Maharaja Hari Singh.

Kashmir at Independence

On the eve of India's independence, Kashmir was India's largest Princely State. Adding to its significance were its contiguous territorial borders with the newly independent states of India and Pakistan, and common frontiers with China and Tibet. Impending British withdrawal from India and the emergence of new political and social formations foreshadowed change in the old order. Sensing, though not sensitive to, the precariousness of his position, Hari Singh's first instinct was self-preservation. For over two months he prevaricated between acceding to the dominions of India or Pakistan, briefly toying with the idea of working out an association with Pakistan, if Pakistan would agree to leave his throne intact.[12] Meanwhile resistance against Hari Singh was spearheaded by Sheikh Abdullah whose party, the All India Muslim Conference, subsequently morphed into the National Conference and launched a Quit Kashmir agitation against Hari Singh, calling for the establishment of representative government. It further declared its intent to end communalism by ceasing to think in terms of Muslims and non-Muslims, and invited all Hindus and Sikhs to participate as equals in the democratic struggle.[13] In a public speech, Abdullah declared that "the time has come to tear up the Treaty of Amritsar . . . sovereignty is not the birthright of Maharaja Hari Singh. Quit Kashmir is not a question of revolt. It's a matter of right" (Bose 1997, 25). For his defiance and resistance, Abdullah was imprisoned by Hari Singh's regime.

The crisis climaxed with the entry of several thousand Pathan tribesmen from Pakistan's North West Frontier Province into the town of Baramulla, on the road towards the capital, Srinagar. Pleading inability to defend his kingdom, Hari Singh acceded to India, on condition that Delhi send troops to defend his territory, and an understanding that this accession was provisional and "conditional on the will of the people being ascertained as soon as law and order were restored" (Noorani 1964, 31). Sheikh Abdullah, who was eventually released by Hari Singh, organised the defence of Srinagar against the invasion with members of the National Conference and the Indian army.

Hari Singh's decision to accede to India was immediately contested by Pakistan. This initial dispute led to the first Indo-Pak war over Kashmir in 1948, and a subsequent 1949 cease-fire supervised by the United Nations. During 1948–49, three United Nations resolutions called upon the governments of India and Pakistan to hold a plebiscite in order to ascertain the wishes of the Kashmiri people and allow them to determine their own future. A.G. Noorani quotes Jawaharlal Nehru who spelt out state policy: "Our view, which we have repeatedly made, is that the question of accession in any disputed territory or state must be decided in accordance with the wishes of the people" (1964, 34). By 1954 however, Nehru veered towards a volte-face on Kashmir by putting forward the dubious argument that Pakistan's entry into the CENTO and SEATO[14] alliances foreclosed the possibility of a plebiscite in Kashmir. By 1956, the volte-face was complete: Nehru virtually ruled out a plebiscite in Kashmir[15] and it was never held. A temporary accession was, in this way, subsequently made 'permanent' by the Indian establishment.

In the aftermath of the 1948 hostilities, a cease-fire line (Line of Control or LOC) was demarcated in July 1949, with roughly two-thirds of Kashmir falling within India and one-third in Pakistan. The territories of Gilgit and Baltistan became part of Pakistan while Jammu, Ladakh and the Kashmir Valley were in India. This division of Kashmir, achieved militarily by India and Pakistan, was subsequently neither affirmed nor reversed. Accordingly, the 1949 LOC that divides Kashmir constitutes the de facto 'border' between India and Pakistan. The rhetorical statement that Kashmir is 'an integral part of India' became the trademark of successive regimes in New Delhi. For Pakistan, Indian appropriation of Kashmir symbolised an unjust and illegal appropriation of a territory peopled by a Muslim majority which, for this reason, it viewed as rightfully hers. These seemingly divergent positions shared one key characteristic: both perceived Kashmir's realities and interests as subservient to their own.[16]

Democracy in Kashmir: promise and betrayal

Sharing borders with China, Pakistan and Tibet, Kashmir includes the regions of Jammu, the Kashmir Valley and Ladakh. Each region contains within it majority religious and ethnic groups, and smaller minorities.[17] The Kashmir Valley, the location of the present crisis, is predominantly Muslim with a small but significant Hindu (Pandit) minority. Post-1947 constitutional provisions limited Indian jurisdiction in Kashmir to defence, foreign affairs and communication.[18] In 1949, the Indian

Constituent Assembly moved to adopt Article 306A as a temporary extension of autonomy to Kashmir, pending a plebiscite.[19] Sheikh Abdullah went on to become Prime Minister in Kashmir's first government, in 1951. The highlight of the Abdullah government's manifesto, "Naya Kashmir", was a land reform programme that conferred ownership rights to (mainly Muslim) peasants who tilled the land, had no security of tenure and were obliged to either migrate to India during the winter season or starve.[20] The reforms led to a redistribution of 230,000 acres of land—a factor that greatly enhanced Sheikh Abdullah's popularity and stature.[21] Subsequently, Prime Ministers Abdullah and Nehru negotiated the Delhi Agreement that ratified Kashmir's autonomy as Article 370 of the Indian Constitution. While Sheikh Abdullah's secular and socialist leanings brought him close to the Nehru administration, his articulation of the independence option (that remained unresolved and, therefore, open to consideration) heightened fears (of Kashmiri independence) within the Indian establishment. New Delhi's increasing suspicion and hostility towards Sheikh Abdullah ended in his dismissal in 1953, provoking widespread protest across Kashmir. New Delhi's imperious attitude towards democracy in Kashmir, and the resentment such a policy generated, foreshadowed the tragedy that followed.

During the unremarkable tenure of Abdullah's successor, Bakshi Ghulam Mohammed (installed by New Delhi), Indian jurisdiction was extended to areas beyond those spelled out in Article 370, and Kashmir was increasingly integrated into the Indian Union. In 1957, under New Delhi's tutelage, the Constituent Assembly of Kashmir adopted a new Constitution that declared: "The State of Jammu and Kashmir is and shall be an integral part of the Union of India." In 1958, a constitutional amendment placed Kashmir under the direct purview of central administrative services; in 1963, it was considered expedient by New Delhi to replace Bakshi Ghulam Mohammed with G.M. Sadiq, whose regime presided over the extension of Articles 356 and 357 of the Indian Constitution to Kashmir, empowering the central government to dismiss an elected state government. Through such legalese, New Delhi eroded the letter and spirit of

Article 370 that it was legally and constitutionally bound to safeguard. As a result, "Kashmir's political arena came to be dominated by politicians installed at New Delhi's behest, and its day-to-day administration gradually usurped by people with no roots among the population" (Bose 1997, 34). The erosion of Kashmir's autonomy and its integration within the Indian Union was thus written into law *without* Kashmiri affirmation. C.P. Surendran summed up the 'legal' charade succinctly: "Clearly, no hegemonic power could be more 'legal' in its efforts to convert a sphere of dominance into territorial acquisition" (1991, 59).

The dilution of Article 370 paralleled legislative sanction for the suspension of civil liberties in Kashmir[22]—an extraordinary measure without parallel elsewhere in India—degrading the integrity of the state and gravely undermining the rights of citizenship. As K.G. Kannabiran notes:

> Freedom of speech, assembly and association in the state could be suspended at any time on 'grounds of security'. No judicial reviews of such suspensions would be allowed . . . What . . . India experienced for a brief period . . . during Mrs. Gandhi's Emergency . . . Kashmir has suffered for . . . years. We cannot deny a people rights that flow out of citizenship, and then expect their allegiance (1990).

After twenty-three years of enforced political oblivion at the behest of New Delhi, Sheikh Abdullah concluded an agreement with Indira Gandhi whereby Kashmir's 'special status' became a mere formality. In a 1975 agreement between both leaders, Kashmir was "made a constituent unit of India . . . legitimising the usurpation of the right of self-determination and thereby making India and Pakistan the arbiters of Kashmir's destiny" (Bose et al 1990, 35). With the legal incorporation of Kashmir into the Indian Union, the option or possibility of self-determination virtually ended.

For all it was worth, the 1975 Accord did, however, ensure Kashmir's first reasonably free and fair elections in 1977, which voted in an administration headed by Sheikh Abdullah until his death in 1982. In the ensuing 1984 elections, Sheikh Abdullah's son, Farooq Abdullah, won a decisive mandate despite a concerted communal campaign by Mrs.Gandhi centred on the alleged secessionist, anti-national 'threat' posed by minorities in Punjab (read Sikh) and Kashmir (read Muslim). Under tremendous pressure in the aftermath of her ill-fated assault on the Golden Temple in Amritsar,[23] and in panic against growing opposition unity (that included Kashmir's Chief Minister Farooq Abdullah) to authoritarian politics and the dismissal of duly elected state governments by her regime, Mrs. Gandhi played her final, fateful card in Kashmir—in 1984, she dismissed Farooq Abdullah's legitimately elected government.

New Delhi's subversion of democracy in Kashmir preceded Farooq Abdullah's fence-mending with New Delhi—a step he subsequently rationalised as acceptance of a reality whereby Kashmir's political future was contingent on New Delhi's approval. Farooq's preference for abandoning principle in order to gain power evoked widespread Kashmiri resentment, since his alliance was with the very (Congress) party that had so cynically undermined democracy in Kashmir. He returned as Chief Minister, but at the cost of considerable erosion in the political and moral base of the National Conference and the legacy of his father.

An immediate outcome of Farooq's disastrous rapprochement with New Delhi was the formation of a broad coalition of political groups under the banner of the Muslim United Front (MUF). Though the MUF did not have a clear-cut ideology, it represented a cross-section of disaffected youth, illiterate working-class people and farmers who expressed anger against family rule, corruption and the lack of development.[24] In the ensuing (1987) elections, Farooq Abdullah's National Conference won a majority of seats amidst widespread allegations of rigging. These allegations were never investigated, and the arrest of several MUF leaders fuelled public resentment and anger. Sten Widmalm quotes Abdul Ghani Lone, leader of the People's Conference, who summed up Kashmiri anger against 'democracy' in Kashmir:

> It was this [subversion of democracy] that motivated the young generation to say 'to hell with the democratic process and all that this is about' and they said, 'let's go for the armed struggle' (2002, 80).

As simmering resentment transformed into mass rebellion, the regime in New Delhic responded with centrally-backed military repression. In one of the most infamous and gruesome incidents, unprovoked firing by military forces at a large unarmed demonstration in Srinagar, in January 1990, ended in over one hundred deaths. Kashmir slipped under the shadow of militarily-backed central rule—marking its descent into a state of violence and chaos from which it is yet to emerge.

Militarisation in Kashmir

> Ours is a vibrant, living democracy. The people's voice rules through the legislature. The rule of law prevails. Our courts of justice are vigilant protectors of the rights of the individual. Our press is free. Ours is a great secular democracy in which every individual of every community is an equal Indian, equal in the enjoyment of civic and political rights.
>
> *Prime Minister Rajiv Gandhi*, 1987 [25]

> Today, the ruling party is faced with the rising discontent of the people . . . and the people are more conscious than before. The government is looking for a way out of this impasse . . .. It is only through war that the government can smoothly suppress all civil liberties . . .. An ex-Chief Minister warned the nation that the 'politics of agitation is wholly irrelevant in Parliamentary democracy—when the very stability and security of India are at stake'. . . . In the meantime, India has been quietly shopping for arms around the world and readying the war machine at home.
>
> *Committee for the Protection of Democratic Rights 1987*, 207 [26]

State claims to democracy and its simultaneous subversion of it at home symbolised the discrepancy between rhetoric and reality at the turn of the 1980s. The emphasis on external defence highlighted the contradiction of a state whose eroding legitimacy within contrasted with its consolidation of military power without. The link between both was summed up by a citizen's report on war and civil liberties which expressed the fear that "a war psychosis is sought to be created to divert people's attention from the problems at home" (Committee for the Protection of

Democratic Rights 1987, 207). The concerns were not unfounded; during the late 1980s, India held large-scale military exercises in close proximity to the Pakistan border in Rajasthan, generating fears of a military confrontation between the two countries.[27]

However, it was in the domestic arena that war continued unabated. By 1990, democratic channels to articulate popular grievances in Kashmir were no longer available. The same year witnessed an armed insurrection against the state led by a section of Kashmiri youth for whom an independent Kashmir, or its merger with Pakistan, were perceived as the means to safeguard Kashmiri cultural identity and ensure a better political future for its citizens. The slogan of *azadi* symbolised not just popular resentment and protest against the denial of democracy in Kashmir, but also 'freedom' from Indian rule over the Valley and restoration of the dignity that the Kashmiris felt had been violated by the Indian state. Kashmir's rebellion added to the crises in Punjab, Assam and the north-eastern states. The state's failure to address the grievances of the Sikhs, the Assamese, the Mizos or the Nagas derived from a centralisation of power, a rigid and hierarchical ideology of 'national' unity and a lack of democratic accountability. In this respect, and to this extent, Kashmir was no different from the latter. Indeed, Kashmir had a history of manipulation by successive regimes in New Delhi that fostered Kashmiri grievance over decades.

This chapter focuses on the interface between militarisation's domestic (institutional) and external/military (Pakistan) dimensions on the one hand, and the subjective experience of this intersection for Kashmir's citizens and society, on the other. I reiterate the analytical importance of gender by discussing that the *process* of militarisation in Kashmir is not limited to its domestic (institutional) or external (military) dimensions; it penetrates Kashmir's social fabric in ways that reinforce gender hierarchy. Before proceeding with the discussion, however, I delineate three points that relate to militarisation in Kashmir and to the main arguments made in this section.

The first point concerns the *origins* of militarisation in Kashmir, which is the result of unwarranted intrusion by central authority that distorted the institutional balance between the central government and the state. The conflict in Kashmir may be traced to the government's efforts to *centralise* power at the expense of democratic processes and institutions.[28] Militarisation in Kashmir, therefore, must be understood in terms of the collective discontents generated by an undemocratic *central* order and its associated hegemony of 'national' unity that transformed its greatest fear (of secession) into an ironic, self-fulfilling prophecy.

The second point relates to Kashmir's *external* dimension, that is its 1948 accession to India, contested by Pakistan, which has, since then, been subject to a continuing military rivalry between both countries. Against the unresolved India-Pakistan dispute over the *territory* of Kashmir, Kashmir's rebellion against the *Indian* state served to inflame the former. Accordingly, while militarisation *in* Kashmir (like Assam, Manipur or Nagaland) has *indigenous* roots, it simultaneously differs from the latter in terms of being invested with an 'external' dimension. By highlighting Kashmir's external dimension, I do not suggest moral equivalence between the two; the responsibility for Kashmir's tragedy lies *primarily* with the Indian state and, secondarily, with Pakistan. As Cohen notes, "Pakistan's role was not the decisive factor in starting the uprising, although a critical one in sustaining it" (2001, 217). It is, however, necessary, to acknowledge the *exploitation* of Kashmiri grievance by Pakistan, and the profound influence of this on Kashmir's citizens and society.

The third point concerns the inside/outside[29] dynamics of militarisation in Kashmir, particularly the way in which the mobilisation for *external* defence (of Kashmir's territory) served to consolidate state power *in* Kashmir. The construction of the Kashmiri revolt as a threat to 'the nation' legitimised a violent nation-state building exercise in Kashmir, even as its simultaneous representation as a Pakistan-*instigated* 'terrorist' conspiracy against the Indian state reduced Kashmir's struggle to a matter of 'national' (external/territorial) defence. This inside/outside duality transformed Kashmir into the most heavily militarised region in the world.[30] Over half a million Indian soldiers are deployed to suppress the rebellion within Kashmir, *and* secure the frontiers of the Indian state.

Kashmir: between democracy and nation

> **Q.** What is your understanding of the bomb blasts that have
> been taking place (in Kashmir)? There have been reports that
> this is on account of the frustration among the youth because
> they are denied democratic rights, including free and fair elections.
>
> **G.J. Pandit** (Director General of Police): This is not correct.
> What has happened is that these anti-national elements, in
> collaboration with the neighbouring country, thought of
> creating a Punjab-like situation in the Kashmir Valley.
>
> *Frontline* 1989[31]

The emergence of the Muslim United Front during the 1987
elections, as a conglomeration opposed to both the Congress in
New Delhi and the National Conference in Kashmir, threatened
both dispensations. The MUF manifesto did not mention
secession but stressed the need for a solution to all outstanding
issues according to the Simla Agreement,[32] and assured voters it
would work against political interference from Delhi.[33] Kashmir's
Chief Minister, Farooq Abdullah—by now firmly aligned with
New Delhi—threatened to jail MUF leaders "for some time so
they get a taste of it" (*Indian Express* 1987),[34] which he eventually
did. Although the Congress-National Conference combine won
the 1987 elections, their victory was marred by allegations of
widespread rigging. The highest ever turnout—75 per cent of
the electorate voted[35]—could not retrieve Kashmir's last chance
for a democratic alternative or redeem the faltering credibility of
the Indian state. "The rigging", noted journalist Tavleen Singh,
"was blatant. . . In the constituency of Handwara, for instance,
Abdul Ghani Lone's traditional bastion, as soon as counting
began on March 26, Lone's counting agents were thrown out of
the counting station by the police" (1995, 102).[36] While the
impact of electoral malpractice on the eventual outcome remained
uncertain, 1987 was a turning point for politics in Kashmir. In
the eyes of Kashmir's opposition parties and its citizens, the
election was perceived as fraudulent and illegitimate. The
implications of a contested mandate for politics in Kashmir were
grave; the general post-1987 consensus was that democratic
politics offered no hope for the redressal of Kashmiri grievance.

Among those for whom 1987 became a reason to forsake electoral politics was future militant leader, Yasin Malik.

Yasin Malik, current president of the Jammu & Kashmir Liberation Front (JKLF), was a polling agent for the MUF during the 1987 elections, and was among those arrested by the state. For Malik, the political system itself was flawed. He describes his disaffection vis-à-vis 'democracy' in Kashmir:

> Each Kashmiri is today aware of how the 1987 elections were rigged, destroying the last hope that Kashmiris were clinging on to, dreaming of getting their right through the so-called democratic process. . . We had lost all hope in opposing any oppression by means of demonstrations, since we were arrested before these could be staged. That is when I and my colleagues decided to take up guns for the protection of Kashmiri masses and for our fight for independence and also for bringing the issue of Kashmir, which we believe is a dispute, into the world limelight (1994, 2).

By 1990, the form and scale of popular discontent in Kashmir gained considerable momentum and assumed a distinctly anti-state disposition. Acts of sabotage by militants—led by the JKLF at this stage—provoked retaliation by the military, more often against civilians in the vicinity than against militants themselves.[37] Srinagar, wrote Tavleen Singh, "resembles a war zone . . . their [military and paramilitary] presence in the empty, silent streets is even more ominous and pervasive" (1990). Against popular defiance of state authority, it was "the khaki-clad, self-loading rifle toting jawan [that] impose[d] the authority of the state" (*The Hindu* 1990).[38] At night "while the capital's streets remained eerily silent except for the occasional patrol car or the CRPF/ BSF truck, in the distance, almost without pause . . . sounds of protest from mosques . . . to defy curfew orders were audible" (Smita Gupta, 1990).

Against the ban on public gatherings, popular support for the rebellion was reflected in mass defiance of state-imposed curfew and the complete observance of calls for *hartals* (strikes) by militants. In a report on his visit to Kashmir, the journalist Shekhar Gupta wrote: ". . . the ordinary Kashmiri . . . in the past few weeks . . . has not just been a witness . . . [but] also a participant in the protest movement, and increasingly with a new spirit of defiance" (*India Today* 1990).[39] Journalist Meera Sharma described the popular mood in Srinagar: "The cry for freedom echoes and re-echoes across the Valley almost without pause . . . they all speak as one, 'Go and tell them in India—we don't want roads, jobs, development, concessions—only freedom'" (*Indian Express* 1990).[40] Shekhar Gupta quoted an officer of the Central Reserve Police Force in Kashmir: "In the past you fired one shot in the air and they disappeared. Today you kill one demonstrator, then a second, and yet the mob keeps coming at you" (*India Today* 1990).[41] Women and school children joined men in mass protests and marches in Srinagar. A senior state official admitted: "We have been forced to close down schools on numerous occasions owing to the protest potential" (*The Hindu*, 1990).[42] In an exceptionally vivid account, Smita Gupta captured popular support for the movement:

> But it is at Nowshera that we get a ringside view of what to all appearances is a liberation movement. Young men, old men, women, teenagers, march in an unending stream through the streets in complete defiance of the prohibitory orders that are in force. They are coming from Ganderbal and Kangan, 25 kms. from Srinagar and their destination is Lal Chowk in the heart of the city [of Srinagar] . . .. Women, peeping out of the homes that overlook the street, softly echo the slogans being shouted. It is the most incredible sight.
>
> *The Independent* 1990[43]

Schofield quotes *The Guardian*, London, which described what reportedly was the largest demonstration in the Kashmir Valley in 1990, when 400,000 Kashmiris marched to the United Nations Military Observer Group in Srinagar to hand in petitions demanding the implementation of the UN resolutions.[44] On March 1, 1990, a massive crowd, estimated at one million, took to the streets in Srinagar in defiance of curfew orders, during which 40 people died in firing by the security forces.[45] In an interview to journalist Shiraz Sidhva, Dr.Abdul Ahad Guru, a neurosurgeon at the Sher-e-Kashmir Medical Institute, Srinagar and a member of Kashmir's professional intelligentsia, summed up the mood in Kashmir: "We are determined to have our own country. And I have faith in my people . . . I have nothing against the people of India. I am against the Indian government" (1991).

Kashmir's challenge to the authority of the Indian state that Smita Gupta characterised as "a war between the masses and the men in uniform", was dismissed by its Governor as "not an issue of freedom but of improper development" (*The Independent* 1990).[46] The representation of Kashmir's uprising in administrative terms, however, offered no way out for the Indian state, except to rule and retain it by force. This mailed fist response was, paradoxically, counterproductive in that it reinforced the very sentiments that it was meant to eliminate. The contradiction between official representations of the crisis and the situation on the ground was bridged by the imposition of state censorship. According to Meera Sharma:

> It first withdrew curfew passes to all journalists and photographers, shut down and closed the Central Telegraph Office, confiscated all film rolls and finally ordered foreign media out of the state on the ground that their continued presence in Kashmir was 'prejudicial to the security of the state.' Since then . . . restrictions on the free movement of journalists continued—except those who [were] willing to dish out government propaganda (*Indian Express* 1990).[47]

As the military enforced authority on the streets of Srinagar, popular resistance against militarily-backed central hegemony began to be cast in 'national' terms in New Delhi. Against a *general* crisis of state legitimacy, the invocation of an endangered 'nation' was an expedient and effective means for political elites to evade the issue of state accountability in Kashmir. The use of the (Kashmiri) 'ethnic other', in this instance, assumed double-edged potency: Kashmir's revolt was not only represented as a threat to 'national' unity; it was simultaneously constructed as incontrovertible proof of Kashmiri (read Muslim) disloyalty towards the Indian state, in connivance with the historical enemy, Pakistan. In short, Kashmiri *grievance* at the denial of democracy in 1987 that paved the way for the 1990 rebellion, was submerged within a 'national' narrative that reinvented the latter as a Pakistan-*led* Islamist conspiracy to splinter the Indian nation. Accordingly, a political struggle that was about justice and (the denial of) democracy, came to be represented and viewed in parochial, 'national' terms.

Arguing that the consequence of a democratic mandate in Kashmir would threaten the 'unity' of the Indian federation, Prime Minister Vishwanath Pratap Singh declared that if it came to a choice between local-level democracy choosing self-determination, or the preservation of the Union, he would choose, and fight for, the latter.[48] India was at war in Kashmir, and at stake was not democracy, but the 'unity' and 'integrity' of 'the nation.'

The tenuous hold of the Indian state over Kashmir was a propitious moment for the *entire* political spectrum to arrive at a 'national' consensus on Kashmir. The characterisation of Kashmiri resistance as an 'anti-national,' Pakistan-led terrorist insurgency reverberated *across* the Indian polity. Kashmir's Chief Minister, Farooq Abdullah—whose discredited regime and alignment with the central government was one of the principal reasons for the revolt—claimed that the source of popular discontent in his state lay across the border. Accordingly, he expressed his resolve to "strike against Pakistan and Pakistan Occupied Kashmir (POK) as Israel did in Lebanon" (Khayal 1989, 30). Kashmir's Governor, Girish Saxena (in effect New Delhi's nominee in Kashmir) declared: "We are fighting a guerrilla war on our soil thrust on us by Pakistani war-mongers in their bid to grab the Kashmir Valley" (*The Hindu* 1990).[49] The then Prime Minister declared in Parliament that, "Pakistan wants to achieve its aim of Indian Kashmir becoming a part of Pakistan without having to go to war" and urged Indians to be "psychologically prepared" for it (Clad and Ali, 1990).[50] The President of India, Giani Zail Singh, appealed to Indians to "rally round to save *the nation* in its moment of crisis" (*The Hindu* 1990, emphasis added).[51] In a visit to the headquarters of the Indian Army's Northern Command in Jammu, Dr. Raja Ramanna, Minister of State for Defence, called upon army men "to be in combat readiness to meet any challenge to the *sovereignty and integrity* of the country" (*The Hindu* 1990, emphasis added).[52] In March 1990, an all-party motion passed in the Rajya Sabha called on "Indian patriots to set aside their ideological and political differences and act unitedly for defending the *unity and integrity* of the country" (Bose et al 1990, 42, emphasis added).

The leader of the Bharatiya Janata Party, Atal Behari Vajpayee, counselled Kashmir's Governor to "crush militancy" (Joshi 1990);[53] on its part, the Communist Party of India declared that "there are no two opinions regarding the fact that insurgency in Kashmir should be suppressed with a heavy hand" (*The Hindu* 1990).[54] For the Communist Party of India (Marxist), Kashmir represented the "challenge from extremism" that mandated mobilisation of all "pro-national unity, anti-separatist forces" (*The Hindu* 1989).[55] As one national daily noted with some satisfaction:

> The very fact that parties as different in their political approach as the Bharatiya Janata Party (BJP), the Communist Party of India (Marxist) and the National Conference, could agree on a common resolution reflects the overwhelming *national* consensus on the Kashmir question (*Indian Express* 1991, emphasis added).[56]

The 'national' consensus blunted and appropriated the moral and political edge of Kashmir's struggle, allowing political elites to escape accountability for their political failure in Kashmir. The remarkable consensus for militarisation in Kashmir must, accordingly, be understood in the context of a polity whose invocations of 'the nation' paper over its own notable lack of commitment to democratic process. Even more remarkable, perhaps, was the endorsement of the 'national' consensus in one of the most important components of Indian civil society, namely, the press. An editorial in *The Times of India*, declared:

> By stating clearly and loudly that the status of Jammu and Kashmir is not negotiable, the entire political class of the country has left the secessionists in no doubt of its determination to fight them to the bitter end (1991).[57]

Rita Manchanda quotes India's leading newsmagazine *India Today*, whose unequivocal endorsement of state policy in Kashmir mirrored the imagery of an endangered 'nation', instead of questioning the politics that had, in fact, brought 'the nation' to such a pass:

> In Kashmir, where the Centre has invested 70,000 crores in subsidies, not to speak of the blood of Indian soldiers in two

wars, the nation faces what is the gravest challenge to the idea
on which its integrity is moored. There are no soft options left.
Any temporary reverses must not be allowed to invert the process
of sustained reclamation. The country can no longer afford to
behave like a tenant on notice to vacate somebody else's property
(1990, 26).

Mainstream characterisations of Kashmir as a threat to
'national unity' reflected a public discourse where the replacement
of civilian government by militarily-backed central rule and the
suspension of citizenship rights, was neither criticised nor
challenged; on the contrary, militarisation was *justified* as law-
making violence. The (mis)representation of Kashmir's crisis as a
Pakistan-*led* secessionist-cum-terrorist-cum-fundamentalist
conspiracy against the Indian state—reinforced by Pakistan's
support for the revolt—eliminated the crucial distinction between
the centre's failure in Kashmir and the political mileage derived
from this failure by Pakistan. Anyone who questioned the analogy
between Kashmir and Pakistan was, accordingly, dubbed 'anti-
national.' To quote Manchanda again: "In the present climate of
patriotic jingoism where propaganda has taken the place of news,
an individual who dares question whether all militants are trained
by Pakistan invites the accusation of being anti-national or a
foreign agent" (1990, 26).

The across-the-board 'national'(ist) consensus on Kashmir
assumed that brute force would keep the Kashmir Valley within
the Indian Union, yet the overwhelming sentiment in the Valley
was ranged firmly against the status quo. As James Clad noted,
"the trouble was that virtually no Kashmiri Muslim, any longer,
wished to remain in India" (*Far Eastern Economic Review* 1990).[58]
The imposition of coercive central rule in the Valley coincided
with a ban on public gatherings and the suspension of civil
liberties.

For its part, Kashmir's militant movement affected daily life
in the capital Srinagar, where a series of bomb blasts, sniper fire,
sabotage and strikes caused considerable civic and administrative
disruption. Acts of subversion by militants prompted greater
repression by the state. The movement for *azadi*, led at this stage
by the Jammu & Kashmir Liberation Front, successfully

challenged state authority, yet the organisation's secular claims were tarnished by its killing of Kashmiri Pandits and unarmed civilians.[59] Beyond the mass mobilisation for independence, the JKLF leadership faced the question: What next? Although the future of the movement for *azadi* seemed ambiguous,[60] events across Kashmir's western border pre-empted further development on this front.

In contrast to the 'national' consensus (in India) regarding Pakistan's support for the revolt in Kashmir, the movement for *azadi* evoked alarm rather than elation within the Pakistani establishment. For "if a Muslim majority state of Kashmir could seek independence, what message would it send to restive Sindh, Baluchistan and the North West Frontier province [in Pakistan]?" (Noorani 2000). Pakistan's motivation to intervene in Kashmir was fuelled not so much by ideological support for *azadi* as by its discomfiture and deep fear of Kashmiri nationalism that could, possibly, threaten its own political status quo. The primary *intent* of the Pakistani state, therefore, was to *usurp* rather than support the movement for *azadi*. Accordingly, as Kashmir's young men turned towards Pakistan—a state that rhetorically upheld Kashmir's right to self-determination—for assistance against the Indian state, they negotiated an establishment with rather different perceptions and designs regarding their struggle. As Robert Wirsing notes:

> A conscious policy decision appears to have been taken very quickly in Islamabad, in fact, to curb the *independence* sentiment that clearly lay at the foundation of the movement. In early February 1990, a meeting was held in Islamabad, with Prime Minister Benazir Bhutto in the chair and with the Chief of the Army Staff, General Aslam Beg, and the President and Prime Minister of Azad Kashmir in attendance. They considered the possibility that the uprising could boomerang on Pakistan, and that Pakistan could lose not only Jammu and Kashmir but the Northern areas as well. They decided they had to curb the *azadi* forces, meaning they would not equip them and not send them into the Valley (1994, 122–123, emphasis in the original).

Accordingly, at the very moment when the movement for *azadi* was at its height in the Valley, the Pakistani establishment—

notwithstanding its rhetorical support for Kashmiri self-determination—moved against the JKLF and its cadres. Pakistan's intervention led to the decline of the JKLF and its line that favours an independent Kashmir, and the concomitant rise of militant factions that supported either a theocratic state or Kashmir's merger with Pakistan. Not only did Pakistan successfully marginalise the JKLF, it simultaneously supported a rival, Hizbul Mujahideen, whose ideology of denominational nationalism and indiscriminate use of violence diminished the JKLF.

In this way, Pakistan successfully appropriated a struggle against state tyranny in Kashmir to reinvent it in denominational terms—a policy that thoroughly undermined the moral and political cause of the very people it championed. Pakistan's intervention provided the Indian state with the opportunity to reduce Kashmir's struggle to one between (secular) India and (fundamentalist) Pakistan.[61] This distortion cast Kashmir's citizens—already under formidable military siege—as not just disloyal to India, but worse, in league with the enemy state across the border.[62] Manzoor Ahmed Butt, a fifty-seven year-old *shikara* owner, and resident of Srinagar, stopped rowing when asked what he thought of the Kashmiri dilemma. In the falling twilight, with his figure silhouetted against the craggy mountains, Butt reflected:

> I did not think of politics very much really . . . In the 1980s things were not too good, but not very bad either. But they took a turn for the worse by 1989–90. See how much we have suffered . . . look around here . . . so much is destroyed. I used to work in a bakery in Safakadal which was burnt down in 1992. With three children and an extended family, I have faced difficult times, hard times. I had to leave Srinagar for a period of time . . . they were arresting people without warrant . . . After suffering so much at Indian hands, I felt that Pakistan was a natural ally, a supporter in our struggle against injustice but . . . now I see it is not that simple. They [India and Pakistan] use Kashmir for their own benefit . . . so who can say which is better or good? . . . I am not sure whom I would prefer . . . [laughs] . . . neither is for Kashmir or the Kashmiris . . . Maybe this is what the problem is . . . that we [Kashmiris] are confused . . . we do not know whom to turn to.[63]

Salman Rushdie summed up Manzoor's dilemma perfectly: "Pity those ordinary, peaceable people, caught between the rock of India and the hard place Pakistan has always been" (1999).

In sum, while it would be a mistake to overlook or deny the role of the Pakistani state in supporting a section of the movement for *azadi*, it would also be an error to impute Kashmir's insurrection against the *Indian* state to Pakistan. India's denial of democracy in Kashmir presented Pakistan with an alibi to utilise Kashmiri disaffection for its own ends. Having made this point, it is necessary to acknowledge that the influx of arms, *mujahedin* fighters and 'Islamic' ideologies from across the Line of Control exerted a profound influence on the political and societal dynamics of militarisation in Kashmir. Accordingly, although this analysis places militarisation in Kashmir firmly within the parameters of the centralised and militarised (Indian) state and its attendant hegemony of 'national unity,' it also examines the influence of Pakistan's involvement in Kashmir on Kashmir's citizens and society.

The political formation that spearheaded a secular movement for independence could not survive the joint onslaught of the Indian and Pakistani states. India's policy of militarised repression, imprisonment of JKLF's political leadership and cadres, and a ban on the organisation was matched by Pakistan's ruthless pursuit of the JKLF through the Hizbul Mujahideen. The divergent motivations and interests of the Indian and Pakistani establishments ironically converged to create the political space for a militancy which—in the years that followed—neither state could subdue or control. The political neutralisation of the JKLF did not render the scenario any less alarming for India or Pakistan. The Indian state had to contend with the local anger and resentment of a people wronged, and an Islamist militancy with a partisan agenda and a formidable capacity for armed combat. Pakistan's success at marginalising the JKLF was shortlived, for it must contend with the task of controlling the very forces it unleashed in Kashmir—forces that threaten Pakistan's own polity. As the struggle for *azadi* was appropriated by advocates of pan-Islamic jihad, Kashmir's *people* became victims of a brutal, militarised conflict over which they have little control. Waged in their name, and on their behalf, by two militarised states,

Kashmiris pay a grievous price for a resistance that amounts to daily survival against occupation by the world's fourth largest military, and the ruinous effects of a violent and parochial Islamist militancy.

As militarisation in Kashmir reinforced popular support for *azadi*, it evoked greater repression by the state. The simultaneous attempt to secure Kashmir without, and to enforce the 'national' idea within Kashmir, resulted in intersecting streams of violence in the societal domain. A range of literature[64] is testament to Kashmir's enduring human rights tragedy. It is not my intention to reiterate the *scale* of this tragedy; rather, I attempt to highlight its myriad *forms*, particularly the ways in which militarisation permeates across and into Kashmir's society and shapes and influences citizens' lives. In order to do so, it is useful to begin with a brief description of the setting.

Kashmir: state of fear and fear of the state

In a society and polity that we have in India, there is no way an administration can think of tyrannising the people into submission.
Girish Saxena, Governor, Jammu and Kashmir, 1990[65]

India . . . is a state-party to the international covenants and to most of the conventions relating to human rights. This indicates the priority India attaches to human rights problems.
Government of India Document, 1993[66]

'Don't tell my father I have died,' he says,
and I follow him through blood on the road
and hundreds of pairs of shoes the mourners
left behind, as they ran from the funeral,
victims of the firing.

From windows we hear
grieving mothers, and snow begins to fall
on us, like ash. Black on edges of flames,
it cannot extinguish the neighbourhoods,
the homes set ablaze by midnight soldiers.

Agha Shahid Ali 2000, 11

The Kashmir Valley is the smallest, albeit the most densely populated, region of the state with a population of approximately four million people. The total area of the Valley is 8,639 square miles.[67] By 1990, the first year of Kashmir's rebellion, there were approximately 150,000 soldiers in the Valley—17 for each square mile and one for every 27 civilians.[68] According to two independent estimates in 1994, there were approximately 400,000 soldiers in Kashmir, representing just under half or 44 per cent of total Indian army strength.[69] A decade later, in 2004, the estimate ranged between 500,000–700,000 soldiers with roughly one soldier for every ten civilians, making Kashmir the most heavily militarised place in the world.[70]

In 1991, members of an all-India fact-finding team described Kashmir as an area under military occupation.[71] Twelve years later, in 2004, there was little difference. Srinagar, the state capital, was like occupied territory with army bunkers in street corners, soldiers patrolling the street and armoured vehicles patrolling roads and highways. Military occupation of civilian areas is a prominent and almost permanent feature of the Valley; the military occupies civil buildings, migrant houses, office buildings, hotels, cinemas, industrial areas, college hostels, university guest-houses, orchards, agricultural land, private buildings and so on.[72] To drive home the message of military power and presence, military bunkers are pasted with slogans hailing victory to Mother India (*Bharat Mata Ki Jai*), glorifying the nation-state (*Mera Bharat Mahan*), and military vehicles bear names such as *Agni* (Fire), *Mahakaal* (Calamity), *Toofan* (Storm). Members of the military have little contact with the local population except during searches and interrogations. "In casual conversation they often use the words 'Muslim' and 'terrorist.' There is a sense they are in the Valley not to protect Kashmiris, but to keep them in line. It is a sense the Kashmiris feel keenly" (Blank 1999, 43).

Since 1990, Kashmir has been subject to a slew of legislative provisions, among these the Armed Forces Special Powers Act (AFSPA)[73] and the Public Safety Act (PSA).[74] The AFSPA (Jammu and Kashmir), promulgated in September 1990, declares Kashmir to be a 'disturbed area' and empowers the military to search homes and arrest citizens without warrant, destroy houses and villages and shoot unarmed civilians with the intent to kill. The extraordinary provisions of the AFSPA are further reinforced with the accordance of immunity from prosecution to members of the military who commit any of the above violations. The AFSPA violates the non-derogable provisions of international human rights law, including the right to life, the right to be free from arbitrary deprivation of liberty, and from torture and cruel, inhuman or degrading punishment as enshrined in the International Covenant on Civil and Political Rights (ICCPR) to which India is a signatory. The AFSPA also violates of Article 21 of the Indian Constitution.[75] The Public Safety Act[76] allows detention up to a period of two years without trial and contravenes India's own Constitutional provisions, the Geneva Convention, and Articles 9 and 14 of the ICCPR. These extraordinary measures were justified as being necessary to restore 'state authority.' In 1990, Governor Jagmohan declared: "this is not repression . . . the situation is such [that] the authority of the state . . . has been challenged [and] has to be restored" (*Indian Express* 1990).[77] Restoring state authority, however, centred more on civilian repression than on institutional revival. A decade later, in 2000, writer Pankaj Mishra noted upon his visit to the Valley: "Human rights violations by the military, instead of being punished, became the accepted means of reasserting Indian authority over the state" (2000a). He quoted an officer of the paramilitary outfit, the Border Security Force: "Isolate the Muslims in Kashmir and then we will have a *free hand* to deal with them" (2000a, emphasis added). The demand for a 'free hand' is particularly ironic in a context where the assertion of state 'authority' is synonymous with violence and terror.

During January 19–20, 1990, about 400 people were dragged out of their houses in Habbakadal, Srinagar, in a midnight raid by the military, and without the knowledge of the Divisional Commissioner of Srinagar. During a protest against the arbitrary arrests by 20,000 people the following day, paramilitary forces gunned down more than a hundred unarmed protestors at what has since become known as the infamous Gowkadal massacre.[78] Forty-two year-old A. was among those who lost her husband that day. Sitting in her one-room tenement from just across the bridge where the tragedy took place, she recalled the horror that has haunted her for fourteen years. She does not think of the tragedy that befell her in terms of the high politics of Kashmir, or indeed even in terms of the struggle for *azadi*; her life was shattered by the arbitrary arrest of her twenty-year old nephew, Riyaz, who never returned, and the subsequent death of her husband who went to protest Riyaz's disappearance:

> My nephew was among those taken away by the military in Habbakdal . . . we tried to find out where he was but there was no information . . . it was a tragedy for my sister and our family . . . he was such a young and good boy. We don't know what he had done . . . if only they would tell us. There were many people in the demonstration the next day. . . We were protesting injustice but I lost my husband . . . [cries] they were shooting to kill . . . I have had such a hard time living and bringing up my children. My life ended that day. I am not very well educated so I cannot earn much money. We only wanted a better life and justice but we have had to bear severe injustice. Is this what we get for asking for justice? Are we not human beings?[79]

A citizen's report documented the testimony of a survivor of the Gowkadal massacre, revealing chilling contempt on the part of state forces for the bloodshed and suffering inflicted by them on citizens whom they are legally and morally bound to protect:

> As I lifted my head, a CRPF man shouted: 'He's still alive!' I pleaded: 'I am a government officer. Please don't shoot!' The officer shouted abuses at me and said: *'Islam mangta hai?'* (Do you want Islam?) and fired back at me. . . . Another paramilitary moved up to me and shouted: *'Tum sala zinda hai—mara nahin?'* (You're still alive—not dead yet?) and aimed his sten gun at my chest. . . The other officer said 'He will die soon.' . . . Soon after a truck was brought . . . a tarpaulin was thrown over us, and two security forces sat upon it. . . After some time, the tarpaulin was lifted and we saw a Kashmiri constable, who discovering us alive, said: 'My God! There are living bodies here . . .' We later heard he had suffered a heart attack (*India's Kashmir War* 1990, 6–7).

In the same year, Shiraz Sidhva describes the fate that befell young Parvez Ahmed Khan in Srinagar. "They chased him into a stream and pushed him into the water with their rifle-butts screaming: *'Azadi chahiye? Wahi milegi'* (You want freedom? That is what you will get) . . .. We recovered his body . . . later, recalls Ghulam Ahmed his close friend, sadly. There was nothing we could do to save him" (1990). The story of fourteen year old Nazeer Ahmed Sofi, is no different. Ayesha Kagal reports that in March 1990, young Nazeer had gone to take lessons from a neighbourhood teacher when there were gunshots and commotion outside. "Nazeer ducked under the bed. When the Central Reserve Police Force (CRPF) broke down the door Nazeer, hidden in the first room of the ground floor, was hauled out and shot" (Kagal 1990).

The state's attempt to impose 'authority' was not limited to individuals or families but extended into forms of collective punishment. The imposition of indefinite twenty-four hour curfews in Srinagar during the early 1990s, for months on end, was a measure without precedent elsewhere in India. Curfew relaxation—if allowed—started at 5 a.m. when it was still dark and cold, and ended at 9 a.m. making it impossible for ordinary citizens to buy daily supplies, prevented those needing medical attention from reaching a hospital, and inflicted enormous hardship on poor, daily-wage labourers.[80] Frequent and prolonged 'crackdowns' were another form of collective punishment. Barbara Crossette of *The New York Times* witnessed one such 'crackdown' in Batamaloo, Srinagar:

> For three days in March the people of Batamaloo . . . were victims of India's war against the independence movement. They call it 'the crackdown,' and it can happen without warning anywhere. . . An area is surrounded, shops are closed, people are confined to their houses or made to stand for hours, other houses are ransacked, women abused, graveyards dug up, mosques violated. . . . In Batamaloo, where more than 100 young men were rounded up on March 27, mothers came out the next day to wail in rage and panic . . . When they began to march, they were driven back with tear gas and blows from rattan poles. By mid-morning, one woman was dead and twenty hospitalised (1991).

There was little change in the situation in the Valley during the 1990s and into the twenty-first century. Thirty-three year old B., an illiterate resident of Khanyar, her parents-in-law and members of her extended family, recalled their nightmare of a midnight raid in March 1997 when, according to them, officers of the 20th Grenadiers regiment burst into their small two room tenement in the heart of Srinagar:

> It was around two o'clock in the morning. We were asleep. They [the military] came in and locked all of us up in one room with the children. We could hear them beating my husband in this [gestures towards the adjoining] room. We pleaded with them and tried to convince them that my husband was not a militant. . . We belong to Kokernag and came to Srinagar to earn a living. We are poor daily wage earners and do not have much money . . . nor was my husband a militant; he was not involved in politics. . . . But all our pleas were in vain [cries] . . .. That was the last time we saw him. . . . Later, the military came and asked us for money. They said they will let my husband go if we give them money. Our family has paid Rs. 15,000 to the military but my husband is still missing. We are surviving on a single income since then. I have three young children and it is so hard for us.[81]

Unable to hold back his grief, B.'s father-in-law pleaded:

> It has been seven years since my son's disappearance. We don't want compensation but just the truth. . . First we are punished for being Kashmiri . . . we lost our son because he is Kashmiri . . . now we suffer a second punishment because we are poor and have no one to turn to . . . [cries].[82]

Raw grief engulfs those who have lost their children. Over tea, amidst silent tears, Parveena Ahanger holds a photograph of her young son, seventeen year old Javed Ahanger, who went missing in 1990. Parveena is a housewife who has the additional burden of taking care of her husband whose illness has worsened since Javed's disappearance. Parveena and her family do not know when or where he was detained, nor is there any record of Javed's arrest. She has visited jails in Kashmir and across India but is unable to get any information about him. Parveena describes her struggle to secure judicial justice against the illegal and arbitrary disappearance of her son by the military:

They took away my son for no reason. I have been doing all I can to find out the truth about him. One former inmate of Badami Bagh [military cantonment] said he had seen Javed there. I secured legal permission to visit Badami Bagh to see my son. I took clothes and food but when I reached there at the appointed time, the military authorities refused to allow me to enter . . . I want the army officers responsible for the disappearance of my son to be punished . . . Although the Srinagar High Court has issued warrants against the culprits they have never been produced before the court or prosecuted . . . The Indian army offered me ten lakh rupees not to file a case against the culprits, but I refused.[83]

Parveena's search for her son and the prosecution of those responsible for his disappearance continues.

Among its numerous documented cases of wilful abuse, the Jammu and Kashmir Coalition For Civil Society (JKCCS) describes the arbitrary murder of Afroza's husband, Tahir, who was apprehended from his house in Sopore on the night of 11–12 September 2003, just after his marriage ceremony, by members of 22 Battalion of the Rashtriya Rifles (RR). Tahir never returned alive. After handing over Tahir's body to his family, the military declared his murder to be a 'mistake'. An intervention by India's National Human Rights Commission (NHRC) which took *suo motu* cognisance of the crime, could not secure justice for Afroza and Tahir's family, since the NHRC does not have powers of jurisdiction over the military. In her moving personal testimony to JKCCS, Afroza said: "My life is ruined. I can never forget the moment when the RR arrested him and I could not show any resistance as I was a one-day bride . . . I became a widow even before knowing marriage" (Imroz 2003, 3).

Parvez Ahmed Radoo, a PhD aspirant from the Valley, was arrested upon arrival in Delhi in September 2006, and is presently lodged in Ward No. 1, Barrack No. 2, in Tihar Jail on charges of militancy that are yet to be proved. Parvez's faith in the Indian judicial system is severely eroded; he has written to K.G. Balakrishnan, Chief Justice of India, to request a fair trial and justice from the courts.[84] Farooq Ahmed Khan, an engineer from Anantnag, has spent twelve years in the same jail on alleged charges of terrorism that are yet to be proved in court. Khan and his family have appealed to President Pratibha Patil for justice, which in their view, must be forthcoming, "if India calls itself a democratic country."[85]

These are but a few of a vast number of ordinary martyrs of the attempt to 'reassert' state 'authority' in Kashmir through the 1990s and into this century. These victims did not brandish Kalashnikovs or AK 47s, nor were they killed during relentless combat. They are ordinary citizens who were direct or indirect victims of the state's drive to restore 'law and order' through illegitimate means, backed by judicial decree. The trials and tribulations of ordinary Kashmiris do not hit the national headlines in New Delhi, yet the individual and collective anguish and anger they generate keeps the fires of *azadi* smouldering. According to an independent poll conducted in the Kashmir Valley in 1995, 72 per cent of respondents were in favour of independence.[86] In June 2008, in the wake of a mass agitation against the transfer of forest land to the Shri Amarnath Shrine Board, tens of thousands of Kashmiris brought the Valley to a virtual standstill; their protests were interspersed with anti-India and pro-independence slogans, evoking memories of similar protests during the early 1990s.[87]

Before our meeting in his office, S.—an employee of Kashmir's State Human Rights Commission—had to ascertain my bonafides with a hostile paramilitary picket posted at his office. In a gentle tone that belied the intensity of his feelings, S. voiced his experience of, and opinion on, militarisation in Kashmir:

> I am neither for India nor Pakistan . . . I wish for independence after experiencing this hell but I know that is impossible. . . . The military occupation of Kashmir has been an exercise in collective humiliation and denigration. I have lost count of the number of times I have been stopped, even detained by the military on suspicion of being a terrorist. . . . Showing them my official card does not help. . . . The military want to use the situation to humiliate us. Every time they stop me, I lose my self-respect, my dignity. Many times they humiliated my wife, but I had to keep silent because I was scared they might arrest me and humiliate my wife further. . . . I have witnessed young

teenagers being taken away by the military but I did not intervene for fear of retribution towards my own family. . . . I feel a sense of guilt and helplessness. I want to, yet cannot help people. What change can you bring about in this situation? Who can bear this prolonged assault on men, women and children in Kashmir?. . . No one can raise their voice against the army . . . is this the way you [India] wish to rule us? By the gun?[88]

After eighteen years of unrelenting violence, the ongoing diplomatic entente between India and Pakistan has not altered the situation for Kashmir's citizens.[89] Inpreet Kaur notes:

> No day passes when the people of the Kashmir Valley or the hilly Muslim-majority areas in Jammu do not bury half a dozen of their loved ones who have perished in the continuing violence. . . Sand bunkers continue to mark Srinagar and its surroundings. The Disturbed Areas Act (1990) and Armed Forces Special Powers Act (1990) continue, granting the Indian security forces a free hand (2006, 15).

State violence parallels violence by militant groups who are guilty of kidnapping, killing and raping of civilians—both Hindu and Muslim—and alleged informers whom they accuse of supporting the Indian government.

> Militant groups—which continued to obtain arms and training from Pakistan—stepped up their attacks, murdering and threatening Hindu residents, carrying out kidnappings and assassinations of government officials, civil servants and suspected informers, and engaging in sabotage and bombings (Gossman 2000, 272).

Members of militant groups have executed military men in retaliation for the increase in custodial deaths, and have also attempted to enforce their own interpretation of 'Islamic values' such as the burqa and a ban on abortion.[90] But it is difficult to obtain reliable information regarding violence and sexual abuse by militants because civilians are reluctant to speak of it for fear of reprisal.

Brutal as militant violence is, it cannot justify state violence, any more than state violence can justify militant violence.[91] The essential focus, however, is the *political context* of militant violence. *Citizens* have created the state, not the other way round, and have rights vis-à-vis the state, including the right to life, dignity and civil liberty. Violence by militants does not, in any way, absolve the state from its fundamental duty and responsibility to protect citizens. Militant violence in Kashmir, itself a *consequence* of state action, cannot be equated with violence by the state. The state, in other words, remains the *principal* focal point vis-à-vis citizens' rights. As jurist Patanjali Vardarajan notes in his report on Kashmir:

> The argument . . . that human rights groups are in dereliction of their duty in not condemning militants . . . must be condemned as the cynical diversionary tactic that it is. . . . The focus of human rights is the state . . . citizens have rights . . . in relation to the state. The *state* is legally, politically and morally duty bound to protect those rights. . . . The state violates *human rights*, militants violate *law* (1993, 28, emphasis in the original).

A glimpse into Kashmir's judicial crisis reveals how the power of impunity accorded to state forces erodes the integrity of the state and extinguishes hopes for justice and accountability for Kashmir's citizens.

Judicial paralysis

The extraordinary powers invested with the military in Kashmir are augmented by an institutional context that confers sweeping immunity on the military and makes it mandatory for a prosecutor to seek permission from the central government before initiating criminal proceedings against a soldier. In 2005, the Jammu and Kashmir government made almost 300 requests for permission to prosecute public servants, including members of the military; none were granted.[92] Since 1989, not a single member of the military has been prosecuted or convicted for a criminal offence in Kashmir.[93] The burden of legislatively sanctioned public unaccountability is also borne by the National Human Rights Commission and its local counterpart, the State Human Rights Commission (SHRC), both of which lack powers of scrutiny and/ or jurisdiction over the military. Their recommendations are nonbinding and neither can intervene in cases pending in the courts. Justice Mir, Chairperson of Kashmir's SHRC, headquartered in Srinagar, highlighted the limited mandate that prevents his institution from demanding accountability from the state/ military, for violations committed by the latter:

> We try our best to deal with the task at hand. However, ours is only a recommendatory body, we can make recommendations to the government but we do not have the power to initiate legal proceedings against those responsible for unlawful violence against citizens. We can, and have, recommended ex-gratia payments to victims of human rights violations and their families, but our mandate does not go beyond this. . . . This itself is an enormous task, given our meagre resources.[94]

More than a year later, in October 2005, Justice Mir said there was no major change in the rights situation. He termed the Commission a "dead horse" whose recommendations were ignored by the government.[95] With the breakdown in the rule of law, the courts in Kashmir are unable to exercise restraint on the administration. For instance, in a 1990 ruling, the High Court in Srinagar directed Kashmir's Governor to list all people detained after 6 April, 1990. The Governor refused to respond on the ground that the Court had "trespassed into issues of state security" (*Far Eastern Economic Review* 1990).[96] Members of the Bar Association of Srinagar are unable to pursue cases of human rights violations where no, or improper, First Information Reports are filed by the police. On their part, police sources plead inability to file FIRs saying they are under instructions from 'higher authorities' not to do so.[97] Those that are admitted face inordinate delays in response by the state. In 1993 there were 7,000 habeas corpus petitions pending in the Kashmir High Court, making it virtually impossible for the Valley's three judges to respond to them.[98] In 2006, according to the President of the Jammu and Kashmir High Court Bar Association, there were 60,000 habeas corpus petitions filed by individuals since 1990 and 8,000 cases of enforced disappearance.[99] In a statement in the state legislative assembly in February 2003, Chief Minister Mufti Mohammed Sayeed admitted that 3,744 persons had gone missing in Kashmir during 2000-2002 *alone*.[100]

The writ of habeas corpus is gravely undermined by the state's unwillingness to *acknowledge* custody of the 'disappeared'. "There is a method in these disappearances," observed Parvez Imroz, APDP member, according to whom:

> The law enforcement agencies arrest people during raids, routine patrolling and search operations. When the relatives approach the security officials, they usually receive assurances that their relatives will be released shortly. That never happens. After a few visits the relatives are told that the people they are looking for were not even arrested. The local police almost never file a First Information Report against the security forces.[101]

Legal redressal for thousands of cases of enforced disappearance, therefore, remains paralysed even as an unknown number of detainees are under state detention. Under the Public Safety Act (PSA) alone, the government detained 2,700 people between 2002 and 2006. In 2006, 607 cases of habeas corpus were instituted in the High Court. In 2008, 117 cases of detention under PSA were instituted in the Srinagar High Court from January 1–April 23. According to former High Court Bar Association president and senior counsel, Mian Abdul Qayoom, detainees were languishing in jails and the government did nothing to release them.[102]

In its (2004) report to the Jammu and Kashmir High Court, a nine-member team headed by the High Court Bar Association, noted:

> The scores of inmates who are suffering from a fear psychosis that they are not ready to talk. . . Detainees have turned into mental wrecks who require psychiatric consultation and treatment for their rehabilitation. . . . The team found many juvenile detainees. Trial courts have already acquitted them and there are no cases pending against them. And yet they are kept under . . . detention. . . . The state Home Department issued a written order in July 2000 not to honour court orders seeking their release (Ashiq 2004a).

Interrogation centres run by military and paramilitary forces are beyond judicial scrutiny,[103] making it virtually impossible for Kashmir's citizens to ascertain the whereabouts or welfare of those

who are in custody or have quite simply 'disappeared'. It is not
any easier for lawyers either. In March 2008, the High Court
directed the jail authorities in Jammu, Delhi and Uttar Pradesh
to facilitate interviews of Kashmiri detenus by a team of lawyers
from the Kashmir High Court Bar Association. On March 17,
2008, the Bar team headed by its president, Nazir Ahmed
Ronga, was not allowed to meet the detainees in Jammu's Kot
Balawal jail (Greater Kashmir 2008).[104] The mandate of the
International Committee of the Red Cross (ICRC) to detention
centres in Kashmir is restricted,[105] while repeated requests by
the United Nations Special Rapporteur on Torture and by
Amnesty International to visit Kashmir have met with official
refusal.[106]

In one of the most poignant testaments to state terror and
Kashmir's judicial crisis, 68-year-old Hafiza Begum and 72-year-
old Shafiq Ahmed sat in their small courtyard amidst unwashed
utensils and a neglected garden, tears streaming down their
anguished faces, their voices choked with unfathomable grief.
Shafiq Ahmed is a retired employee of the State Transport
Corporation; Hafiza Begum is a housewife. They lost their one
and only son, Mohammed Hanif, on August 19, 1991. He was a
student at Amar Singh College and did not return home that
evening. "He was only 25 when he disappeared," said Hafiza
handing me an old black-and-white photograph and a photo-
identity card of her son. Shafiq Ahmed said:

> This year he would have been 38. Our life is ruined; we have
> known only anguish and torment. . . . He would have been a
> support in our old age, but we have to now fend for ourselves
> and face life alone. I am too old to work and do not keep well.
> . . . In the beginning we had some hope but now, after thirteen
> years, our hopes are all but extinguished

Have they asked the military or the courts? "Yes," said Hafiza,

> We went to the military authorities many times but they said they
> have no information and denied taking him into custody. We are
> too old and tired to pursue that any more. . . . We have registered
> my son's disappearance with the government authorities but have
> not heard anything. We just want to know the truth. If he is

dead, we want to receive his body . . . this endless wait is killing
. . . [cries].

When I asked Hafiza and Shafiq about their son's views regarding
the situation in Kashmir, they recalled Hanif's anger at events in
1990:

> We don't know if he was affiliated with any political party; he
> never talked politics with us, but he supported the demand for
> independence. . . . His friends said he was detained by security
> forces during a 'crackdown' while returning home from
> college. . .

"Tell your government in Delhi", pleaded Shafiq, holding my
hand as I took leave, "Please tell them . . . tell them of what has
happened here."[107]

By 2001, there were more than 35,000 civilians under
detention in Kashmir.[108] Twenty-nine year-old D.'s husband
Mushtaq, a resident of Tengpora, on the outskirts of Srinagar,
has been missing for seven years. Mushtaq's family is economically
underprivileged, with little knowledge of law or legal procedure.
Their small, cold, two-room tenement with bare floorboards and
dim lights is part of an entire row of similar dwellings. The
neighbourhood is without streets, sanitation or lighting. Its
inhabitants are primarily poor, working-class people. Mushtaq
has two children and lived with his parents. His wife, D., has left
her children with her in-laws while she lives with her family.
According to her:

> On 10 June 1998, there was an operation in this area
> [corroborated by D.'s neighbours who described a similar
> operation during the same night]. They [soldiers] came in and
> took away my husband saying they needed to ask him some
> questions . . . they said they would release him after that. But we
> never saw him again. We are not in a position to initiate any
> action against the army . . . we do not have the money to pay
> legal costs, nor do we know whom to approach. We have been
> to the army headquarters many times but they do not give us
> any information. . . . Some time ago a human rights group
> noted our complaint. . . . I do not think that helped for there is
> still no news of my husband.[109]

In a report upon their conclusion of a visit to Kashmir in 2004, members of Lawyers without Borders (LwB) and the Interchurch Peace Council (IKV), The Netherlands, quoted the High Court of Jammu and Kashmir, Srinagar, that summed up Kashmir's extraordinary judicial crisis:

> The administration . . . appear[s] to have thrown to the winds the rule of law, there is a total breakdown of the law and order machinery. . . . Even this Court has been made helpless by the so-called law enforcing agencies. Nobody obeys the orders of this Court. Thousands of directions have been given to top administrative and law enforcing agencies who have not even responded. . . Statements of judges insisting on respect for the rule of law are neglected, critical judges are intimidated or even maltreated and risk being transferred or even dismissed.[110]

A European Union Parliamentary delegation that visited Kashmir in 2004 described it as "the world's most beautiful prison".[111]

While dominant understandings of militarisation vis-à-vis Kashmir are monopolised by military-militant encounters, gun battles, bomb blasts and the Indo-Pakistan nuclear impasse over Kashmir, relatively little attention is paid to the profound and lasting damage inflicted by the just mentioned intersecting streams of violence on Kashmir's citizens. V. is a 26-year-old college student and a resident of downtown Srinagar[112]—a working-class area that bore the brunt of the state's counter-offensive. Her father runs a small printing-press business, her mother is a housewife and her brother is a high-school student. V's parents do not belong to any political party. They are dreamers of ordinary dreams—finding gainful employment, educating their children and looking for a suitable partner for their daughter. Standing on a wooden balcony overlooking the street below with rows of tightly-packed houses—several destroyed beyond recognition—on either side, sliced by narrow streets and warrens, V. talks in a low voice, frequently glancing over her shoulder to ensure we are not within hearing distance of anyone:

> I grew up here in the 1990s and my childhood memories are of . . . fear and violence. Those charred houses [points to three houses in the facing row] . . . they were gutted by the military

who said there were Pakistani militants inside . . . those people became refugees and left for Sopore. . . . They belonged here and they were not bad or wrong people, but they were angry and had joined politics. . . . I witnessed *mukhbirs* (informers) who would come here in army jeeps with darkened windows during a crackdown, and point out men who were driven away in military vehicles and never came back home. I remember a truck with human corpses that drove in one evening in 1992, and the cries and wails of families who found their loved ones' bodies riddled with bullets . . . there was so much grief and suffering . . . [silence] [cries]. . . . Some were people of this very neighbourhood with whom I grew up. . . It was terrible, painful . . . I lost my own cousin brother [Z] . . . he lived across from this lane. He went to Pakistan and returned in 1993, was arrested soon after and we never saw him again [long silence].

His father, my uncle, is not educated and we all fear retaliation from the military . . . so we never approached them. . . . My father thinks he is dead but does not say as much to my uncle and aunt . . . they are already disturbed and depressed. . . . The military raided our house in March 1994 when I was fifteen years old. They ransacked this house, emptied canisters of oil and rice on the floor and stamped their boots on it. . . . They asked us about militants and threatened my father . . . it was terrifying. . . . We have lived through all this. I feel dead inside. I don't want to think any more, of the future, of life, of anything. . . . I look forward to the night when I can stop thinking and sleep.[113]

V.'s story is one among countless others that testify to mental and emotional trauma, apart from material and physical destruction. The human and social costs of militarisation in Kashmir are borne by Kashmir's citizens and society, not by its militants.

Pakistan's intervention in Kashmir meant that the Indian state's attempt to consolidate 'authority' *within* Kashmir paralleled the rituals of *external* defence (of Kashmir's territory) against Pakistan.[114]

Inside/outside the world's most beautiful prison

The emergence of Islamist militancy coincided with the diversion and proliferation of light weapons from what is termed the Afghan pipeline—a system formerly used to channel weapons to the Afghan resistance against the erstwhile Soviet Union. Pipeline weapons made their way into Kashmir via Afghan fighters as well as through Pakistan's military and intelligence establishment and were used in hit-and-run tactics against patrols, pickets, convoys or bunkers of the Indian army in Kashmir.[115] The Islamist offensive against what it perceives as the 'Hindu' state of India[116], is particularly ironic in terms of its ignorance of the culture and traditions of a people whose cause it claims to champion. In a parallel irony, the Islamist onslaught enabled successive regimes to reduce the struggle for *azadi* to an issue of 'terrorism' and territorial defence. The conflation of Kashmir's domestic (political) dimensions with its (interstate) territorial dimensions de-legitimised Kashmiri grievance, transformed the aggressor (the state) into a victim (of terrorism), and deprived its real victims, Kashmir's citizens, of justice and citizenship rights.

Militarisation in Kashmir coincided with militarisation for external defence that was prompted, in part, by the former.[117] Pakistan's exploitation of Kashmiri grievance heightened tensions between both countries. By the mid-1990s, Israel replaced the Soviet Union as India's largest arms supplier, with India set to purchase a range of military hardware from Israel estimated at over US$ 1 billion.[118] The India-Israel military relationship had special significance for Kashmir, where 3,000 soldiers of a new Special Forces group were being trained by Israeli specialists to fight separatist militants,[119] while an Indian defence team travelled to Israel to study the four-tiered barbed wire system in Gaza with an eye to its construction on the Line of Control.[120] The attempt to 'secure' Kashmir's territory, however, is at the cost of the physical security of its citizens. According to a report by Medicins Sans Frontières (2006) on Kashmir, in the period 1989–2005, people reported experiencing violence such as crackdowns, frisking by security forces, round-up raids in villages, the destruction or threat of destruction of property, illegal detention, torture, and an unusually high incidence of sexual violence.[121]

By 1998, the analogy between Kashmir, 'terrorism' and 'national' defence assumed nuclear overtones, with the Indian state linking Kashmir to its self-proclaimed nuclear weapons status. In the wake of the Pokharan II nuclear tests, Union Home Minister L.K. Advani urged the Pakistani government to "realise the change in the geo-strategic situation in the region and the world" (Ram 1999, 3 n 5). The attempt to retain the domestic status quo in Kashmir by 'geo-strategic' means, however, did not enhance the 'security' of the Indian state either in narrow military terms, or from the point of view of a wider human security perspective.[122] On the contrary, nuclearisation raised the risk of conventional war escalating into nuclear conflict, a danger that was apparent during the 1999 Indo-Pakistan military confrontation in Kargil and in 2002, when India mobilised over 500,000 troops and its three armoured divisions along the 3,000 km frontier with Pakistan, placed its navy on 'high alert' and deployed its nuclear-capable missiles. Pakistan reacted in kind, concentrating forces along the Line of Control. The deployment was the largest since the 1971 military conflict between the two rivals;[123] the actual 'target' of these manoeuvres was not an abstract 'enemy' but the people of Kashmir, India and Pakistan.

Violence and counter-violence

A significant dimension of the state's counter-offensive in Kashmir has been the cultivation of 'renegades'. Renegades are former militants who subsequently work under the patronage and control of state agencies. According to human rights scholar, Patricia Gossman:

> The security forces made systematic use of these irregular militias, in effect subcontracting some of their abusive tactics to groups with no official accountability. Wearing no uniforms, their members could not be easily identified. There was no one to whom civilians could register complaints about their behaviour (2000, 275).

Approximately 1,500 renegades remain on the government's payroll and "are now the most dreaded people in the Valley, more than the *jihadi* guerrillas, more than the army and police officials

in remote areas or . . . soldiers in their bunkers" (Mishra 2000).
Renegades work in conjunction with state-led anti-insurgency
outfits. Their nameless, faceless violence is as brutal as that of
their political masters. During a long conversation, 40 year old
E.—a JKLF ex-militant who spent over a decade in prison—
explained the state-renegade connection:

> See, suppose they [the state] want to target me, or any other
> person. They have their surrendered militants in their camps.
> . . . They direct Kashmiri surrendered youth to kill a person.
> . . . He is a Kashmiri. He kills me. What is reported in the
> media? That this person has been killed by militants themselves.
> Although I am not killed by militants but militants working with
> [state] agencies, official statements and media claim the person
> has been killed by militants. . . . In this way they manage all
> these killings by renegades in Indian military camps.[124]

The state-renegade nexus is a particularly dangerous one. By out-
sourcing violence and abuse to its former adversaries, the state
remains unaccountable for the cycle of anonymous killings
executed under its patronage and tutelage. Not surprisingly, the
military-renegade connection has helped the former kill large
numbers of militants. Abhay Sapru quotes the diary of a Special
Forces officer of the Indian army who described a joint operation
with renegades in Kashmir:

> I am sitting in ambush in the north Kashmir hills with a few
> surrendered militants from the al-Barq [a militant group] group.
> We haven't had a kill for over a month and the pressure to deliver
> is intense. We see our man coming down the track . . . quite
> oblivious to the fragility of his life. Our rifles roar in unison and
> the man falls. I disarm him. . . . I wonder if I can slit him from
> ear to ear, payback for something I had seen done to our men
> during a raid in Doda. . . He is dying and requests politely to be
> put out of his misery. One of his former comrades obliges. His
> bravery moves us. My soldiers spontaneously salute the dead
> man (2004, 35).

Armed and invested with legislative approval and buttressed
by support across influential sections of Indian civil society, there
is little official reticence regarding extra-legal tactics employed

by state agencies in Kashmir. "For government officials, there could be nothing better than this turn of events . . . they can't stop smiling. A senior state official in Srinagar expressed satisfaction at the job done by renegades: 'Oh, they are definitely making our job easy. We have no reason to complain' " (Jha 1995).

Militants are not the only targets; the state-renegade nexus has targeted journalists and human rights activists who are critical of violations committed by the military. In return, the military and civil authorities ignore killings and kidnappings committed by renegades.[125] In 1997, 19 journalists travelling to a press conference in south Kashmir were kidnapped by members of the Jammu and Kashmir Ikhwan—a counter-insurgent renegade group funded by Indian security. The captors were released upon orders from New Delhi. In his description of the ordeal, Surinder Singh Oberoi, one of the kidnapped journalists, noted that "Our captors departed gleefully, unlicensed weapons in hand" (1997, 1).

Ethnic fragmentation

The killing of Kashmiri Pandits during the early years of the conflict and the rise of Islamist militancy heightened fear and insecurity within the community. Of the total population, comprising three per cent of Kashmiris, approximately 100,000 Pandits from the Valley have moved to Jammu, Delhi and other locations since January 1990.[126] Whether the Pandit exodus reflects a degeneration of the struggle[127] or is a consequence of Islamist militancy, or both, the fact remains that Kashmir's Pandits, and by extension, Kashmir's secular fabric and traditions, have paid a heavy price. The Valley's Muslims tend to view the Pandit exodus as a state-led conspiracy to discredit them. While there is some truth in this allegation, particularly during the tenure of Governor Jagmohan, the migration was undoubtedly influenced by events in the Valley. As Veena and Sunita from Pulwama, who reside in Srinagar, recalled:

> Pandits and Muslims coexisted peacefully, with cordial relations between both communities. After 1990 however, relations became strained due to fear. There were posters and we received letters from both the JKLF and the Hizbul Mujahideen

threatening Pandits and asking them to leave. It was frightening.
Our family decided to leave the village and we packed all our
belongings even though our Muslim neighbours pleaded with us
to stay. . .[128]

In her moving memoir on Kashmir, Sudha Koul, a Pandit from
the Valley, reflects how Kashmir's Pandits became victims of
circumstances beyond their control:

In any case, as less than three per cent of the population, it really
does not matter to anyone in India or Pakistan or Kashmir what
we Pandits want, and we will pay with our very existence for
that. Our history has taken a terrible turn through no fault of
ours. . . . We are now an endangered species, destined for a
scattering from our homeland. . . . The trouble is that like the
Muslims, we Pandits call only the Valley of Kashmir home. . . . If
we cannot carry our mountains, our lakes and our fish with us,
we don't want to go (2002, 140).

L., a 28 year-old Muslim resident of Rainawari, Srinagar, recalled
the fear experienced by his Pandit neighbours:

There were many Pandits living in this locality. We had coexisted
peacefully until the troubles began. They [Pandits] could not
believe that the people next door, with whom they had grown
up, were now so hostile towards them . . . there was palpable
fear among them. Pandits were visibly scared when people in the
neighbourhood started participating in demonstrations and raised
religious slogans. One Pandit was killed by militants. When my
uncle protested, the militants threatened to kill him if he
intervened.[129]

Amitabh Mattoo, a Pandit academic, notes Kashmir's cultural
loss in the wake of the Pandit exodus:

The Pandits were the literati of the Valley; they were teachers,
bureaucrats, doctors and lawyers. Within the community were
also a hierarchically lower occupation group of *buhurs* (small
traders), *wazas* (cooks), and *kaandurs* (bakers). These groups
formed the backbone of what was once an efficient and purposeful
community. This functional network has vanished from the Valley,
and the Muslims too are feeling the loss (1993).

There are however, a small number of Pandits, estimated at 17, 860, who chose not to leave and have stayed on in the Valley.[130] In Mattan, south Kashmir, for instance, a young school teacher, Jyoti, continues to live with her Muslim neighbours. "This is the only home I've known. These are the only friends and neighbours I have ever had and they've been very good to us—so why should we leave?"[131] As is always the case, it is the less well-off Pandits who have suffered the most. The tragedy of Kashmir's Pandits—a consequence of the larger tragedy of Kashmir's Muslims—was politicised to press home the point that Hindus too were victims of the violence in Kashmir. Gautam, a Pandit refugee in Jammu, told Pankaj Mishra he felt

> betrayed by . . . politicians, especially the Hindu nationalists, who had held up the community as victims of Muslim guerrillas in order to get more Hindu votes, and then done very little to resettle them, find jobs for the adults and schools for the young (2000a).

The Pandits, however, are not the only ones who have been forced into exile from the Valley of Kashmir. A Federation Internationale Des Ligues (FIDH) delegation that visited Pakistan found that till March 1, 1993, a total of 8,304 refugees were registered with Pakistani authorities. According to the FIDH report:

> The most striking observation that the delegation made was that entire villages appear to have sought refuge in Azad (Pakistan administered) Kashmir. They arrived, as is the pattern on foot, traversing inhospitable mountain tracks and running the gauntlet of hostile Indian security forces empowered, by military command and by legislation, to shoot to kill. The refugees told of many casualties in the course of their crossing. . . . Nearly a thousand refugee families (or four to five thousand individuals) were not registered and were in all likelihood being sheltered by relatives (Jaudel et al 1993, 9).

Over the years, this number has multiplied. According to a Human Rights Watch (2006) report, 30,000 Kashmiri Muslims have fled to neighbouring Pakistan since 1989.[132] Other Kashmiris are less fortunate. Keppley Mahmood wrote of her visit to

Muzaffarabad on the Pakistani side of Kashmir:

> . . . [where] a blackboard by the banks of the Jhelum river keeps
> count as Kashmiri bodies float down from across the border
> [from India]. When I visited in January 1997, the grim chalk
> tally there was at 476. Given the deep mythic significance of
> India's rivers in the Hindu tradition, this defilement is especially
> telling. 'The largest democracy on earth' has polluted its sacred
> waters with the bodies of tortured citizens (2000, 72).

There is yet another category of "quasi refugees"—described by
the Pakistani authorities as "Line of Control Affectees"—who
are "the inhabitants of settlements on the Pakistani side who have
been displaced . . . by the intermittent skirmishes at the Line of
Control . . . there are about 4,875 families, or 24,375 people"
(Jaudel et al 1993, 11). According to an independent estimate,
45,000 people are displaced along the Indian side of the Line of
Control and cannot return home despite the ceasefire.[133]

Notwithstanding their travails, both Pandits and Muslims
share a desire to end their enforced exile. Dolly, a Pandit
languishing in one of the refugee camp in the plains, yearns to
return to the Valley: "I love Kashmir and I dream of the day
when I will be back there" (*Sada-e-Aman* 2003). Blank quotes
Raja Izhar Khan, a refugee who crossed over into the Kamser
refugee camp in Muzaffarabad, Pakistan, with his whole village
after killings, beatings and gang-rapes by Indian security forces:
"We Kashmiris used to get along fine . . . any religion, side by
side, no problems." None of them has applied for citizenship in
their host country. "We are only waiting here," says Raja Khan.
"We want to go home" (1999, 52). Notwithstanding their
divergent tragedies, Pandit and Muslim exiles from Kashmir
remain united in their yearning for a place they may never see,
and a time that may never return.

A bruised civil society

Kashmir's society and culture pay a heavy price for eighteen years
of unrelenting violence. Over a thousand school buildings have
been gutted and all sports stadiums closed.[134] Two hundred and
sixty-two out of a total of 585 schools in the Valley are either

occupied by the military or converted into centres for interrogation and torture.[135] A Medicins Sans Frontières survey in two blocks of Budgam and Kupwara districts in 2005 noted that 15.5 per cent children were unable to attend school for fear of violence, while 16.3 percent had difficulties studying due to lack of teachers and study material.[136] Staff and students at the University of Kashmir are reluctant of speaking openly against the military or the militants; criticism has, on occasion, had serious, even fatal consequences.[137] No definitive study on the Kashmir question had been undertaken because of pressures by the government and militants; free expression is not possible.[138]

Militarisation seriously impaired the state of community health and health care systems in Kashmir. There was a sharp depletion in the number of doctors as Kashmiri Pandit doctors fled the Valley and other physicians and surgeons departed for the Gulf. The attrition rate for doctors and nurses in Kashmir is high; female doctors posted in rural areas leave for fear of humiliation by security forces, as a result of which there are virtually no medical facilities for women in the countryside.[139] Behind Kashmir's roll of death is a society profoundly scarred by the trauma and grief of thousands of families who have lost family members. In a report on Kashmir's crisis of mental health, Medicins Sans Frontières (2006) emphasised the psychiatric and psycho-social crisis in Kashmir and the imperative need for state agencies to address the cycle of violence and abuse.[140] Women are among the worst casualties; most patients are women aged between 16 to 25 years.[141] Sudha Ramachandran quotes Shobhana Sonpar, a clinical psychologist, who has worked in Kashmir:

> Women account for most of the cases of depression, anxiety, post-traumatic stress disorders and psychosomatic illnesses. This is because they are targets of sexual harassment and assault. They also carry the burden of having to fend for themselves and their children following the death or disappearance of the husband or son (2003a, 25).

In 1980, Kashmir had the lowest suicide rate in India; presently, it is among the highest in the world.[142] More women in Kashmir are driven to suicide as compared to men.[143] The Valley's landscape is dotted with granite and marble slabs of what locals term as

'martyr's graveyards'—of known and unknown citizens who have
perished in the relentless cycle of violence; there are currently
5000 such graveyards across Kashmir.[144] In 1989, Srinagar had
seven tomb-makers; now there are more than twenty-five. All are
doing good business.[145]

Kashmir's rich cultural legacy has not been immune to the
ravages of militarisation. In 1994, in what was widely believed to
be an assault on Kashmir's cultural heritage, the Madinat Ulum—
a library containing 16,000 priceless books and many invaluable
manuscripts in Srinagar's famous Hazratbal mosque in Srinagar—
was burnt down.[146] A year later, in 1995, the fifteenth century
carved-wood shrine of Kashmir's patron saint, Sheikh Nooruddin
Noorani, built by Zainul Abedin—medieval Kashmir's most
famous king—was gutted during a gun battle between security
forces and militants at Chrar-e-Sharief. In 2004, the 105 year-
old building of the Islamia school—Srinagar's oldest educational
institution and a heritage building—was gutted in a fire,[147] as
was Srinagar's tourist reception centre, an important historical
landmark that housed a priceless collection of original
photographs of Kashmir by the legendary photographer Henri
Cartier-Bresson, which were also destroyed.[148]

Kashmir's leading intellectuals are also among the casualties
of militarisation. Dr. Farooq Ashai, doctor and documentor of
cases of torture and extra-legal killings, was killed in 1993 by the
CRPF.[149] Dr. Jalil Andrabi, founder and Chairperson of the
Kashmiri Council of Jurists, filed several thousand habeas corpus
petitions, campaigned for the rights of detainees in Kashmir's
prisons and 'interrogation centres' and sought information from
the state on the status of missing people.[150] He was killed in
1996 by soldiers of the Rashtriya Rifles; questions regarding his
killing in Parliament elicited vague, evasive replies.[151] Dr. Abdul
Ahad Guru, a surgeon and an articulate critic of human rights
abuses by state forces, a member of Srinagar's professional
intelligentsia, and a member of JKLF's Governing Council, was
gunned down in 1992 by "a pro-Pakistan militant who regarded
the doctor as un-Muslim and a *gaddar* (traitor) for daring to
suggest that Kashmir might not axiomatically belong to Pakistan"
(Bose 2000, 102). Among Kashmir's most poignant losses was
that of socialist and trade union activist Hriday Nath Wanchoo,

whose documentation of cases of torture, extra-judicial killings and disappearances made him too dangerous for the Indian state. Wanchoo was a Hindu and his work was particularly embarrassing because he could not be dismissed as a militant.[152] He was shot dead in 1992 by a militant of the Hizbul Mujahideen, released by state authorities to execute the killing, who, in turn, was murdered by the military.[153] The tragedy of Kashmir's intellectuals is an enduring loss for Kashmiri society. Kashmir's intelligentsia who fell to the gun subscribed to an inclusive, humane and just vision for Kashmir, a vision for which they eventually paid with their lives. Their loss mirrors the depth of the tragedy for Kashmir, especially for Kashmiri Muslims, well summed up by a Kashmiri Pandit:

> The Kashmiri Pandits have lost nothing except their homes. We have been able to protect our education and intelligentsia. The Kashmiri Muslims on the other hand have lost their education, their intelligentsia and their leaders—by the gun (Oberoi 1997).

The establishment's focus on Pakistan-abetted ('cross-border') terrorism in Kashmir and international concern directed towards militarisation over Kashmir—important as both are—have obscured the tragedy of the Valley's citizens and stripped it of its political context, namely, the state-sanctioned violence, abuse and powerlessness visited upon the Kashmiri people. So relentless and remorseless is the focus on 'cross-border terrorism' and 'national' defence, and so cynical the exploitation of Kashmiri grievance by successive central regimes, that the appalling and disproportionate violence against Kashmiri civilians and society for almost two decades is rationalised and accepted as legitimate state policy. Pakistan-sponsored terrorism in Kashmir is condemnable, and the prospect of war over Kashmir, chilling. However, *both* dimensions flow from *local* political grievance *in* Kashmir that the Indian state has consistently failed to address. As militancy and 'cross-border' terrorism decline and fears of war recede, Kashmir's military occupation continues, as do the disappearances, extrajudicial killings, illegal detentions, sexual abuse and violence against civilians. The Armed Forces Special Powers Act, the Public Safety Act and the impunity accorded to the military are still in place, Kashmir's judiciary remains dysfunctional, and the Valley's citizens continue to be denied basic democratic rights and freedoms. For precisely this reason, even as India and Pakistan maintain a ceasefire on Kashmir's border and move towards better diplomatic and economic relations, with greater movement of people and goods across the LOC, and significantly lower levels of military-militant violence, as Pandits return home and tourists flock to Kashmir's gardens, lakes, houseboats and ski-resorts, there is little change in the *Valley's* accumulated legacy of grief, loss, trauma, anger and despair; its citizens still wait for justice, dignity and human rights. The irony and meaninglessness of the changed scenario for the Valley's residents was captured in the words of a local journalist who wrote upon a much publicised inauguration of Srinagar's tulip garden by Sonia Gandhi, in April 2008, coinciding with the release of a report by the Association of the Parents of the Disappeared on missing and disappeared persons, and the discovery of mass graves: "While going through the report, one realises the horror of the situation we Kashmiris are living in . . .. The view of the tulip garden and the . . . graves of the nameless persons; how can the two be reconciled?" (*Rising Kashmir* 2008).[154]

Notes

[1] Ashoka (268–231 B.C.) was one of India's great kings whose empire included the greater part of north-western India, including present-day Kashmir.

[2] "It was the Brahmins (Pandits) on whom Hinduism had the strongest hold and who had the most to lose by conversion to Islam. Accordingly, while many of the lower castes became Muslim, a small number of the Brahmins— eleven families according to some authorities—remained steadfast, and managing to escape death, secured the survival of their caste till more favourable times restored their prosperity and influence. . . . This accounts for the curious situation today whereby the Hindus of Kashmir are almost entirely Pandits." James P. Ferguson, *Kashmir: An Historical Introduction* (London: Centaur, 1961), p. 32.

[3] Ibid. pp. 33–34.

[4] Ibid. p. 50.

[5] The Dogras were Rajputs from central India, from where some migrated to the north. Among them were Gulab Singh's ancestors who, in the eighteenth century, settled in Jammu.

[6] The Valley was sold for a sum of Rs. 75,00,000 that approximated to £

500,000. Alastair Lamb, *Kashmir: A Disputed Legacy 1846–1990* (Karachi: Oxford University Press, 1991), p. 8.

[7] Francis E. Younghusband, *Kashmir* (London: 1917), p. 181.

[8] Victoria Schofield, *Kashmir in Conflict: India, Pakistan and the Unending War* (New Delhi: Viva Books by arrangement with I.B. Tauris, London, 2004), p. 17.

[9] Younghusband, *Kashmir*, pp. 178–9.

[10] "The people of Poonch had little in common with the Valley or indeed with Jammu. They were Pathans and had close relations with other Pathan regions of north-west India and eastern Afghanistan. Poonch formally became a part of Jammu and Kashmir during 1935–36—a point of resentment for its Muslims who never reconciled themselves to being subjects of that state." Lamb, *Kashmir*, p. 14.

[11] The Princely States were not formally part of British India as their territory was not annexed by the British. This particular aspect of British hegemony meant that in return for their recognition of, and allegiance to, the British Crown, the latter recognised the authority of these rulers over their respective fiefdoms.

[12] Sumantra Bose, *The Challenge in Kashmir: Democracy, Self-Determination and a Just Peace* (New Delhi: Sage, 1997), p. 26.

[13] Alastair Lamb, *Crisis in Kashmir: 1947 to 1966* (London: Routledge and Kegan Paul, 1966), p. 31.

[14] The CENTO and SEATO were United States-backed military pacts against the Soviet Union and its allies.

[15] A.G. Noorani, *The Kashmir Question* (Bombay: Manaktalas, 1964), pp. 66 and 72.

[16] For an astute critique of state-centric approaches to Kashmir, see Eqbal Ahmed, 'A Kashmiri Solution for Kashmir,' *Himal South Asia*, Vol. 9, No. 8, 1996, p. 16.

[17] Ladakh constitutes the largest area of all three regions and is home to Ladakhi Buddhists and a small Shia Muslim minority; Jammu is largely Hindu with Sikh, Muslim, Dogra, Pahadi and Gujjar minorities; the Kashmir Valley is largely Muslim with a small Pandit (Hindu) minority.

[18] The jurisdiction of the Supreme Court of India did, however, extend to Kashmir.

[19] "The Constituent Assembly was meant only to give a representative government to Kashmir and was not intended, likewise, to be an alternative to a plebiscite." Noorani, *The Kashmir Question*, p. 47.

[20] Schofield, *Kashmir in Conflict*, p. 74.

[21] "If one takes into consideration the small population of Jammu and Kashmir at the time, this may be considered the most extensive land reform program in India ever." Sten Widmalm, *Kashmir in Comparative Perspective: Democracy and Violent Separatism in India* (London: Routledge Curzon, 2002), p. 182, n. 68.

[22] India's constitution guarantees judicially enforceable fundamental rights, including the right to freedom of speech, political affiliation and against

arbitrary arrest or detention. Fundamental rights, however, are not inalienable, and may be suspended (Article 357). In the wake of Kashmir's 1990 uprising, civil society organisations were raided, political parties and public gatherings banned, with widespread use of preventive detention and blatant disregard for the right to habeas corpus. The ban on political parties has since been revoked, but the ban on public gatherings, free speech, the right to be free from unlawful detention, and the right to a fair trial remain suspended. The Jammu and Kashmir Public Safety Act (1978), the Jammu and Kashmir Criminal Law Amendment Act (1983), the Terrorism and Disruptive Activities Act (1987), (in force in Kashmir till 1995), together with the Armed Forces Special Powers Act (Jammu and Kashmir), contravene, respectively, the right to be free from arbitrary detention, the right to political affiliation and opinion, the right to freedom of speech and the right to life. For more details see *Blood in the Valley*, pp. 94–99 and p. 101, and Schofield, *Kashmir in Conflict*, pp. 170–172.

23 In 1984, Mrs. Gandhi ordered the storming of the Golden Temple in Amritsar by the Indian army—allegedly to remove militants—an operation that ended in large civilian casualties and her eventual assassination.

24 See Bose, *The Challenge in Kashmir*, p. 45.

25 Speech by Rajiv Gandhi, August 13, 1987. 'A Citizen's Guide to Rajiv Gandhi's India', People's Union for Democratic Rights (1987) in A.R. Desai (ed.), *Expanding Governmental Lawlessness and Organised Struggles* (Bombay: Popular Prakashan, 1991), p. 319.

26 Report by Committee for the Protection of Democratic Rights, 1987, Ibid. p. 207.

27 Sen Gupta, 'India in the Twenty-first Century', p. 301.

28 See Gossman, 'India's Secret Armies', p. 261. As Abdul Aziz, resident of Kashmir, remarked to Victoria Schofield: "We were trying to change the political framework by democratic and peaceful methods, but we . . . failed in this. . . . The people of Kashmir got disgusted and disappointed and disillusioned." Schofield, *Kashmir in Conflict*, p. 138.

29 See R.B.J. Walker, *Inside/Outside: International Relations as Political Theory* (Cambridge: Cambridge University Press, 1993), p. 63 and pp. 151–152.

30 "The Indian troops-to-Kashmiri people ratio in Kashmir is the largest soldiers-to-civilian ratio in the world." Junaid Ahmed 2002. http://www.zmag.org/content/SouthAsia/junaid_ahmed_kashmir.cfm. Accessed March 24, 2004. See also Pankaj Mishra, 'Death in Kashmir', *The New York Review of Books*, Vol. 47, No. 14, 2000.

31 'They are on the Run', *Frontline*, April 15–28, 1989.

32 The Simla Agreement was signed between India and Pakistan in 1971 in the wake of the Bangladesh war, and resolved to settle outstanding issues between both countries by peaceful means. The Agreement endorses the Line of Control (LOC) as the de facto border between India and Pakistan.

33 Schofield, *Kashmir in Conflict*, p. 137.

34 Farooq Abdullah quoted in 'Farooq Takes Tough Stand on MUF', *Indian Express*, April 4, 1987.

35 Chandrashekhar Dasgupta, 'Jammu and Kashmir in the Indian Union: The Politics of Autonomy', in R. Dossani and H.S. Rowen (eds.), *Prospects for Peace in South Asia* (Stanford: Stanford University Press, 2005), p. 250.

36 "Every election since, except two (in 1977 and 1983 and the first in 1957) was marked by corruption and deceit." Sumit Ganguly, *Kashmir: Portents of War, Hopes for Peace* (Cambridge: Cambridge University Press, 1997), p. 39. "Independent accounts speak of intimidation of voters with doubtful loyalty, attack on polling agents, curious stoppage of counting whenever opposition candidates were in the lead, summary rejection of candidates' complaints and midnight announcement of results. Either by design or accident, delays of over ten days in announcing the results occurred in constituencies where the MUF was leading." *The Hindustan Times*, April 15, 1987.

37 For instance on October 1, 1990, in Handwara, in retaliation for the killing of one BSF soldier, 300 houses and shops were gutted with 14 civilian casualties. See 'Kashmir: Nursing a Shattered Dream', *The Hindustan Times*, August 22, 1993.

38 'Valley where Normality is Enforced', *The Hindu*, September 8, 1990.

39 'Kashmir Valley: Militant Siege', *India Today*, January 31, 1990.

40 'Why is Kashmir Burning?', *The Indian Express*, February 11, 1990.

41 'Kashmir Valley', *India Today*, January 31, 1990.

42 'Valley where Normality is Enforced', *The Hindu*, September 8, 1990.

43 'Storm over Srinagar', *The Independent*, February 17, 1990.

44 Schofield, *Kashmir in Conflict*, p. 150.

45 Ibid.

46 Jagmohan, Governor, Jammu and Kashmir, 1990, quoted in Smita Gupta, 'Storm over Srinagar'. *The Independent*, February 17, 1990.

47 Meera Sharma, 'Why is Kashmir Burning?' *The Indian Express*, February 11, 1990. "News reports might be datelined Srinagar, but they were little more than handouts drafted by the state's then Governor, Jagmohan." Rita Manchanda, 'Facts and Propaganda', *Far Eastern Economic Review*, July 19, 1990. See also Nils Bhinda, 'The Kashmir Conflict (1990–)' in Michael Cranna (ed.), *The True Cost of Conflict* (London: Earthscan Publications, 1994), p. 62.

48 James Clad and Philip Bowring, 'Limits of Tolerance', *Far Eastern Economic Review*, May 17, 1990.

49 'Security Forces Foiling Plans of Militants: Saxena', Girish Saxena, Governor, Jammu and Kashmir interviewed in *The Hindu*, September 14, 1990.

50 James Clad and Salamat Ali, 'Will Words Lead to War?' *Far Eastern Economic Review*, May 24, 1990.

51 President Zail Singh quoted in 'Bid for National Stand on J&K,' *The Hindu*, March 6, 1990.

52 Dr. Raja Ramanna, Minister of State for Defence quoted in 'Tight Security for Kashmir Bandh', *The Hindu*, February 11, 1990.

53 Arun Joshi, 'BJP-JD Rift over Kashmir', *The Hindustan Times*, September 8, 1990.

[54] Statement of Mr. M. Farooqi, CPI leader and Secretary at a press conference in Jammu, quoted in 'Security Forces Foiling Plans of Militants', *The Hindu*, September 4, 1990.

[55] Statement of Harkishan Singh Surjeet, member, CPI(M) quoted in 'Change in Kashmir', *The Hindustan Times*, December 26, 1989. In 1991, Mr. Surjeet attributed the conflict in Kashmir to "Imperialism, especially U.S. imperialism" that was "bent upon destabilising the country and is working for its balkanisation." Harkishan Singh Surjeet quoted in 'The Need for a Political Approach in J&K', *The Hindu*, July 26, 1991.

[56] 'Unambiguous Signals', *The Indian Express*, November 15, 1991.

[57] 'Moves on Kashmir', *The Times of India*, November 15, 1991.

[58] James Clad, 'Valley of Violence: The Deep Chasm between Kashmiri Muslims and India', *Far Eastern Economic Review*, May 24, 1990.

[59] The JKLF was responsible for the killing of Lassa Kaul, director of Doordarshan (state television station), Srinagar; H.L. Khera, General Manager, Hindustan Machine Tools (HMT); Mushirul Haq, Vice Chancellor, University of Kashmir, and his secretary Abdul Ghani. It was also responsible for the kidnapping, rape and killing of Nurse Sarla Bhat.

[60] Bose et al., *India's Kashmir War* (New Delhi: Committee for Initiative on Kashmir), 1990, p. 27.

[61] "Such an effort is a . . . recreation of the enemy in the shape of India's choice. A force that fights for Kashmiri nationalism would be difficult for India to de-legitimise morally. It would be difficult to argue before the world in defence of India's war against such a people. But a force that fights for unification with Pakistan is an easier target in this sense, especially because the West fears[s] pan-Islamism these days. India therefore prefers a Kashmiri fundamentalist over a Kashmiri nationalist. . . . That Pakistan is also interested in the same transformation brings about the strange unity of aims between these two supposed enemies." *Blood in the Valley, Kashmir: Behind the Propaganda Curtain: A Report to the People of India* (Bombay: Lokk Shahi Hakk Sangathana, 1995), p. 63.

[62] See Sumantra Bose, *Kashmir: Roots of Conflict, Paths to Peace* (New Delhi: Vistaar Publications, 2003), pp. 112–113.

[63] Personal interview with Manzoor Ahmed Butt, Dal Lake, Srinagar, September 23, 2004.

[64] Among others, *The Human Rights Crisis in Kashmir: A Pattern of Impunity* (Asia Watch and Physicians for Human Rights 1993); *Kashmir Under Siege* (Asia Watch May 1991); *The Crackdown in Kashmir* (Human Rights Watch, 1993); *Behind the Conflict: Abuses by Militants and Indian Forces in Kashmir* (Human Rights Watch, 1996); Asia Watch and Physicians For Human Rights: *Rape in Kashmir—A Crime of War* (1993); *India's Kashmir War* (Committee for Initiative on Kashmir, 1991); Patanjali M. Vardarajan, *Kashmir: A People Terrorised*, Rapport (Paris: FIDH, 1993); *Blood in the Valley* (Lokk Shahi Hakk Sangathana, 1995); *Undeclared War on Kashmir* (Andhra Pradesh Civil Liberties et al, 1991); *Wounded Valley, Shattered Souls* (The Indian People's Tribunal on Environment and Human Rights,

1997); *Grim Realities* (Andhra Pradesh Civil Liberties et al, 2001); *Behind the Kashmir Conflict: Abuses by Indian Security Forces and Militant Groups Continue* (Human Rights Watch, 1999); and *Everyone Lives in Fear* (Human Rights Watch, 2006).

65 'There is a Definite Change of Mood', Jammu and Kashmir Governor Girish Saxena interviewed by Shiraz Sidhva, *Sunday*, October 26, 1990.

66 Government Document cited in Vardarajan, *Kashmir: A People Terrorised*, p. 84.

67 Ministry of Home Affairs, Government of India. http://mha.nic.in/ove.htm. Accessed November 7, 2005.

68 *Undeclared War on Kashmir* (Bombay: Andhra Pradesh Civil Liberties Committee, Committee for Protection of Democratic Rights, Lokk Shahi Hakk Sangathana, Organisation for Protection of Democratic Rights, 1991), p. 10.

69 Nils Bhinda, 'The Kashmir Conflict', p. 66.

70 Etienne Jaudel et al., *Violations of Human Rights Committed by the Indian Security Forces in Jammu and Kashmir* (Paris: Federation Internationale Des Ligues Des Droits De L'Homme, 1993), p. 4; See also Pankaj Mishra, 'These Murders Take a Toll on Kashmiri Tolerance', *The Guardian*, London, July 22, 2002; *Wounded Valley, . . . Shattered Souls: Women's Fact-Finding Commission Probing Army Atrocities on Women and Children in Kashmir* (Bombay: The Indian People's Tribunal on Environment and Human Rights, 1997), p. 18.

71 *Undeclared War on Kashmir*, p. 10.

72 Sarwar Kashani, et al., *The Impact of Violence on the Student Community in Kashmir* (New Delhi: Oxfam India Trust: The Violence Mitigation and Amelioration Project, 2003), p. 16; see also *Wounded Valley*, p. 18.

73 "The AFSPA has its roots in British colonial legislation dating back to the 19th century and is based on a 1942 colonial ordinance intended to suppress the Indian independence movement." *Everyone Lives in Fear: Patterns of Impunity in Jammu and Kashmir*, Vol. 18, No. 11(C) (New York: Human Rights Watch, September 2006). http://www.hrw.org/reports/2006/india0906/. Accessed November 23, 2007.

74 Under the PSA, fundamental legal safeguards under international law are routinely violated, including the right to be brought promptly before a judicial authority; to communicate with counsel of one's choosing; and to be charged and tried without undue delay. In 1990, the PSA was amended to exempt state authorities from providing detainees with reasons for their arrest. It also allowed for the shifting of detainees outside the state, thereby undermining efforts to establish their whereabouts and enormous hardship in the quest for habeas corpus. See Schofield, *Kashmir in Conflict*, p. 171 and *Blood in the Valley*, p. 97. Even though the Terrorism and Disruptive Activities Act (TADA) in Kashmir lapsed in 1995, detainees continued to be charged under TADA on the claim that the crime was committed before TADA was repealed.

75 According to Article 21 of the Indian Constitution, no person may be

deprived of life or personal liberty except according to procedure established by law. See also Amnesty International, 2005. Briefing on the Armed Forces (Special Powers) Act, 1958. http://web.amnesty.org/library/print/ ENGASA200252005. Accessed May 30, 2005.

76 Once the PSA detention order expires, new charges are brought against the detainee with s/he being rearrested on 'new charges' for a period of two years. As a result, detainees may be held indefinitely without trial. See *Behind the Kashmir Conflict*, op. cit., p. 2.

77 Pushp Saraf, 'NC Bid to Regain Credibility', *Indian Express*, February 9, 1990.

78 See Bose et al, 'India's Kashmir War', pp. 5–6.

79 Personal interview with A. Gowkadal, Srinagar, June 30, 2004.

80 Vardarajan, *Kashmir: A People Terrorised*, p. 7.

81 Personal interview with B. Khanyar, Srinagar, June 15, 2004.

82 Personal interview with X. Khanyar, Srinagar, June 15, 2004.

83 Personal interview with Parveena Ahanger, Batamaloo, Srinagar, March 23, 2004. Simultaneous translation from the Kashmiri by Tahir Ahmed Mir. Parveena is one the founder members of Kashmir's Association of the Parents of the Disappeared (APDP) in 1994.

84 'Trauma in Prison: Surreal Story of KU PhD aspirant,' *Kashmir Times* (online edition), April 24, 2008.

85 'Kashmiri Engineer Completes 12 Years in Delhi Jail', *Greater Kashmir*, May 24, 2008.

86 "Contrary to popular notions, the average Kashmiri does not seem worn down by the years of hardship. An overwhelming majority of people (72%) polled put it down on paper that they are determined to dig their heels in for a long haul," saying "categorically that it is independence alone which can bring peace in the violence-riven Valley." Altogether 504 adults were interviewed in Srinagar, Sopore, Baramulla, Bandipora and Anantnag during the second half of September 1995. 'Till Freedom Come', *Outlook*, October 8, 1995.

87 See for instance M. Tasim Zahid, 'Kashmir Out on Roads: Tens of Thousands Want Land Back', *Greater Kashmir*, June 28, 2008 and Khalid Gul/Malik Salam, 'Massive Protests Rock South Kashmir: Districts too on Boil', *Greater Kashmir*, June 28, 2008.

88 Personal interview with S. Dal Gate, Srinagar, March 17, 2004.

89 European Parliament, 2004, *Summary Report of the Visit of the Ad Hoc Delegation of the European Parliament to Kashmir: December 8–11, 2003 and 20–24 June 2004*, p. 5. Grateful thanks to Marjan Lucas for this information.

90 Asia Watch and Physicians for Human Rights, *The Human Rights Crisis in Kashmir*, op. cit., pp. 147–149 and 160–162.

91 Grateful thanks to Mary Kaldor for drawing my attention to this point.

92 Human Rights Watch, *Everyone Lives in Fear* (2006). Under the provisions of the 1993 Human Rights Protection Act, the Commission may seek a report from the central government but cannot independently

investigate the case itself. http://www.hrw.org/reports/india0906/6.htm#Toc144362293. Accessed November 23, 2007.

[93] In March 2006, Chief Minister Ghulam Nabi Azad told the Jammu and Kashmir assembly that disciplinary action had been taken against 134 army personnel, 79 members of the Border Security Force and 60 policemen, without providing any details regarding the perpetrators, the nature of their crimes, or whether any of the latter had anything to do with human rights abuse. "In short, the Indian security forces continue to hide behind the shield of immunity provisions in Indian law and the lack of political will in New Delhi to address the critical human rights situation in Jammu and Kashmir." Ibid.

[94] Personal interview with Justice Mir, Chairperson, State Human Rights Commission, Dal Gate, Srinagar, March 16, 2004.

[95] Basharat Peer, 'It Could be Follow-on for Mufti', *Tehelka*, October 8, 2005.

[96] James Clad, 'Valley of Violence', *Far Eastern Economic Review*, May 24, 1990. In 1991 Governor Saxena "admitted that hundreds of people were being arrested on suspicion [that was] *arbitrary, but added that the government had powers to do so under TADA*. . . . He admitted that the government had not filed replies to . . . habeas corpus petitions which require the government to produce the people if they are in its custody." *Undeclared War on Kashmir*, p. 30, (emphasis added).

[97] Vardarajan, *Kashmir: A People Terrorised*, p. 24.

[98] Ibid. Barbara Crossette quotes Justice Bahauddin Farooqi, former Chief Justice of the Jammu and Kashmir High Court, according to whom, in 1990, there were 3000 petitions pending in Srinagar alone. See Barbara Crossette, 'Srinagar Journal: In Kashmir's Enchanted Valley, War Breaks Spell', *The New York Times*, October 5, 1990. See also *Wounded Valley*, p. 12.

[99] *Everyone Lives in Fear*, Human Rights Watch, 2006.

[100] Ibid.

[101] Parvez Imroz, Member, Jammu and Kashmir Coalition of Civil Society, quoted in Fayaz Bukhari, 'Dying Day by Day: Taking Stock of Mental and Social Health'. *Himal South Asia* (November 2002).

[102] All figures in this para from *Greater Kashmir*, April 23, 2008.

[103] The Disturbed Areas Act and the Armed Forces Special Powers Act permit the military and paramilitary forces to operate their own network of detention and interrogation centres.

[104] 'Bar Allowed Access to Tihar to Interview Detainees about Their Condition', *Greater Kashmir*, April 2, 2008.

[105] The ICRC has to seek and obtain government approval for visits to jails in Kashmir. A member of the ICRC expressed concern at the mental condition of detainees and declined to comment on instances of torture in detention centres. He admitted that, "Several activists in the Valley have voiced their disillusionment with the work being carried out by the ICRC. They believe that the token presence of the ICRC helps New Delhi gain international legitimacy for its policies in the Valley vis-à-vis the political prisoners." See

'Carrying the Cross' Georgios Georgantas, member, ICRC team to India, interviewed by Humra Quraishi, *The Times of India*, September 24, 2002.

[106] Amnesty International Release ASA 20/016/1996. 28 March. Available from http://web.amnesty.org/library/Index/ENGASA200161996? open&cof+ENG-IND. Accessed May 30, 2007.

[107] Personal conversation with Hafiza Begum and Shafiq Ahmed, Batamaloo, Srinagar, June 11, 2004.

[108] Surinder Singh Oberoi, 'Fear and Loathing in Kashmir', *The Washington Quarterly*, Vol. 24, No. 2, 2001, p. 196.

[109] Personal interview with D, Tengpora, Srinagar, June 27, 2004. Simultaneous translation from the Kashmiri by Isaq Nehvi.

[110] Press Statement on return of IKV/Lawyers Without Borders delegation to Kashmir, The Hague, dated June 7, 2004. Grateful thanks to Marjan Lucas for this information.

[111] "The EU report refers to Jammu and Kashmir as 'Indian-occupied Kashmir' and expresses concern at the huge military presence with approximately one soldier to every ten civilians. . . . Furious with a 'biased' . . . report by a European Parliamentary delegation, whose leader called Jammu and Kashmir 'the world's most beautiful prison' India withdrew official patronage to such visits. . . . The Government of India rejected the report by the Parliamentary delegation headed by John Cushanan of Ireland, saying its understanding was 'inaccurate'". See 'India Withdraws Patronage to EU Visits in J&K,' *The Times of India*, August 21, 2004.

[112] Location withheld to protect identity.

[113] Personal interview with V. April 25, 2005, Srinagar. Location withheld to protect identity.

[114] "Troop deployment crossed the 5,00,000 mark with three divisions of the Indian army, 1,20,000 paramilitary forces, 50,000 Rashtriya Rifles (a division of the Indian army), even as the number of militants operating in Kashmir went down from a high of 10,000 in 1992–93 to less than 5,000 post-1996–97, and today it is said to be less than 3000. . . . Thus it is the massive Indian military presence that confronts Kashmir." Gautam Navlakha, 'Limits and Scope of Dialogue', *Spotlight* (2004), Vol. 23, No. 39. http://www.nepalnews.com/contents/englishweekly/spotlight/2004/apr/apr16/viewpoint.htm. Accessed March 31, 2007.

[115] *Arms and Abuses in Kashmir* (New York: Human Rights Watch, 1994), p. 3.

[116] See Rizwan Zeb, 'Pakistan and Jihadi Groups in the Kashmir Conflict' in W.P.S. Sidhu et al (eds.), *Kashmir: New Voices, New Approaches* (Boulder, London: Lynne Rienner, 2006), pp. 65–79.

[117] Human Rights Watch, *Arms and Abuses in Kashmir*, op. cit., p. 4.

[118] Edward Luce and Harvey Morris, 'India and Israel Ready to Consummate Secret Affair', *The Financial Times*, September 4, 2003.

[119] South Asia Monitor Newsletter, (Washington D.C.: Centre for Strategic and International Studies), 2003.

[120] See Vijay Prashad, *Namaste Sharon: Hindutva and Sharonism under US Hegemony* (New Delhi: Leftword Books 2003), p. 51; see also Soumya K Ghosh, 'Hi-Tech Border Fence Import from Israel Likely', *The Hindustan Times*, January 27, 1995.

[121] 'Valley of Nightmares,' South Asian Human Rights Documentation Centre, January 29, 2007. HRF/158/07. http://www.hrdc.net/sahrdc/hrfeatures/HRF158.htm. Accessed April 28, 2008. The findings of the MSF report are also highlighted in Shujaat Bukhari, 'Threat of Physical Violence Looms in Kashmir', *The Hindu*, December 25, 2006.

[122] Admiral L. Ramdas, 'Nuclear Weapons and National Security' in Ramana and Reddy (eds.), *Prisoners of the Nuclear Dream*, p. 71.

[123] All facts and figures in this para regarding the 2002 India-Pakistan military stand-off are from 'Kashmir Crisis,' *Globalsecurity.org*. http://www.globalsecurity.org/military/world/war/kashmir-2002.htm. Accessed September 23, 2006.

[124] Personal Interview with E., JKLF spokesman. JKLF Office, Maisuma, Srinagar April 2, 2004.

[125] Pankaj Mishra, 'Kashmir: The Unending War', *The New York Review of Books* Vol. 47, No. 16, p. 7. For a first hand account of how renegades feel they have won the war for the politicians but have been denied their due, see Jonah Blank, 'Fundamentalism Takes Root', *Foreign Affairs* (1999), Vol. 78, No. 6, pp. 47–49. For an analysis of violence by renegades see, *India's Secret Army in Kashmir: New Patterns of Abuse Emerge* (New York: Human Rights Watch, 1996), Vol. 8, No. 4 (C), pp. 15–26.

[126] A similar figure is quoted in *India's Secret Army in Kashmir*, p. 9 and Bose, *Roots of Conflict*, p. 120.

[127] In 1994, the JKLF admitted to atrocities by militants that had alienated the people. See Schofield, *Kashmir in Conflict*, p. 173.

[128] Personal interview with Veena and Sunita, Barbarshah, Srinagar, July 7, 2004.

[129] Personal interview with L. Rainawari, Srinagar, April 20, 2004.

[130] Sonia Jabbar, 'Hindu Minority Refuses to Bow out of Kashmir.' *Asia Times Online*, April 5, 2000. http://www.atimes.com/ind-pak/BD05Df01.htm. Accessed November 15, 2004.

[131] Ibid.

[132] Human Rights Watch 2006. http://www.hrw.org/reports/2006/india0906/. This figure is also cited by Parwini Zora and Daniel Woreck, 'HRW Documents Repression in Kashmir,' World Socialist Web, December 1, 2006. http://www.wsws.org/articles/2006/nov2006/kash-n30.shtml. Accessed November 23, 2007.

[133] Although the security situation has improved since the ceasefire, reports from the Akhnoor and Poonch regions reveal that thousands are still displaced. Many people remain in the camps because they no longer have access to their fields due to the fencing along the Line of Control, or because their fields have still not been de-mined as promised, and they therefore have no

way to earn a livelihood in their home villages. See 'India: Large Number of IDPs are Unassisted and in Need of Protection,' International Displacement Monitoring Centre (IDMC). http://www.internal-displacement.org/8025708F004CE90B/(httpCountrySummaries)/82626CB2EB1759D9C12572C90029A4EF?OpenDocument&count=10000#sources#sources. Accessed June 2, 2008.

134 Surinder Singh Oberoi, 'Kashmir is Bleeding,' *Bulletin of the Atomic Scientists*, Vol. 53, No. 2, 1997. http://www.mtholyoke.edu/acad/intrel/crisis/bul.htm. Accessed November 7, 2005.

135 See *Wounded Valley*, p. 18.

136 Shujaat Bukhari, 'Threat of Physical Violence Looms in Kashmir?' *The Hindu*, December 25, 2006.

137 Kamal M. Chenoy, 'On Human Rights Violations', Summary Presented at the conference on Kashmir organised by the Kashmir Foundation for Peace and Development, September 30–October 1, Srinagar, December 2000. Reprinted in *Seminar* (496). http://www.india-seminar.com/2000/496/496%20report.htm. Accessed February 27, 2006.

138 Rehana Hakim, 'Kashmir's Endless Autumn', *Countercurrents*, November 18, 2004. http://www.countercurrents.org/kashmir-hakim181104.htm. Accessed June 16, 2005.

139 *Grim Realities* 2001, p. 41.

140 Report by Medicins Sans Frontieres (2006) summarised by South Asia Human Rights Documentation Centre, New Delhi. 'Valley of Nightmares: Mental Health in Kashmir Needs Urgent Attention'. HRF/158/07, January 29, 2007. http://www.hrdc.net/sahrdc/hrfeatures/HRF158.htm. Accessed January 30, 2008.

141 Izzat Jarudi, 'The People of Kashmir', *MIT Journal of Undergraduate Research* 6, 2002, p. 24.

142 Peerzada Arshad Hamid, 'Deathly News, What Else?', *Tehelka*, July 21, 2007.

143 Of the 167 suicide deaths registered at the SMHS hospital, Srinagar, during 1998, 92 were women and 75 men; in 1999 the total was 208—144 women and 64 men. Between April–March 2001, altogether 567 suicides—377 women and 190 men—were registered by the hospital. See Bukhari, 'Dying Day by Day'.

144 Peerzada Ashiq, 'Death is Still a Livelihood in Kashmir', *Tehelka*, June 26, 2004.

145 'Death is Still a Livelihood in Kashmir'.

146 Vardarajan, *Kashmir: A People Terrorised*, p. 50.

147 Shujaat Bukhari, '105-year-old school in Srinagar burnt down', *The Hindu*, July 6, 2004.

148 See Justin Huggler, 'We Were Pinned Down by Fire as a Gun Battle Took Place in the Heart of Srinagar', *The Independent*, London, April 7, 2005. http://www.commondreams.org/headlines05/0407-06.htm. Accessed November 31, 2007.

149 *Blood in the Valley*, p. 100.

[150] See Sumantra Bose, 'Kashmir 1990–2000: Reflections on Individual Voices in a Dirty War', *Development* Vol. 43, No. 3 (The Society for International Development and Sage Publications, 2000), p. 101.

[151] Ibid. p. 102.

[152] Gossman, 'India's Secret Armies', p. 273.

[153] Ibid. p. 274.

[154] Imtiyaz Ahmed, 'Giving Flowers is Pointless', *Rising Kashmir*, April 26, 2008. In keeping with the 'national' obsession, the garden at Siraj Bagh was rechristened Indira Gandhi Memorial Tulip Garden.

4 Gender and Militarisation in Kashmir

Wars today are called civil, revolutionary, drug, gang, feudal, ideological, but they are linked by the fact that they refuse easy oppositions that had marked, in fact, constituted, the War Story . . . Low-intensity conflict may spill into a non-militarised zone, but people still need to believe in the separation of space into dangerous front—men's space—and danger-free home—women's space . . . People's beliefs, hopes and needs notwithstanding, the reality, or better the realities, of nuclear age wars fly in the face of such distortions. Those who continue to function in terms of black and white categorisations . . . long for a world . . . that never existed.

Miriam Cooke

But the reports are true, and without song: mass rapes in the villages, towns left in cinders, neighbourhoods torched. Power is hideous like a barber's hands. The rubble of downtown Srinagar stares at me from the *Times*.

Agha Shahid Ali

As a discipline concerned with the prevention with war, IR analyses represent Kashmir as an essentially male arena. Gender is assumed to have little or no significance in a disciplinary hierarchy premised on normative constructs of state 'security'/defence. Underpinning the state-centric paradigm of International Relations is a public-private dichotomy that assumes gender to be beyond the realm of international politics. Mainstream analyses on Kashmir, accordingly, fail to examine the intersection between inter-state military processes on the one hand, and social transformations on the other. It is not my intention to review the extensive IR literature on Kashmir; rather, I address what, arguably, is a significant *limitation* in IR analyses on Kashmir. At a time when civilians, especially women, are at the centre of military conflict, the significance of gender as a category of analysis can hardly be overstated.

A somewhat similar limitation characterises political analyses on militarisation *in* Kashmir where the state is assumed to be the central category of analysis. The state, however, is not a neutral, reified entity, but a dynamic process embodying the institutionalisation of social relations.[1] Accordingly, while both men and women are victims of state violence, violence itself tends to be gender specific. As Cockburn notes, "In . . . political terror, the instruments with which the body is abused in order to break the spirit tend to be gender differentiated and, in the case of women, to be sexualised" (2001, 22). If at all acknowledged, political analyses consider rape and sexual abuse against women as part of the *general* violence against civilians. The point is not that one is worse than the other; rather that the gender specificity of rape as a crime against women as *women* is not a sequel, but a constituent,[2] of militarisation. State-centric analyses that focus on the military *vs* militant stand-off obscure the gender dimensions of militarisation in Kashmir; gender transformations cannot be assumed to be peripheral simply because they occur in the social realm; they are inextricably linked to institutional processes with important political implications for women.

Both IR and political analyses ignore militarisation's social fabric *and* the gender relations that embody the latter. In this respect, both frameworks are inconsistent with militarisation's empirical realities. An emphasis on gender is not synonymous with the denial of militarisation's external (military-strategic) or domestic (institutional) dimensions; on the contrary, gender analyses illustrate that state and inter-state military processes are embedded in the social and cultural realities of the population at large. By demonstrating the interrelation between violence at the international, national and family levels,[3] gender highlights its own significance as an *integral*, rather than a separate, category of analysis. Indeed, in this respect gender illustrates precisely *why* militarisation's analytic frame must not be compartmentalised into mutually exclusive national/international, military/civil or social/cultural categories, but must be viewed and analysed as an inter-related whole.

The salience of gender, however, comes with the caveat that it is neither desirable nor possible to generalise. Both men and women experience direct and indirect violence associated with military conflict. While men are disproportionate victims of direct violence (extra-judicial killing, illegal detention, torture, enforced disappearance), violations experienced by women occur mostly in the sphere of economic, social, sexual and cultural rights. Violence against women may not always be gender specific; it may be influenced by factors such as class, ethnicity or geographic location.[4] Notwithstanding this important clarification, the *political* significance of gender vis-à-vis militarisation cannot be overstated because it exposes it as a multi-dimensional, multi-layered process that exerts profound and lasting influence on the lives of male and female citizens and on relations between them. By including women in its narrative and analytic frame, a gender analysis demonstrates that women are not marginal to, but at the heart of, contemporary military conflict.

In her analysis on Kashmir, Kavita Suri notes that a gender analysis must

> break down stereotypes of women as passive recipients of conflict ... and see them as having an active role. Indeed, many women have acted with courage amid the conflict, deserving praise but going unnoticed even in the eyes of their own people (2006, 82).

Mainstream narratives vindicate Suri's point, focused as they are on Kashmir's military-militant dimensions. The argument regarding gender, however, goes *beyond* reclaiming women's agency or highlighting women's 'active' role. Gender analyses of militarisation are not only about women; rather, they illuminate what Marysia Zalewski appropriately terms the "*political* nature of the private realm" (1995, 347, emphasis added) that demonstrate the intrusion of state (and inter-state) military processes into 'private' social spaces and the targeting of a constituency that the military is legally bound to protect. A gender analysis demonstrates that the exploitation of sexual difference by the military is integral to the project of (militarily-backed) nation-state building in India; in so doing, it highlights the failure of a vital institution of the state to protect female citizens and, by extension, the contradiction between state claims to democracy and legitimacy in Kashmir on the one hand, and the absence of one of its fundamental provisions, the physical security and sexual integrity of citizens, on the other. Further, a gender analysis highlights the transformation of social and cultural realities in ways that reinforce gender hierarchy. Women's increased economic and sexual vulnerability as a result of the loss of male kin members, the political marginalisation of women, together with the reinforcement of regressive gender stereotypes, demonstrates that the process of militarisation "re-patriarchalis[es] society and gender relations in general" (Albanese 2001, 1000).

Gender analyses are thus not as much about women, as they are about demonstrating that militarisation is a process where meanings and interpretations of sexual difference are manipulated and exploited. "That there are [sexual] differences is undeniable; but what really matters, in terms of the effects on people's lives, is how those differences are interpreted and acted upon" (Zakewski 1995, 344). The significance of a gender analysis, therefore, derives not so much from 'adding' women as from reclaiming women's subjectivities in order to challenge the public-private dichotomies that construct militarisation as an exclusively institutional/masculine domain. Accordingly, while women's absence from dominant narratives on Kashmir must, as Suri rightly asserts, be redressed, the analytical task of gender is not merely to make women 'visible,' but to highlight the *political* salience of sexual difference in the context of militarisation in Kashmir. Remembering and reinscribing gender in the narrative on militarisation is therefore not only an empirical and theoretical obligation, but an act of resistance, of remembering and writing experiences that women are not supposed to have had.[5]

The following discussion is divided into three sections. The first section focuses on women's role in Kashmir's struggle for *azadi* which, I argue, remains hostage to a patriarchal politics. I describe how Kashmiri women's identification with, and participation in, the struggle for *azadi* is at odds with their marginalisation in formal politics—a contradiction which I ascribe to the gender politics underpinning the movement.

The second part focuses on the Indian state's counter-offensive in Kashmir—directed as much at Kashmiri men as at Kashmiri militants—highlighting the implications of this onslaught for Kashmiri women. I illustrate how Kashmir's landscape of dead, 'disappeared' or missing men deprives women of traditional male support and protection, a deprivation that heightens Kashmiri women's economic, social and sexual vulnerability. I subsequently focus on the appropriation of rape as a weapon of war by the military in Kashmir that raises crucial questions regarding state legitimacy and accountability. I then discuss what I call the cultural politics of gender underpinning militarisation in Kashmir, namely, the exploitation of social constructions of sexual difference within Kashmiri society, the instrumental use of gender by Kashmir's Islamist militancy, and the implications of both for Kashmiri women. I conclude by arguing that the gender dimensions of militarisation in Kashmir exemplify the illegitimacy of such a policy, and the need to re-imagine the idea of state and nation in ways that can prevent the killing, abuse and rape of citizens.

Azadi: a popular sentiment

> [Kashmiri] women have been killed in crossfire, shot in public demonstrations, blown up in grenade explosions or in shelling along the Line of Control and raped by security forces, by anti-government militants and by pro-government militants.
>
> *Rita Manchanda*

According to Manchanda, there are two narratives about women in the Kashmir conflict. The first derives from a human rights discourse where women figure as victims of direct (state) and indirect violence that transforms them into widows, half-widows of the disappeared, or bereaved mothers of lost sons and children. The second centres on the conventional patriarchal ideology of the Kashmiri struggle in which women symbolise the Grieving Mother, the Martyrs' Mother and the Raped Woman (2001, 43). The representation of Kashmiri women as victims rather than survivors does not correspond with women's subjective experience and removes them from the *political* canvas of militarisation. Militarisation in Kashmir is synonymous with a state of total war that is not confined to 'public' military-militant encounters or the extra-legal offensive against Kashmiri men; it breaches conventional civil-military spatial distinctions and permeates domestic 'private' spaces presumed to be beyond the realm of war/militarised conflict.

The first phase of militarisation during the early (1990–91) years of the popular mobilisation was most visible in the capital city of Srinagar. Among the thousands who marched in the streets of Srinagar were many women who were active participants during the most spontaneous phase of the struggle. Women's identification with the struggle drew them into a public sphere where they were at the forefront of mass protests and agitation. As a national daily reported:

> More and more Kashmiri Muslim women—mainly college and school students—are decrying the 'Indian occupation' of Jammu and Kashmir and alleged atrocities by security forces against local people. Thousands of them, in separate groups, poured onto streets in Srinagar on three days last week and clashed with police or made determined bids to march to the United Nations Military Observer's office seeking the world body's intervention to help solve the Kashmir dispute (*The Hindu* 1990).[6]

Kashmiri (Muslim) women's resistance assumed a cultural expression, with militants being the focus of public adulation. Rita Manchanda notes it thus:

> Women would break out into a *wanuwan*, the traditional Kashmiri song of celebration, intertwining couplets in praise of local *mujahids* (militants). Cutting across class, mothers, wives and daughters all came out to join the swelling processions which congregated nightly in the neighbourhood mosques. . . . It was an activism rooted in [women's] cultural role as mothers, wives and sisters. . . . Heavily swathed in burqas or in voluminous head-scarves, mothers, wives and daughters came pouring out into the streets, their voices joining those of the men in the cry for *azadi*. . . . In January 1990, every evening as dusk fell and rivers of people flowed through the streets towards the mosques, women were in the forefront, their voices excitedly shouting,

'*marde mujahid jag ab, vakt shahadat aya hai!*' (Oh, you holy fighters, rise and awake! The time of your martyrdom has come) (2001, 50–51).

Although this particular articulation centred on a (gendered) binary of sacrificing mothers and heroic sons, most women need not necessarily have had male kin affiliated to militant groups. Rather, women's support derived from their *political* solidarity for the movement for *azadi*.[7] G., a twenty-five year-old student at Government College for Women, Srinagar, recalled the mood of defiance that swept across the city in 1991:

> I was young then . . . I remember evenings walking with my parents in very large demonstrations. No one from my family was a militant or politician. My father is a teacher and my mother had a government job. Both my parents and members of my extended family, including female relatives, took part in public demonstrations. They felt India was discriminating against Kashmiri people . . . [and] supported the struggle for an independent Kashmir because we . . . suffered so much injustice . . . I remember walking [with my parents] as soldiers with rifles looked on.[8]

The movement for *azadi* had strong resonance amongst Kashmiri Muslim women and simultaneously afforded them an opportunity for political self-expression—an experience that was liberating. M. is a sixty-year-old senior teacher at Government College for Women, Srinagar, from an educated middle-class family, whose son was detained by the military without charge in Srinagar's notorious Papa 1 military camp in 1991. M. recalls the memory of mass protests during 1990–1991:

> We [women] participated in demonstrations for freedom and self-determination out of a sense of the great injustice and subordination of Kashmir's Muslims. The historical memory of injustice is strong and is enhanced by the present conflict. I belong to a generation where social norms and conventions were strong and women's participation in public life was low. The situation [militarisation] in Kashmir changed that, women have been drawn outside . . . into public roles. I walked with hundreds of women and men in 1990 during protests against the Indian government.

> There were . . . many women . . . in these demonstrations and a
> feeling of, what should I say . . . comradeship and camaraderie,
> a feeling that we were all there because of a shared vision for the
> future.[9]

But activism was not confined to public protest.[10] Beyond pitched
battles in the streets and warrens of Srinagar, women served as
couriers, provided militants with food and shelter and took care
of the injured.[11] In instances where a young man was picked up
by the military, women protested at security bunkers in order to
secure his release.[12] They acted as guards in the narrow alleyways
of the city, sounding an alert and blocking the advance of military
forces in order to allow militants to escape. Instances of women
using the burqa to smuggle arms and explosives to militants were
not uncommon, and it was women who organised food supply-
lines during the unprecedented curfew of over six months in 1991,
when it was too risky and dangerous for men to go out.[13]

   Z. is a forty-nine year-old lower middle-class housewife in
Srinagar's crowded downtown area. She is a high-school graduate
who could not pursue further education due to marriage, financial
constraints and the preoccupations of raising a family. Z. is joined
by P., a forty-six year old neighbour and maternal cousin from a
similar background, who lives a few houses down the block. P. is
a graduate and primary school teacher. In a conversation about
their lives and opinions regarding the struggle, Z. and P. share
their memory of women's activism during the early 1990s.
For Z., the identification with, and support for, the political
struggle for *azadi* was inextricable from the struggle to protect
her family:

> I want to begin by saying that this struggle was not as it is today
> . . . it has changed a lot. In the beginning, in 1990–1991, women
> participated in public protests against the Indian government.
> The arrival of security forces however, was catastrophic and
> synonymous with large-scale arrests and detention of men, verbal
> and physical humiliation of women. . . . We were crushed under
> overwhelming force . . . and scared at what was happening. We
> were tossed into a war on all fronts. . . . The struggle against
> injustice in Kashmir is also a struggle to protect ourselves, our
> homes, our sons and husbands, our families, safeguard our honour

and dignity . . . this is no ordinary war, we are still protesting injustice while trying to keep together.[14]

P.'s compulsions for resistance were, like Z.'s, political and personal:

> The first time I protested was when my husband was imprisoned in 1990, when the troubles started. I had to cope with my job and I had three small children with no support at home. . . . I have supported the demand for *azadi* ever since that year because for me, my husband's arrest was not a result of any wrong-doing on his part but the Indian government's refusal to respect Kashmiri people. I joined public protests out of a sense of duty towards my husband and obligation to all those who were facing injustice. . . . We would cook and send food and messages for men in jail, provide moral support and information about what was happening. . . . If we came to know of a crackdown beforehand, we would warn men and arrange with friends and family to shift them to a safer zone. . . . We comforted and supported women and families whose husbands and sons were taken away or had disappeared.[15]

Z. and P. are not affiliated to any political group. Their engagement with the movement for *azadi* derives from their own understanding and lived experience of the situation that testifies to not just a keen political understanding of the crisis, but their multiple roles within it. Indeed, it was these multiple roles that preserved family and community, and greatly facilitated the general resistance against state hegemony. As Manchanda notes, "Women faltering in the support of the struggle would have seriously crippled the movement" (2001, 52).

Women's public roles merged with their traditional domestic roles as the latter became politicised in the effort to protect and preserve the family against formidable counter-offensives by the state. Vijayan M.J., a human rights activist associated with a civil society group in Srinagar, described it thus:

> A serious crisis developed post-1991. Any man between the ages of 15–70 years was considered a militant . . . many a time women escaped this stereotyping. Women had to run the family. Most of the men had to go underground . . . especially in areas like

Pahalgam where virtually all men were living in the forest. This was in a place like Pahalgam which is a renowed tourist resort. . . . Women's participation in public protests is interesting not only because they do this in order to save the male members of their family . . . but also, of late, have started playing the family-running role. . . . So this is also one of the reasons why they come to the forefront of a demonstration. . . . They are now involved with families . . . the realities of families. . . . More than half the time you are living without the man in the house.[16]

Militarisation created a situation where the management of survival and women's domestic roles became politicised,[17] yet there is little public acknowledgement of their role. C., a thirty-one year-old (male) supporter of *azadi* attributed this to the public-private dichotomy[18] and cultural constructs of gender:

The movement for *azadi* has the support of women, it has the support of women in my family. Women's participation in the struggle surpassed expectations. We could not have done without it. . . . But women cannot expect similar roles and positions as men. It for men to fight battles and women to support them . . . this [Kashmir] is a traditional society, women are educated [and] and have professions, we are not against that but, in a traditional culture such as ours, women's place is primarily within the home and family.[19]

While the attempt to retain combat as a fundamental and decisive marker of the public-private dichotomy is not unique to Kashmir, its significance relates to the unstated, albeit manifest, reluctance of Kashmiri men to accept women as *political* equals. C.'s views are a pointer to the fact that Kashmir's secular and relatively liberal social ethos is imbued with a distinct patriarchal attitude, resistant to the idea of women's equality. Its benign patriarchy secures compliance by restricting women's agency; an implicit, albeit omnipresent, threat of potential social censure inhibits women from initiating individual/group action. As Nusrat Andrabi, former Principal of Srinagar's Government College for Women, reflected:

It is a situation of [a] male–dominated society for centuries and the same is applicable here. We have women in law, education and medicine . . . [yet] women don't get mobilised here. . . . I myself tried to analyse this. We have no self-help groups. We don't have women's political parties, women's social groups . . . or groups for women's literacy, helping women. . . . I don't know whether it is the continuous insecurity and uncertainty of the political environment, or this political scenario. What it is, I can't understand. . . . It is not oppression, but the fear of social censure.[20]

Kashmir's social conservatism has been reinforced by militarisation. In a public interview, Mehbooba Mufti of the People's Democratic Party (PDP), acknowledged the marginalisation of women in contemporary politics where, according to her:

The barriers to women's participation have become almost insurmountable today. Very few Kashmiri Muslim women have permission from their families to join politics. To go and meet all kinds of people—militants and security forces included—without protection is unimaginable for them. As for the active women among the Kashmiri Pandits, they have either fled to Jammu or Delhi or are practically invisible (Chopra 2002).

It is in this context that we must situate women's absence within the echelons of Kashmir's militant factions. None of the militant organisations has women in their respective executive bodies.[21] Upon being asked about this absence in Kashmiri politics, Javed Ahmed Mir, ex-Vice President of the JKLF maintained: "Women aren't sure what they want. They do not have clear ideas" (Ramachandran 2003c, 36).

A notable exception to the trend is the Muslim Khawateen-e-Markaz (MKM), an all women's group that joined the movement for *azadi* after the Gowkadal massacre.[22] The MKM has members in Kashmir's six districts, with a main office in Srinagar. It is the only women's group that is a constituent of the Hurriyat Conference (an umbrella of Kashmiri political parties and militant factions) and is aligned with Ali Shah Geelani's Jama'at-e-Islami party. The MKM undertakes humanitarian and human rights work across Kashmir. In 2004, MKM's President, Anjum Zamrood, was under state detention.[23] Her absence, according to the organisation's Vice President, Yasmeen Raja, curtails MKM's political activism, particularly with regard to its investigations of sexual abuse against women in remote rural areas. In a conversation about MKM and its activities, Yasmeen Raja reiterated her own, and MKM's, frustration at the prohibitive political restrictions in force in Kashmir, that thwart the organisation's efforts at raising public awareness regarding state violence against women:

> We try to make women's voices and experiences visible. We talk about human rights . . . and seek to highlight cases of human rights violations against women. . . . We receive a lot of cases of violations against women . . . they are heartrending. . . . We would like to go from door to door but we lack the energy and resources to do so. . . . It is difficult for us to travel for work because the police restricts our travel. Yet, we travel by horse-cart, truck and bus to reach our destination. We sometimes manage to stage a protest for ten minutes before we are arrested. We work mainly in the villages. Kunan Poshpora, Chhanpora, Rangret. . . . As soon as we hear of a case we go there and try to raise the issue in public. However, there is no space for freedom of expression here in Kashmir, for as soon as we step out to do so we are arrested. They don't even care to read what is written on our banners as they are more concerned with stifling our protest. The police bundle us into vans and we are driven away. That is how our protests end. It is frustrating and disheartening. Sometimes I feel our only crime is to be Kashmiri.[24]

In a passionate and moving monologue, Masooda, a 32 year-old member of the MKM from the city of Pampore, testified not just to the catastrophic aftermath of militarisation for her and her immediate family, but also its spectacular failure in creating 'Indians' out of Kashmiris:

> I am an educated woman, a post-graduate. I lost my husband who was an advocate. He was 32 years old. He was killed by renegades of the 17th regiment under the command of one Punya. . . . The regiment that raided my house was under orders of the army. When his body was returned, his face was missing. . . . I went insane when I saw my husband's disembodied corpse.

They went into my house and killed my husband with an axe in front of my children. . . . Why do this in front of my children? What crime had they committed? Can you imagine what my children went through? . . . The Superintendent of Police said they would arrest the men, but that never happened. . . . Since then, I have been asking the government: *kya yahi hai aina-e-hind* [does this mirror the face of India]? Is this what your [Indian] government is all about? . . . As long as I have strength, I shall go on fighting the case. . . . We are not Indian, we are in favour of independence . . . we have an abiding hatred of the Indian occupation.[25]

The MKM claims that there are hundreds of cases of rape or sexual abuse by the military, and in 2004 the organisation was working on 75 cases. When asked about its affiliation with Syed Ali Shah Geelani,[26] a projected 'hardliner' in establishment circles, its Vice President stated: "We have favoured Geelani Saheb, but in case he makes an error we shall refute him and hold him accountable . . . the future of Kashmir rests with us, the people."[27] The interaction with women of the MKM in their office took place in a cordial atmosphere; its members reasonable and composed in the face of the violence and humiliation they have experienced and described.

Women's political activism, however, remains secluded from mainstream politics. The Jama'at-e-Islami, some of whose members support Kashmir's accession to Pakistan, has what it calls female "close sympathisers" and supporters, but no woman is part of its central executive council (*majlis-e-shura*).[28] The record of Kashmir's secular parties is no different. The political acumen of Shabnam Lone (daughter of the slain People's Conference leader, Abdul Ghani Lone, and a lawyer by profession) makes her eminently placed to lead her father's party, yet it was eventually her brothers who inherited its reins.[29] Mehbooba Mufti is an articulate President of the People's Democratic Party, yet her position derives more from her father's political eminence than from any real opportunity afforded by Kashmir's political class to Kashmiri women. In the absence of female politicians, women's concerns and aspirations remain hostage to a male-dominated Kashmiri polity and a patriarchal militant leadership for whom gender is secondary[30]—a relegation that has obscured but not obliterated the concerns of Kashmiri women.

Women's general support for the struggle is infused with scepticism and anxiety regarding the movement's position on women. J., a lecturer from the University of Kashmir, on condition of strict anonymity, voiced the contradiction between Kashmiri women's support for *azadi* and its political implications for them:

> Women were expected to and did support the demand and movement for *azadi* but even as we did so, it was clear that the social hierarchies were still very much in place. . . . With few exceptions, militant groups are silent or not taking a clear position on issues concerning women—particularly the views of Islamist militants. . . . I am not talking about violence here, but silence. What does it suggest?[31]

J.'s point regarding men's silence was echoed by Mehbooba Mufti of the People's Democratic Party. In a more pointed reference to the gender politics underpinning the *azadi* movement, Mufti castigated the silence of Kashmiri men in the wake of a campaign for a dress code for Kashmiri women—a silence that not only implicated Kashmir's male-dominated political parties and militant groups, but also Kashmiri society:

> When something tragic happens to men, women come out. In Haigam,[32] women faced bullets and two of them were killed while protesting against security forces. But now, when such a tragedy [campaign to enforce a dress code] has struck women, our menfolk are silent. Society should not treat this merely as a women's issue.[33]

The contradiction between women's involvement in the mobilisation for *azadi* on the one hand, and their political marginalisation on the other, is a painful one. Much like their lack of public concern regarding women's marginalisation from contemporary politics in Kashmir, Kashmir's male politicians and militant leaders, as well as Kashmir's society, remain largely indifferent to the fate of female survivors of indirect violence by the state.

A world of widows

As the counter-offensive of the state targeted the social base of the movement, namely, Kashmir's civilians, the people felt powerless in the face of the assault mounted by security forces who were no longer hounding militants, but looking upon the entire Kashmiri people as enemies.[34] Victoria Schofield quotes Jagmohan, Kashmir's Governor in 1990: "Every Muslim in Kashmir is a militant. . . . All of them are for secession from India. . . . The bullet is the only solution for Kashmir" (2004, 154). In 1996, any (male) Kashmiri found without an identity card was liable to be dragged to a military interrogation centre to prove he was not a Pakistani or Afghan militant—or become one more 'infiltrator' killed in a shoot-out while trying to cross the border.[35] A resident of Batamaloo, Srinagar, told an independent citizens' delegation that young boys and men were routinely taken away and subsequently charged with being terrorists.[36] According to an independent estimate in 2001, approximately 30,000 men had been killed, with approximately 4,000 believed to have 'disappeared' or in illegal detention.[37]

According to the Association of the Parents of the Disappeared, in 2000 there were approximately 20,000 widows in Kashmir and at least 1,000 half-widows whose husbands have 'disappeared' with no trace of their whereabouts or existence.[38] Kashmir's landscape is dotted with hamlets and villages of widows; like Sheikh Mohalla, Ganderbal, a ten-family strong hamlet with 11 widows, 30 orphans and just three men.[39] Or Dardpora, a village in north Kashmir, that has lost over a hundred young men and is home to 122 widows and almost 300 orphans.[40]

The prolonged, often permanent, absence of male family members is particularly detrimental for women from weaker socio-economic backgrounds, where the absence of male kin has severe economic implications. It has been argued that the lower-middle class was more directly involved in the public mobilisation for *azadi* and therefore subject to greater repression by the state.[41] For this reason, but also despite it, women from economically weaker backgrounds are particularly vulnerable to, and influenced by, the state offensive against Kashmiri men.

It has been eight years since K.'s husband, Mushtaq Ahmed

Khan, was taken into custody by the military in 1997. K. is 32 years old, illiterate and lives in a two-room dwelling with nine other members of her husband's family. According to her:

> It was 14 April, 1997, late at night. We were sleeping. . . . The soldiers knocked and pushed open this door and came in. . . . They took away my husband, Mushtaq. He was not a militant. There was no charge against him . . . he was simply taken away . . . I have no idea where he is or what happened to him. I have four children. I am staying with my in-laws but it is very hard, since there are ten of us in the family and we are surviving on just Rs. 1500 earned by my brother-in-law who works as a daily labourer. I have not received any compensation by the government. I do not have money and cannot afford the expense of repeated trips to government offices. For me this endless wait is killing. I feel my husband must be dead. I just want his dead body and official declaration of his death. . . . I also worry about the future of my children. I would like to work so I can afford to get them educated but I am not educated myself. I don't know how I can earn some money . . . [cries]. I don't know what will become of us. . . . It is good that I can stay here because I cannot go back to my own family. But I am not sure if my brother-in-law will continue to support me after he marries and has his own family . . . I don't know what lies ahead.[42]

The chances of half-widows remarrying are slim—especially if they are married to ex-militants. Like R., whose husband Merajuddin Dar, was picked up by a Border Security Force (BSF) vehicle in 1997. In a dimly lit room with bare floorboards, R. narrates her story:

> My husband was an ex-militant who gave up arms and ran a local grocery shop. In April 1997 he was taken into custody by members of the Border Security Force when they raided our home at night. They took him away in a BSF vehicle. . . . I am still waiting for my husband, though the military authorities deny taking him into custody. I live in my parent's place now. I cannot continue living with my husband's family. They already have a financial problem because there is little money to feed themselves as they are old and do not work. . . . Besides, I have had to leave

my children with my in-laws because I cannot afford to pay for their expenses myself nor can my own family. . . . I do not want to re-marry because of my children. What will happen to them if I do? I might lose my children. . . . I feel I should wait for my husband. . . . Maybe he will come back. . . . I went to the army to ask about my husband. . . . One officer threatened to arrest me. Since then, I feel insecure going out of the house. I am unable to decide what to do. . . . I have so many anxieties.[43]

Since their husbands have not been declared dead officially, half-widows are not entitled to ex-gratia payment by the state. Until 1997, they could not consider remarriage because of conflicting interpretations regarding the mandatory period of waiting under Muslim law.[44] The loss of a husband is compounded by fears regarding custody of children and/or desertion by in-laws. More corrosive still is the psychological price paid by broken families—constant agony and trans-generational trauma that, over time, can develop into mental disorders.[45]

The situation of widows and half-widows of militants is far worse because they are directly associated with violence through their husbands. Wives, mothers and sisters of militants are particular targets of harassment and face routine questioning and harassment from security forces. Nobody wants to be seen associating with militants' families.[46] Even for half-widows who have some means of employment, the future is fraught with multiple anxieties. Twenty-four year-old Q. is a secondary school graduate. Her husband was an auto-rickshaw driver who disappeared in 2000 while driving in Srinagar. Q. has no information about his whereabouts; she thinks he is dead even though his body has never been recovered. She works as a domestic help to make ends meet:

I earn some money but it is not enough. I have been trying to get compensation from the government but it is a cumbersome procedure. I do not have proof of my husband's death so my case is not very strong. There is little time for me to pursue this since I will then have to stop working which means I lose whatever income I have at present. I cannot afford to do that. I hope to earn enough money to send my child to school. I don't want to go back to my parent's house since they cannot afford to take care of me and my child. My husband's family is not in Srinagar so I cannot stay with them either. I have to face life alone.[47]

Employed half-widows like Q. are nevertheless better off than uneducated, unemployed widows in rural Kashmir for whom the loss of a husband can mean destitution.[48] A survey of five villages in Kashmir's Baramulla district in 2002 listed 8,000 pending applications for compensation.[49] This figure reflects the *scale* of the gendered fallout of the state's attempts to impose 'law and order' in Kashmir. The plight of Kashmir's widows and half-widows is not a 'women's' issue; it is inextricably linked to the enforced disappearance/detention and/or unlawful killing of men by the state. The lack of accountability regarding the 'disappeared' is further magnified by coercive repression in instances where citizens organise for public protest. As Parveena Ahanger, co-founder of the APDP, says:

> There were many innocents who happened to be children. They were lifted from their homes and schools, from shops. Their parents have been waiting for their children for years. Whenever we have tried to raise our voices for our missing children or demonstrate on the roads, soldiers and people in uniform have beaten and dragged us away to police stations and jails. . . . After I became a member of APDP the military came to inquire about my links with other organisations.[50]

With the ban on public gatherings firmly in place, it is not difficult for state authorities in Kashmir to stifle and thwart public protest by citizens like Parveena or, for that matter, by women from the Muslim Khawateen-e-Markaz. The issue of state accountability vis-à-vis Kashmir's widows has been largely ignored by the mainstream media.[51] In contrast to state apathy and indifference towards widows in Kashmir, fear of a public exposé *outside* Kashmir prompts swift and effective intervention by the state. In 2006, a video documentary "Waiting," depicting the ordeal of Kashmiri women whose husbands have disappeared in the custody of troops, was denied a certificate for screening by the Central Board of Film Certification at the Mumbai International Film Festival. The film's producer-director, Atul

Gupta, and co-director, Shabnam Ara, underlined official (and civil) hostility to the film: "We were threatened and pushed around by military authorities and faced hostile crowds who were suspicious of us."[52] In their letter of protest, film-makers and festival delegates wrote to the Union Minister for Information and Broadcasting: "The issue of the half-widows will not disappear by suppressing the freedom of expression and flow of information which is the cornerstone of any democratic society," they said.[53] The state's unwillingness to countenance public debate regarding Kashmir's widows is symptomatic of the profound lack of public accountability that also, simultaneously, places Kashmiri women beyond the pale of the official War Story. In Kashmir's conservative society, moreover, the absence of male presence and support renders widows vulnerable to social censure. Q., quoted earlier, spoke of her concerns and anxieties as a single woman:

> Although I am single in the sense that my husband is missing, I am judged by people and society as a married woman. People do not think well of me, they suspect what I may be doing. A single woman is vulnerable. . . . I have to go out and meet unknown people. . . . I have been trying to learn how to file an FIR on behalf of my missing husband which involves meeting people, including men [lawyers] whom I am not acquainted with. . . . I had to go to the police and military authorities for information regarding my [missing] husband. I felt terrified when I did because I was afraid that my neighbours and acquaintances may think I am an informer for the police or . . . military. . . . Some women have been killed for being informers. . . . I fear for my child. There is no trust among people and a lot of suspicion. I feel vulnerable, less confident in the absence of my husband.[54]

The social policing of widows induces its own set of anxieties. When Shobhana Sonpar, a clinical psychologist, asked widows in Kashmir "how their lives were different now, the tenor of their response was that they had to be much more careful *following* their widowhood, because they were now that much more likely to be the object of speculation and slander" (DasGupta 2000, 39, emphasis added). For others, the situation is even worse. Peerzada Ashiq describes the dark and depressing world of Shafiqa

Badiyari, a 24-year-old half-widow living in a one-room Srinagar shanty, for whom the sorrow and suffering of widowhood is exacerbated by the predatory advances of men:

> By day she works as a maid, and at night she resorts to the comforting numbness of sleeping pills. . . . The army picked up her husband four years ago and since then he has been missing. 'Goons come to me and offer money in return for sex', said Shafiqa, tears streaming down her cheeks (2004b).[55]

For many widows who wish to remarry there are no grooms, while extreme circumstances force others to turn to prostitution.[56]

Even as individual trauma and economic insecurity are the most immediate outcomes of widowhood, its social experience is mediated through a sequential gender bias. Widow remarriage, although permissible under Islamic law, is not always socially acceptable. Kashmiri society places a taboo on remarriage and widows are not acceptable as brides. According to a University of Kashmir study, 91 per cent of widows surveyed had not considered remarriage.[57] Widowhood also has a bearing on women's property rights in Kashmir. According to Muslim Personal Law, if the father-in-law of the widow is alive, neither she nor her children can claim any share in the family property.[58] Widows cite emotional stress, sexual harassment and social undesirability as their major social concerns; at a personal level, widows experience loneliness, physical insecurity and social pressures to remarry.[59] A sample survey of widows across Kashmir's six districts conducted by the University of Kashmir found that 86 per cent of widows were either employed or sustained by relatives, neighbours or NGOs.[60]

A matter of 'honour'

As the political impasse between the Indian state and the people of Kashmir escalated into an illegitimate war between the military and Kashmir's citizens, the distinction between combatants and non-combatants, ceased to exist. In effect, this meant that the state's counter-offensive was not confined to the streets of Srinagar, but extended into domestic spaces as well. The home ceased to be a sanctuary and refuge from violence, with women increasingly becoming specific targets of direct violence by the state. Rape by the military is a frequent occurrence in Kashmir; against the background of administrative and judicial paralysis, there is little reliable information or statistics regarding these offences. Yet, as AsiaWatch/Physicians for Human Rights note in their report:

> There are no reliable statistics on the number of rapes committed by security forces in Kashmir. Human Rights groups have documented many cases since 1990, but because many incidents have occurred in remote villages, it is impossible to confirm any precise number. *There can be no doubt that the use of rape is common and routinely goes unpunished* (*Rape in Kashmir* 1993, 3, emphasis added).

In 1990, Sukhmani Singh investigated sexual violence against women "by the keepers of law and order—the Indian army and security forces stationed in the Valley . . . to curb the . . . terrorist menace" (1990, 33). According to her: "While villages in the interior have witnessed the highest number of rapes, those [in cities] have not been spared either" (1990, 34).[61] Singh asked Kashmir's Director General of Police (DGP) J.N. Saksena to explain the incidence of rape in Kashmir. According to the DGP:

> All these allegations were made two days after the incidents occurred. Nobody came forward at that time. In addition, a large number of senior officers were present that day, so it was not possible that so many rapes had taken place (1990, 35).

Saksena's implication that rape victims report to the very authorities who raped them is ironic, as is his suggestion that the presence of senior officers is an effective deterrent against rape.[62] His denial is not based on evidence, even as it impugns the integrity of its victims. Most tellingly, however, DGP Saksena confirms the use of rape as a proxy weapon of war against 'terrorists'. When asked by Sukhmani Singh: "Why is it that the maximum number of rapes have taken place in Kupwara?" (district), Saksena responded: "Because it is a badly infested terrorist area" (1990, 34). The use of rape as not just an individual, but a form of *collective* punishment effectively dismantles the official War Story; its use as a weapon of war challenges the notion of sexual abuse of women as a *side-effect* of militarisation and underlines the fact that such violence is used to serve *political* ends. The sexual appropriation of Kashmiri Muslim women by the military functions not just as an especially potent *political* weapon, but also as a *cultural* weapon to inflict collective 'dishonour' on Muslim Kashmiri men. In short, rape by security forces in Kashmir is neither incidental nor 'private' but a weapon to punish, intimidate, coerce, humiliate and degrade.[63]

Mainstream narratives of war/militarised conflict are premised on a gendered division of power and labour based on the male (public) space of combat and the female (private) space of home. "War," as Zalewski explains, "is perhaps the arena where division of labour along gender lines has been the most obvious, and thus where sexual difference has seemed the most absolute and natural" (1995, 350). Official acknowledgement of the (illegitimate) sexual violence would not only dismantle these gendered dichotomies; it would thoroughly undermine state authority and legitimacy in Kashmir. Rape here by state forces "*is not a privately-motivated form of . . . abuse . . . but an abuse of power that implicates public responsibility*" (*Rape in Kashmir* 1993, 5 emphasis added). The *political* stakes to keep women *beyond* the pale of the War Story in Kashmir are therefore, exceedingly high; the case of Kunan Poshpora reveals exactly how high they are.

Kunan Poshpora was raided on the night on 23–24 February 1991, during counter-insurgency operations led by soldiers of the 4th Rajput Rifles. According to Amnesty International:

> Reports suggest that hundreds of soldiers, many of whom were drunk, arrived at the village around 11 p.m. The men were taken from their houses and tortured during the night and interrogated about Kashmiri militant activity while large numbers of women, reportedly between aged between 13 and 80 years old, were raped at gunpoint. The incident came to light through a letter dated 7 March 1991 (No.conf/1956–61) from the local magistrate, S.M. Yasin, to the State Commissioner of Kashmir, Wajahat Habibullah. The local magistrate confirmed the allegations after he visited the village on 5 March. He stated that, 'The armed forces had turned violent and behaved like beasts' (Amnesty International Press Release UA 108/91, 1991).

Three months after the actual incident of mass rape in Kunan Poshpora, a one-man Press Council of India team that visited the village (for three hours) declared that women's testimonies, in lieu of the charge of rape by soldiers of the 4th Rajputana Rifles, were "baseless," and deemed supportive medical evidence as "worthless". Its report concluded that charges against the army constituted "a massive hoax orchestrated by militant groups and their sympathisers and mentors in Kashmir and abroad . . . for reinscribing Kashmir on the international agenda as a human rights issue" (*Rape in Kashmir* 1993, 8). Official denials mask, rather than absolve, the culpability of the military. As Shiraz Sidhva maintained, "From its report it is evident that the Press Council team visited Kunan Poshpora with the intention of absolving the army—it is clear that the victims were invariably suspected of lying and exaggerating. They probably did exaggerate, but that is not the same thing as saying that nothing happened" (1991a, 39).

In 1993, Lt. General D.S.R. Sahni, General Officer Commanding, Northern Command, was asked to answer charges of rape by his forces. In his response, he asserted: "A soldier conducting an operation at the dead of night is unlikely to think of rape when he is not even certain he shall return alive" (*Rape in Kashmir* 1993, 17). Twelve years later, the policy of official denial and rebuttal remained unchanged. When questioned about allegations of rape in 2005, Lt.Col.V.K. Batra, Public Relations Officer (Defence), 15 Corps HQ, Srinagar, claimed that they were "largely propaganda with 98 per cent of the cases having fallen through". Upon being asked his opinion regarding those cases where rape had been conclusively established, he sought to trivialise the gravity of the crime by claiming that "rape in Kashmir had lost its social stigma".[64] When I asked him about the incidence of prostitution involving members of the Indian Army, he offered a novel explanation; according to him "since Kashmiri men have become psychotic after cordon-and-search operations and cannot perform, women have to seek satisfaction elsewhere".[65] Col V. at the Indian army's Srinagar Headquarters, was more circumspect. According to him, rape and violence against women are a result of the fact that "our soldiers operate under very stressful conditions".[66] He did not elaborate on the connection between the demands of curbing 'militancy', and the sexual abuse of

Kashmiri Muslim women. As Asia Watch and Physicians for Human Rights note in their report, the Indian authorities are far more interested in shielding government forces from charges of abuse than in the integrity of the investigation.[67]

Rape and its attendant politics of 'honour' implicate state authorities that seek to suppress, discredit or publicly deny sexual violence against Kashmiri Muslim women. Among others, allegations of rape at Chhanpora and Pazipora (1990), Kunan Poshpora (1991), Chak Saidpora (1992), Haran (1992), Theno Budapathary Kangan (1994) and Wavoosa in Srinagar (1997) were neither officially acknowledged nor investigated, primarily because the offence is seldom registered by the local police. For instance, in 1990, in Pazipora, a Station House Officer (SHO) who recorded statements and registered the cases of eight rape victims under Section 376 of the Criminal Procedure Code, came under tremendous pressure from the Superintendent of Police (SP) and the army to close the cases.[68] The trend was corroborated by Vardarjan in his report on Kashmir where he noted that,

> Incidents of sexual assault and rape go un-investigated and unpunished because of pressure exerted by military authorities on the local police not to file a First Information Report on behalf of rape victims (1993, 6).

Backed by legislative decree and shielded from public scrutiny or accountability, denial turns into defiance. In 2001, in their testimony to a citizens' team, three women from Bihota, a village in southern Kashmir, testified that they were raped and then taunted by soldiers of the Rashtriya Rifles: "Where are your human rights protectors? They have gone and nobody can now protect you from us" (*Grim Realities* 2001, 62).[69]

Rape exploits cultural constructions of 'honour'[70] based on the control of female sexuality and strict adherence to norms of virginity and chastity. By violating the 'honour' of women, the military displaces and appropriates the male authority that had hitherto defined and determined this 'honour' to inflict *collective* 'dishonour' (read defeat) on 'the other'/enemy. While rape and sexual abuse of women is frequently used as rhetoric by militant groups, it is rare for individual militants to divulge their own thoughts about it. In a long and profoundly moving monologue, N—an ex-militant of the JKLF—spoke of his anguish at Kashmir's tragedy and, in particular, the humiliation of Kashmiri men through the sexual subjugation of women by the military:

> We have no tears left, they have dried. . . . It is not possible for me to capture in words what has happened to us as a people . . . what we feel. . . The military offensive has crushed us and inflicted great suffering on the people. For me, it is not fighting and dying for the cause that is daunting as it is based on the idea of freedom . . . it is part of the struggle for freedom. I am not afraid of fighting or even death . . . But when the military use women to humiliate us and the family and the community, it is not possible for me, or for any of us to bear this denigration . . . Soldiers rifle through young women's rooms, take out their clothes and taunt their brothers and fathers . . . we can only watch and do nothing. There are among us those who took up arms, who subsequently heard of their sisters' detention at military camps. That is enough to break anyone. It is easy to pick up the gun as the desire for freedom runs deep and strong within . . . yet it is very difficult, almost impossible, against the risk and danger of sexual retaliation at women. I cannot fight if my sister is humiliated or raped . . . [long pause]. . . . I have not spoken of this to anyone. I share this with you only. . . .[71]

Kashmir's militant movement may have successfully challenged the Indian state's monopoly over violence, yet the challenge to monopolised violence wanes in the face of militarily-backed patriarchal violence by the state.

The rape of women in Kunan Poshpora was a powerful, symbolic defeat for the men of the village; yet, the sequential logic and politics of 'honour' transcends its perpetrators to rebound with cruel irony on its survivors. The men of Kunan Poshpora lament the fate that befell their women; yet, when asked whether they would marry women from another village where women had been raped, they were categorical in their refusal; they would not marry anyone from the "village of raped women". As one of Kunan Poshpora's young men said: "*Yeh to izzat ka sawaal hai*"—it was, after all, a matter of 'honour' (Ramachandran 2003, 20). For the women of Kunan Poshpora, the social backlash since 1991 has been relentless. Three years after the incident, no marriage had taken place in the village. All young women, raped or not, were single; all married women who were raped had been deserted. Two husbands did take their wives back, one on the condition that have no conjugal relations; the other that he live in the city away from his wife.[72] For women from underprivileged backgrounds the physical violence and trauma of sexual abuse, together with the stranglehold of 'honour' can become a virtual prison without reprieve. Young and beautiful O., whose house was raided by the military in July 1999, narrated her story in a small, dingy room in Srinagar:

> One night in July 1999 30 vehicles drew up to my house. This house was raided by security forces who were accompanied by members of the Special Operations Group with them. My father and brother were beaten and kept upstairs. Alleging that I and my mother were harbouring militants, both of us were subject to beatings by the military. I was manhandled, administered electric shocks and had my nails prised out [holds out her scarred hands and points to the electric sockets that were used for this purpose]. Subsequently, they brought buckets of cold water and held my head under it to prevent me from breathing. Our physical torture lasted till 3 a.m. The military tried to drag me to their camp but were foiled by women from the neighbourhood who raised an alarm. Since that night of torture and abuse, I have developed a heart and lung ailment and had to undergo costly treatment that we can ill-afford.[73]

But it was when O. wanted to get married that her agony resurfaced:

> Whenever I received a proposal of marriage, the neighbours would inform people who came with the proposal that the military had visited my house. These people in turn would speculate about the nature and timing of my torture and the fact that I was alone with ten to fifteen military personnel in the middle of the night and had been tortured by security forces. Others felt apprehensive, fearing similar treatment at the hands of the military if I married into their family. As a daughter-in-law, they feared I could be subject to further physical abuse by the military that would be

> very humiliating and dishonourable for my husband and his family.
> None of the men considered me worthy of marriage. Now I
> have passed the age of marriage.[74]

She ended up marrying a 60 year-old man, a marriage that turned
out to be disastrous—she is only 27 years old.

> I felt this was a grave injustice and subsequently returned home
> after some time. Now that relationship is over. Thoughts of suicide
> crossed my mind. I read the Qur'an which eventually saved me.
> I finally took a loan to pay my husband Rs. 50,000 and end my
> marriage.[75]

O. had wanted to file a FIR against the military but was
advised against doing so by three (male) militant leaders[76] because,
according to them, "she would face a social problem". The 'social
problem' would be O.'s presence at a military court to testify
against her tormentors—a step which would erode her integrity
further and make her the guilty party. In the absence of male
protection and fearful of the impunity accorded to the military,
O. chose not to undertake legal action against it. After public
outrage had died down, the security forces asked O. not to reveal
what had been done to her. In return they offered her a job. The
Deputy Commissioner visited O.'s house to reiterate the demand
of the security forces. O. declined the offer of a job, but could
not escape the social price demanded from female victims of sexual
abuse:

> I have become an untouchable . . . I do not step out of my house
> for fear of being identified as the woman who was physically
> tortured by the military . . . I don't want to look out of the
> window. . . . This [she whispered amidst tears] is like a prison
> for me.[77]

For women like 40 year-old F., a husband's absence is not
only synonymous with economic hardship and vulnerability; it is
a source of deep anxiety at potential sexual exploitation by the
military. F.'s husband is serving a life sentence in Delhi's Tihar
Jail although she says he has never had a criminal record against
him. Ill health and his prolonged absence pushed her and her
four daughters close to destitution. F. initially took refuge in a

house abandoned by a Pandit family, now she lives in a small tenement on a modest allowance provided by neighbours and well-wishers.

> For three years I was in a very difficult situation. But with the grace of God, we have survived . . . I am wary of the security forces here. . . . Initially BSF and CRPF personnel came very frequently but now their visits are not so frequent. Last time they enquired about my husband. . . . To protect my honour and the honour of my innocent children, I do not reveal that my husband is in jail. Instead, I say he is a wage labourer who has gone to find work. I never divulge the absence of my husband. If they come to know my husband is in jail they might come up with an allegation against me and take me in detention. And then who knows what they might do with my daughters? I have to do this just for the sake of honour, to protect the honour of my daughters.[78]

While it is not possible to quantify the scale of sexual abuse against women by state forces, there is little doubt that it is widespread. In Shopian for instance, in 2003, college girls were molested in broad daylight by security forces, prompting huge demonstrations during which police used tear gas to dispel the protestors.[79] Young girls going to school, collecting firewood or grazing sheep and goats, alone, in the border areas, are routinely sexually harassed.[80] State authorities, however, have sought to deny or downplay such violence. In August 1997, during a visit to the Valley, the chairperson of the National Commission of Women (NCW),[81] Mohini Giri, requested to meet victims of rape and other excesses by state forces, a request that was turned down, with state official Sushma Chowdhry asserting that no incidents of rape had taken place in Kashmir.[82] Military authorities have attempted to mask the violence and brutality of rape by using the term 'misconduct'[83] to describe all such violations. In 2004, an army major accused of raping a woman and her ten year-old daughter in Badar Payein, Handwara, was dismissed from service on account of 'misconduct'. Rape victims who file complaints against soldiers are discredited by military authorities,[84] even as it has used women as informants and as tools to advance its own propaganda.[85] Moreover, violence against women by *militants* has provided a fillip to the propaganda machinery of the military that issues press briefings and releases about the alleged immoral deeds of the *jihadis*; this in turn, serves to justify its own abuse of power against civilians.[86]

A trend that has been reported with increasing frequency since 1991 is that of rape and sexual abuse by militant groups. Both Pandit[87] and Muslim[88] women have been sexually targeted by militants, albeit for different reasons. Rape and sexual abuse of Pandit women is a replay of the politics of honour; their sexual appropriation by Muslim militants a means to inflict individual and collective dishonour and humiliation; and to assert patriarchal power and hegemony in the Valley.[89] Militants have abducted Muslim women and handed them over to a militant leader, leading inevitably to further abuse. In local parlance, these 'abductions' are referred to as forced marriages, highlighting the social ostracism suffered by rape victims, and the code of silence and fear that prevents women and people from openly condemning such abuses.[90] The incidence of women being branded informers and killed by militants has registered a marked increase,[91] especially in the districts of Doda, Rajouri and Poonch.[92] In the face of abject poverty and destitution, becoming *mukhbirs* (informers) is a means of survival for women. Generally speaking, both the military and militants prey upon and exploit the tragedy, sorrow and vulnerabilities of Kashmiri women to advance their respective political agendas.[93]

The cultural politics of militarisation

In a monograph written during his imprisonment JKLF chief, Yasin Malik, acknowledged that "women are raped, physically abused, manhandled, tortured and humiliated". These "innocent women", according to Malik, were victims of Indian military forces that condemn them to "lifelong torture and stigma" (1994, 4); that this 'torture and stigma' is also inflicted by Kashmiri society is an issue that Yasin Malik fails to address. In 2004, in the wake of public outrage against the alleged torture of a teenage girl in Handwara, People's Conference leader, Sajjad Lone, declared in an emotion-laden speech that his party would obtain justice for the victim. After public protests died down, the victim was accused of collusion with the authorities, ostracised and asked by villagers to leave the village.[94] Finding local sources and structures of support is almost impossible. As Afsana Rashid notes:

> It [rape] is related to honour and dignity that should not be there. . . . They are left to fend [for themselves]. There is a small percentage of families who support their daughters in such cases. But . . . in-laws do not accept them. . . . Such victims are unacceptable to society and they are treated more or less as prostitutes. Society never forgives them . . . on the contrary they are victimised by both family and society. . . Incidents of rape mostly get politicised . . . that time many people visit the affected person or the family and sympathise but that is all a momentary phenomena . . . but finally everything ends . . . they are left to suffer. . . . Outside the Valley, rehabilitation centres and women's organisations come forward to help them to come out of the trauma. But here nobody is willing to help (2006).[95]

Kashmir's militant leaders have cashed in on public anger against rape by the military, yet their own patriarchal rhetoric does not in any way alter the social realities of rape survivors. The politics of rape in Kashmir illustrates women's instrumental relationship with the militant movement that has used militarisation's gendered contours to advance its own political agenda, but failed to publicly acknowledge women's contribution to the struggle and done little to affirm the dignity and self-worth of rape survivors.

Kashmir's conservative social context has been further masculinised in the wake of the attempt to crush the militant movement. The threat to women's physical and sexual integrity, the destruction of the traditional family structure, the pressures of economic survival that oblige women to breach traditional roles, and the rise of female-headed households have dismantled traditional sites of patriarchal control and precipitated reciprocal attempts by Kashmiri men to reassert their authority over women. Accordingly, even as Kashmir's gendered tragedy caused many women who were earlier restricted to traditional roles to seek employment, the flip side is the increase in patriarchal control over them and social regulations about how women should behave in public.[96] The permeation of Kashmir's secular struggle with an Islamist ideology has reinforced male domination.[97] Dr. Hameeda Bano, an academic at the University of Kashmir, Srinagar, spoke of the social policing of women, informed by a combination of patriarchal-masculinist dominance and Islamist obscurantism:

> I had so many fights with boys on the campus. I was the warden those days and they came into the hostel to ask girls to wear the burqa. I told them, they are properly clad, we shall not impose anything on them. And by the way, who are you, to sit and judge how people should dress? They said this was not Islamic. . . . Some people came to my house to ask me to request girls to wear the burqa. I told them, I know what the girls are wearing and that's decent enough. . . . Some boys with a gun came into the dining hall. I came out and asked them what they were doing. One of them said they saw a girl wearing a green dupatta talking to a boy. I asked them who gave them permission to enter the girls' hostel premises and police the girls. They replied they were looking for that girl. . . . I asked them to put down their gun. That boy was mad. Such people had guns. . . . I said they had no authority to police girls.[98]

In 1990, one of the smaller militant factions, the Allah Tigers, issued a diktat that women adhere to specific dress codes and refrain from entering beauty parlours. This was part and parcel of an 'Islamic' campaign that also targeted Srinagar's cinema halls and video libraries.[99] In the same year, leaflets were dropped over the walls of Srinagar's Government College for Women exhorting Muslim students and teachers to wear the burqa and Hindus, the bindi.[100] Neerja Mattoo, former teacher and ex-Principal of the college recalls:

> The gun had not yet been used to enforce it [the burqa] [but] when that happened, the scene in 1990 at the college re-opening after the winter break, was completely changed. There were hardly any Pandit students and the view was an unrelieved black, not figuratively, but literally. Almost all the girls were now covered in a burqa of that colour, only some out of religious conviction, most out of fear, which was palpable, rampant (2002, 168).

Srinagar's educated and student community was a constituency that refused to conform to the dress code and condemned its imposition.[101] H., a lecturer from the University of Kashmir, Srinagar, recalled her bitterness and anger at the time:

> Women are not just affected by physical violence, there are other forms of violence too. The dress code by the militants was an insult to our intelligence and dignity. I was opposed to it but it was difficult to voice dissent in the prevailing atmosphere. It made me wonder about the 'freedom' we were fighting for.[102]

The gender politics of militarisation in Kashmir must therefore be understood within the context of an overwhelming and repressive military presence that has reduced secular space on the one hand, and the articulation of a patriarchal resistance that has been overshadowed by its Islamist component, on the other.[103] An informal discussion with students in front of the University of Kashmir's Allama Iqbal Library exemplified this trend; students' anger and resentment at the devastation wrought by Indian hegemony in Kashmir was couched in Islamic terms. While appreciative of my sympathy for the suffering of Kashmir's people, they would not countenance criticism of doctrinaire Islam.[104]

Dr. Hameeda Bano, quoted earlier, recalled her opposition to, and resistance against, the dress code within the shrinking secular space in Kashmir:

> It has not been part of the movement to threaten women but some vested interest groups have come in. [Since] the very beginning, when this armed resistance started . . . there have been some militant groups who have threatened women. . . . The situation [was] very turbulent, all kinds of people with very different kinds of agendas [came in]. . . . Some groups found women to be easy targets. It was not only women; even cinemas were closed. All these things happened. Even today most cinemas lie closed. . . . Women also faced somewhat similar pressures. There was an attempt to enforce a dress code on women by some groups. But Kashmiri women are also very resilient. For a short time, in order to avoid these threats and save their lives, women did toe the line. But once they felt the threat had evaporated, they reverted back to their normal dress. . . . They said I could take off my burqa when I entered the class, but had

to wear it in public. . . . This logic [was] indefensible. That I take
off the burqa when I am in front of my students but others
should be banned from seeing my face. There was neither logic
nor law in this argument . . . I said you are totally wrong. . . . In
1992 and 1993 I used to use the chadar with the dupatta. I was
walking in the campus. There was a whole group of burqa-clad
women in front of me. Suddenly someone threw colour on me.
. . . I never did wear the *abaya* myself. I was scared, of course,
and every time you cannot afford to be defiant.[105]

A discussion with students at Srinagar's Government College
for Women echoed similar concerns regarding the Islamist edge
of militancy:

It was a time of fear and uncertainty. We faced harassment by
the military and felt threatened by the militancy. We were forced
to cover our heads with an *abaya* (scarf). Shirts were replaced
with shalwar-kameez. (Group Discussion)[106]

Upon conclusion of the above discussion, W., a teacher at the
same college, narrated her personal experience:

Green colour was thrown on me. I felt very indignant because I
was more than decently dressed and the colour was thrown by a
young girl. I rang up my brother who was in the Gulf. He sent
me a burqa. I wore it out of fear and self-respect for precisely
three days. Women successfully resisted this imposition.[107]

Women's reproductive freedoms became the subject of
militant decree. Dr. Bilqees Jamila, Head of the Department of
Gynaecology and Obstetrics at Srinagar's Lal Ded Hospital
confirmed that family planning and contraception was reduced
due to a diktat by the militants.[108] In her testimony to a women's
delegation, a senior head of department from the same hospital
recalled banners and leaflets opposing sterilisation and abortion
pasted all over the hospital's walls.[109]

Notwithstanding the daunting challenge posed by Islamists,
Kashmiri women resisted impositions that were inimical to
Kashmiri culture and tradition. In her presentation at a seminar
on women in Kashmir, Qurratul Ain, a Kashmiri schoolteacher,
summed up the significance of a refusal to succumb to social

customs alien to the Kashmiri way of life.[110] At the same seminar, there appeared to be a consensus among those who had witnessed the conflict themselves that the movement, or at least some vested interests within the movement, had tried to restrict the rights and freedoms enjoyed by the women of Kashmir.[111] Notwithstanding the enduring influence of militarisation's cultural politics, its socio-economic implications for Kashmiri women are no less significant.

Female education has been negatively influenced by a general destruction of the educational infrastructure and the occupation of schools by the military. Manchanda (2001, 72) cites a government survey that reflects increasing disparity between male and female dropout rates for school-going children.[112] The situation is further exacerbated by the threat of sexual harassment and abuse of minor students by the military.[113] College students narrate a similar experience; the threat of sexual violence by the military influences the educational advancement of women; female college students are known to forego their studies and consider early marriage[114]—a trend confirmed by N., a JKLF ex-militant (quoted earlier), which he said was not due to social prejudice against female education, but parental fears regarding the safety and sexual integrity of their daughters:

> Due to the fear of sexual molestation and harassment parents are anxious to get daughters married. This is not because they wish to get rid of their daughters but due to a pervasive air of tension and anxiety regarding young women's sexual integrity in a context where women are targets of military forces.[115]

For other women—particularly in urban areas—the average age at marriage has gone up. According to one of Srinagar's leading psychologists, the rise in the average age at marriage from 28 to 38 years has an adverse impact on women that is reflected in the rising incidence of female depression, mental disorders and suicides.[116] The violence of militarisation is particularly devastating for women who are known to constitute a high-risk group as far as trauma is concerned; the disappearance or death of a loved one worsens an already terrible situation.[117]

Individual fears and anxiety do not always flow from direct violence but from an environment of uncertainty and anxiety. As

I., a student at Srinagar's Government College for Women confided:

> I am not a religious person, I never used to pray. Yet now I do so five times a day because I fear the future. . . . Life is so uncertain. I could die tomorrow and then there shall be no chance for me to do what I do now.[118]

Other students at the college described how religion has been transformed into a psychological refuge in an environment of deep uncertainty and fear: "People have become more religious, with very young people going for the Haj pilgrimage" (Group Discussion 2004).[119] Religion helps individuals cope with personal trauma and tragedy; the mosque has turned into a safe refuge for men, while women visit shrines to deal with their distress.[120]

The new militancy

The second phase of the militancy coincided with the decline of the JKLF and the rise of its principal adversary, the Hizbul Mujahideen (HM) in the mid-1990s. The predominance of the HM and other Islamist militant groups and their redefinition of Kashmiri identity in Islamic terms cannot be attributed *only* to HM's links with Pakistan; other factors, too, contributed towards the consolidation of Islamist influence in Kashmir. There is a close link between the HM and the Jama'at-e-Islami; indeed a great many of the Hizbul Mujahideen cadres are recruits from the latter.[121] Most Jama'at adherents are from Kashmir's educated middle and lower middle-class, who wish to purge and reform Kashmir's Sufi[122] Islam of what in their view are its un-Islamic practices. This factor, together with continued domination of Pandits at the local administrative level, the rise of militant Hindu nationalism in India, and Kashmir's economic crisis that rendered thousands of educated youth unemployed, combined to produce a situation wherein appeals to Islamic solidarity and authenticity fell on increasingly receptive ears.[123]

In addition to these internal factors, three external (Pakistan-based outfits) outfits—the Al Badar Mujahideen, the Harkat-ul Mujahideen (HUM) and Lashkar-e-Toiba (LeT) entered the fray by the mid-1990s. Of the three, the Al Badar Mujahideen had fought in Afghanistan against the Soviet Army as a faction of Gulbuddin Hekmatyar's Hizb-e-Islami, and operated solely in Kashmir. Al Badar members were highly educated young men, uncomfortable with madarsa recruits, whereas the HUM and LeT were offshoots of religious parties in Pakistan.[124] By 1993 these Pakistan-based bodies entered Kashmir as 'guest fighters', and by 1995 dominated all others except the Hizbul Mujahideen. Their commitment to doctrinaire Islam, their representation of Kashmir's struggle as an Islamic *jihad* against 'Hindu' India, and their hostility to women's rights exacerbated a socially conservative and repressive political context. It was against this backdrop that a women's organisation, the Dukhtaran-e-Millat (DM) or Daughters of the Faith, entered the political limelight to promote the burqa as a symbol of Kashmiri, or rather, 'Islamic' identity.

The DM was founded by Asiya Andrabi in 1987, a product of the reformist impulse within middle-class Kashmiri Muslims who perceive Islam in Kashmir to be corrupted by non-Islamic cults and practices. For this section of Kashmiris, Islam is a claim to cultural identity and a form of political assertion that, in its view, is compatible with the modern world. The DM perspective coincides with that of the Jama'at-e-Islami which argues for social reform based on what it considers to be authentic Islamic ideals. Like the Jama'at, the Dukhtaran-e-Millat thinks of Kashmir in pan-Islamic terms, dismissing Kashmir's Sufi traditions as 'alien' to Islam.[125]

In 1990, the DM gave a call for women to march to the United Nations office; it brought thousands of women out into Srinagar's city centre, where their peaceful demonstration was fired upon by the paramilitary battalions of the CRPF and BSF. Dukhtaran-e-Millat utilised the burqa as a means for clandestine operations that included carrying arms, acting as couriers for militants and functioning as decoys.[126] The DM's claim to fame however, derives from its forceful advocacy of the burqa for Kashmiri women, which propelled it into the political limelight.

Historically,[127] wearing the burqa was restricted to women from the elite (*sayyed*) class[128] who, due to reasons of status and class, practised various forms of veiling. For Asiya Andrabi however, the burqa is the beginning of an Islamic social reform movement that, according to her, was unimaginable during the early 1980s:

> To tell you the truth, if you came to Kashmir before 1981 you would not have seen anyone in a burqa. When I went to buy a burqa in 1981, the shopkeeper told me that now even old women don't wear it any longer so we no longer stock burqas in the shop. If you see the situation today, there are of course not 100 per cent women wearing the veil but I would say there are at least 35 per cent. . . Our movement has increasing support among Kashmiri women and a section of Kashmiri men. The movement is going well despite the fact that I have been underground for prolonged periods . . . if these restrictions were not there, we would have met with greater success.[129]

The DM's claim to success, however, seems tenuous in the face of public criticism and stiff resistance to the practice. Although Asiya admits that the Dukhtaran-e-Millat's burqa campaign has faded, she nevertheless maintains: "We don't care about public opinion or about the majority. This happens to be our stand."[130] Though the burqa is no longer being enforced in the streets of Srinagar, the campaign has nevertheless left a lasting social imprint; a group of college students in Srinagar explained its lingering influence thus:

> In the wake of pervasive violence and disruption of education, many young women—primarily from higher income groups—left the Valley to pursue studies elsewhere. For women from economically weaker sections there was no such option. Women from lower income groups did not have the option of leaving. They stayed on and became perceptibly conservative. Use of the headscarf and burqa increased (Group Discussion).[131]

The DM and its politics symbolise the exploitation of a deeply unpopular and increasingly violent military occupation by obscurantist social forces, such as the DM, that the occupation itself has either generated or reinforced. Unrepresentative groups like the Dukhtaran-e-Millat and Kashmir's Islamist militancy thrive in a climate of harsh repression to justify the notion of perpetual war. The link between both was captured in a remark made by Asiya Andrabi to a women's human rights team: "We thank the security forces for their excesses—the more atrocities they commit, the more people will be prepared to take up arms for the struggle" (Dewan, et al 1994, 13). Against the extraordinarily high levels of violence unleashed by a pervasive military presence, the pan-Islamist brigade transforms its greatest weakness—the lack of a popular constituency or mandate in Kashmir—into political advantage.

The motivations underlying the burqa campaign are primarily *political* and for this reason, must not be underestimated. They seek to arrest, if not reverse, all that has been achieved by women in modern Kashmir. Essentially, the DM seeks to undo over five decades of qualitative social change, due to which Kashmiri women in general achieved a fair degree of social and cultural mobility, thereby challenging the institutional structure of the traditional family and enhancing women's participation in public life.[132] The DM's hostility to women's rights exemplifies the dangers of Kashmir's pan-Islamic currents of resistance that are as authoritarian, undemocratic and patriarchal as the state they oppose.

From revolt to jehad: the struggle is corrupted

From 1995 onwards, Kashmir's struggle for *azadi* was overrun by an Islamist militancy that defined Kashmir's struggle in social and religious, rather than political, terms—an agenda that is completely divorced from the aspirations of its people. Bereft of any politics, except that of the gun, Islamist militancy indulges in acts of random, indiscriminate and criminal violence. While Islamist groups enjoy generous patronage from Pakistan, their influence in the Valley is not only a function of their firepower; Pakistan-backed militant groups cannot function in Kashmir without local support—the fact that a section of Kashmiri youth support these groups is often overlooked. The Islamist offensive preys upon the economic insecurity of Kashmiri men to advance its message and goals. By offering young men the best opportunity to make money,[133] Islamists invest Kashmir's poor and unemployed with the power they arrogate to themselves—to kill, extort, abduct and rape. Their anonymous violence has not only blunted the political edge and moral legitimacy of Kashmir's struggle for justice, but also appropriated meanings of gender to advance a patently regressive and patriarchal social agenda.

A militancy that once drew the spontaneous support of Kashmiri Muslim women for what in their eyes was a morally just struggle, is now perceived as corrupt and illegitimate. Women are wary of the new militancy. Y., a shop-assistant in Srinagar, reflected on this turn of events in Kashmir:

> I know we cannot achieve what we want [independence]. India will never leave Kashmir. . . . We shall never be free. I supported the militancy in 1990. Now I do not even know them [militants]. . . . They too have been corrupted with the passage of time. . . . We don't even know who they are. . . . All I know is they have guns. . . . The struggle is over.[134]

For other women, their enthusiasm and support for the militants during the early years has been replaced with disillusionment at the degeneration of a struggle, at the hands of a constituency whose vision of Kashmir is far removed from the aspirations of people. Growing indiscipline within militant ranks has made women turn their backs on militancy, but has not, however, insulated them against militant violence. On the contrary, women's refusal to provide moral and/or material support to the militancy has made them into explicit targets.[135]

Nothwithstanding its lack of popular support, the Islamist campaign has not died down. In September 2000, militants shot and injured two women in a beauty parlour in the heart of Srinagar, for wearing trousers in violation of their self-declared 'Islamic' dress code.[136] A year later in 2001, a relatively unknown militant group called Lashkar-e-Jabbar imposed a deadline for wearing the burqa after a 14-year-old girl, Kulsum Bhat, was splashed with acid in Srinagar as she walked home from school.[137] The call to impose the burqa was supported by the Dukhtaran-e-Millat who asked for an extension of the deadline in order to allow women to visit their tailors.[138]

Since then, the Islamist offensive has shifted to Kashmir's rural areas where it is waged with particular vengeance, exposing women to some of the worst kinds of social and sexual exploitation. In the forested mountain slopes of Surankote (Poonch district), adjoining the border with Pakistan, Muslim women in the twin villages of Marah and Kulali have picked up the gun to resist militants who demand food, shelter and sexual favours:

> Militants who would force us to provide them shelter, food and at times to entertain them physically, were harassing us physically and mentally. If we opposed them they would commit rapes or kill our family members. We wanted to confront them, and the only way to do so was to acquaint ourselves with the basic functioning of guns and grenades. . . . I am proud to fight against . . . marauders who have cheated us of our dignity and honour, says Shamima Akhter, 30-year old commander of an all-women patrol (Gupta 2005).

Female education is a specific target of Islamists. In 2002, posters created by the Harkat ul Jehad Islami (HUJI) in Darhal (Rajouri district) called for female students and teachers to wear the veil, with punishments ranging from mutilation to death. According to village headman, Hadi Noor, several families who continued to send their daughters to school received beatings from members of the HUJI. The girls' uniforms and books were burned, with the warning that their faces would be mutilated if they continued to offend. Parents pulled out class 11 and 12 students from the local secondary school, as a result of which the school's 80-odd girl students were unable to appear for their examinations.[139] At a seminar on women in Kashmir in New Delhi, Shabnam Ara, a young student from the Valley, summed up the tragic irony of the Islamist offensive in Kashmir: "Was this," she asked, "the kind of *azadi* they wanted for Kashmir?" (DasGupta 2000, 35).

Eighteen years of political repression and unrelenting violence has profoundly influenced women's lives in Kashmir. At one end is the cruel counter-offensive of the Indian state that has produced a landscape of widows, half-widows, orphans, bereaved and broken families and a ruined society. In the middle stretches the anguish and hardship of economic survival for Kashmiri Muslim women against an unresponsive state and a chaotic, often unsympathetic social context. Towards the end of the spectrum is the violence, fear and anxiety associated with Kashmir's external dimension and its underlying gender politics, namely, the creeping

Islamisation that threatens the rights and freedoms of Muslim women in Kashmir.

Kashmir's gender dimensions are, nevertheless, inextricably linked with the struggle of Kashmiri Muslims for justice. Eighteen years of occupation and resistance have not eliminated the enduring anger of a people wronged.[140] At the heart of Kashmiri anguish lie those imaginings and longings that are now suffused with unfathomable pain. E. an ex-militant of the JKLF (male) and U., a female JKLF supporter wept as they recalled memories of a struggle that has degenerated and slipped well beyond their grasp:

> U. was there when we started this movement, this struggle on 1 March 1990 . . . [looks at U.]. . . Some leaders betrayed us. That is why I feel emotional. [cries]. . . I spent 14 years in prison. . . From 10 Dec. 1990, I was in prison continuously for an entire decade. We recalled our friends who died, who were our comrades when I was part of the militancy. Friends like Mohammed Siddiq Sofi, Altaf Qureshi, Ashfaq Majid Wani and others. Out of them only some are alive. There are so few of us left from the many who started this revolution. We are alive because we are no longer associated with militancy. That is why we are surviving at present. Otherwise all our friends died. . . . She (U.) mentioned the names of our friends which made me weep. . . . At that point of time, a lot of . . . people supported us. What to speak of girls, women, the elderly and children . . . they all let us in their houses, hid us in their houses. There was no question of shame with young women. There was no hesitation in their support for the mujahideen. But then society has both good people and bad people. Politics is a dirty game. . . . Now when we look back on all that . . . it is painful.[141]

Concluding remarks

To sum up, a gender analysis challenges the public-private dichotomies, the exclusions and the silences that authenticate IR and political narratives on Kashmir. It highlights militarisation as a complex, multi-dimensional and multi-layered continuum of violence that renders women vulnerable to direct and indirect violence by state and non-state agencies, and discrimination within society. By highlighting the violence, chaos, human suffering and social inequality underpinning militarisation over Kashmir, a gender analysis contests the notion of inter-state military conflict as an all-male arena and the fiction of a sanitised, 'national' War Story. In so doing, it raises important questions regarding the moral and political legitimacy of the Westphalian, 'sovereign' state—so central to normative IR theory and to the political imagination of Indian elites—that removes women from the canvas of interstate military conflict and allows those responsible for foreign policy to evade public accountability for its influence on women's lives. More specifically, a gender frame demonstrates that the construct of the unitary, sovereign (Indian) state, and its underlying ideas of 'national' community and one-ness of 'the nation' effectively *depoliticise* and trivialise the state's use of rape as a weapon of war. In the name of 'national' survival, rape by the military is rationalised and legitimised as an inevitable 'side-effect' of militarily-backed nation-state building, and removed from the scope of politics and public accountability. A gender analysis underscores the paradox of the state's claims to 'security' that, in fact, have little meaning when the struggle for bodily integrity is a daily challenge.[142] Direct violence by the military against female citizens highlights the irony of an institution that, in principle, classifies these citizens as 'non-combatants'; a gender analysis exposes a disturbing reality where such violence is *not* a marker of the *general* violence of militarisation, but an embodiment of a state offensive based on the exploitation of sexual difference for *political* ends.

While the state claims to have restricted militant incursions from across the LOC, its massive military mobilisation has been unable to thwart militants' assertion of patriarchal control and dominance over Kashmiri women, or indeed militant violence against them. A gender frame enables us to see that the political agenda of Islamist militancy is advanced through armed combat against Indian soldiers *and* through violence against, and social domination of, Kashmiri women.

Militarisation over Kashmir, however, is inextricably linked with militarisation *in* Kashmir—a crisis rooted in the subversion of democracy by central authority and the denial of citizenship rights to Kashmiris. A gender perspective demonstrates that the inability of institutions to prevent violence against citizens or provide them justice has specific implications for women that are overlooked in mainstream analyses. The lack of democracy and democratic accountability in Kashmir is synonymous with the denial of justice for Kashmiri widows and half-widows; these women may have escaped direct violence by the state but cannot avoid their own social marginalisation, as a result of widowhood, within the family and the larger community. The tragedy of Kashmiri widows demonstrates precisely why the illegitimate state offensive against Kashmiri men has reinforced social hierarchy and women's marginalisation at the local level. It further highlights the failure of Kashmir's militant leadership to criticise societal attitudes towards survivors of rape and sexual abuse that condemns such women to a life of social ostracism and individual trauma. Although these leaders are ostensibly committed to struggling for democracy in Kashmir, democratic rights for Kashmiri women do not figure in their agenda; their disinterest and lack of concern at women's absence within their own political outfits reflects their maintenance of the gendered status quo. Neither the state, nor the militants (whatever their political affiliation), nor indeed Kashmiri society, has any support or solace to offer women driven to destitution, prostitution or becoming informants as a result of militarisation. The tragedies of these women have no bearing on Kashmir's national or international politics and evoke little sympathy from any quarter.

A gender analysis further reveals that in contrast to state violence against men that is publicly acknowledged and challenged through legal/institutional means, no such recourse is available to Kashmiri women, for whom all violations and psychological trauma must be borne in solitude, because there is no legal recourse against forms of violence, discrimination, marginalisation and social censure that occur in 'private' spaces. As Eric Blanchard notes: "Violence at the international, national and family levels is interrelated . . . and takes place in *domestic* spaces beyond the reach of law" (2003, 1296, emphasis added). If there is a general inference to be drawn from a gender analysis, it is that there exists a direct and inextricable relationship between militarisation in Kashmir and women's social subordination. In short, a gender analysis demonstrates the *inseparability* of 'public' (interstate) and 'private' (domestic) spheres of violence.

Finally, such an analysis of militarisation in Kashmir draws attention to the gendered contours of militarily-backed nation-state building and its implications for the state and the military in India. It highlights a deep and corrosive crisis of state legitimacy with a long precedent in modern India. In a letter of protest addressed to Prime Minister Indira Gandhi against her regime's violation of women's rights and dignity in Nagaland in 1971, Kuhovi Jimomi wrote: "The sexual depravity of the Indian army personnel against . . . Naga girls is a tactical move of the *Indian army offensive in Nagaland*" (Desai 1991, 81, emphasis in the original). Thirty-three years later, there was little change in the military's extra-legal offensive against female citizens. In Manipur, in April 2004, Thangjam Manorama Devi was picked up by soldiers of the 17 Assam Rifles from her residence and allegedly tortured and raped before being shot dead, prompting a group of Manipuri women to protest by stripping naked before Kangla Fort, the headquarters of Assam Rifles in Imphal, in July 2004.[143] In the same year, in a report on widespread public protests against the alleged rape of Shabnam Rashid and her mother, Aisha Begum, in Handwara, Kashmir by Major Vijay of 30 Rashtriya Rifles in November 2004, journalist Showkat Motta wrote that Shabnam has become "Manipur's Manorama for Kashmir" (*Greater Kashmir* 2004).[144]

By demonstrating the sexualised contours of coercive nation-state building in Kashmir, a gender analysis notes the disquieting trend whereby state power is wielded through non-representative and illegitimate means. It underscores the illegitimacy of a state whose military violates the dignity and sexual integrity of its citizens and, by extension, the illegitimacy of militarisation in Kashmir. If, in R.B.J. Walker's memorable words, "democracy is a struggle to make the state accountable" (1993, 156) then public acknowledgement of, and accountability for, sexual violence against Kashmir's female citizens is an integral part of the struggle for democracy in Kashmir.

Withdrawing the military from Kashmir would eliminate the principal source of militarisation in Kashmir. Yet, military withdrawal alone will not end the *resentment* that brought the military to Kashmir in the first place. The source of this resentment derives from a centralised, authoritarian state and its fatal fixation with a single 'national' identity. In this normative hierarchy, the aspirations and longings of Kashmiri Muslims can, at best, be described as 'separatist' even as militarised repression—ostensibly in the 'national' interest—so flagrantly undermines the principle of state legitimacy. Miriam Cooke quotes Hannah Arendt to underline the inherent limitation of the centralised, unitary nation-state: "Whatever the administrative advantages . . . of centralisation may be, its political result is always the same: monopolisation of power causes the drying up . . . of all authentic power sources in the country" (1996, 95).

The Indian state can affirm the rights and dignity of Kashmiris by relinquishing its relentless, albeit futile, pursuit of the unitary, centralised imaginary that has generated an endless spiral of state and societal violence in Kashmir, and a bitter military and nuclear rivalry with Pakistan. Kashmir's tragedy underlines the need to develop a plural, non-hierarchical and inclusive concept of the state. By affirming the democratic rights of Kashmir's citizens and reconciling Kashmiri imaginings within a plural concept of 'the nation,' the Indian state can arrest its domestic and external crisis of militarisation. In other words, the disjuncture between state and nation in India—exemplified by Kashmir's crisis of militarisation—is neither a flaw nor an aberration that needs to be obliterated by militarily-backed nation-state building within, or the creation of nuclearised and militarised frontiers without. Rather, India's ethnic and cultural plurality can form the basis of an alternative, plural and democratic concept of state and nation—a theme I take up for discussion in the concluding chapter.

Notes

1 Jill Steans, *Gender and International Relations: An Introduction* (Cambridge: Polity, 1998), p. 68.

2 Catherine MacKinnon, 'Crimes of War, Crimes of Peace', in Stephen Shute and S.L. Hurley (eds.), *On Human Rights: Oxford Amnesty Lectures 1993* (New York: Basic Books, 1993), p. 108; "Although both men and women can be and are raped, causing severe injury to both, in terms of numbers rape is essentially a crime committed against women. Further, women suffer from particular after-effects in rape that are not shared by men." See Christine Chinkin, 'Rape and Sexual Abuse of Women in International Law,' *European Journal of International Law* (Vol. 5, Issue 3, 1994), p. 1.

3 Eric Blanchard, 'Gender, International Relations and Security', *Signs: Journal of Women in Culture and Society* 28 (3) 2003, p. 1296.

4 Irene Tuft, 'Integrating a Gender Perspective in Conflict Resolution: The Colombian Case', in Inger Skjelsbaek and Dan Smith (eds.), *Gender, Peace and Conflict* (London: Sage, 2001), p. 140.

5 Miriam Cooke, *Women and the War Story* (Berkeley: University of California Press, 1996), p. 5.

6 'More Kashmiri Women Turning Militant', *The Hindu*, September 3, 1990.

7 Sudha Ramachandran quotes a woman from rural Kashmir: "Some of us helped the militants because we had brothers in the militant groups. But most of us helped because we were excited about *azadi*." 'Women Lift the Veil on Kashmir', *Asia Times Online*, March 7, 2002. http://www.atimes.com/ind-pak/DC07Df01.html. Accessed January 17, 2006.

8 Personal interview with G., Government College for Women, M.A. Road, Srinagar, March 19, 2004.

9 Personal interview with M., Government College for Women, M.A. Road, Srinagar, March 22, 2004.

10 Manchanda quotes Anjum Zamrood Habib of the women's group, Muslim Khwateen-e-Markaz (MKM): "We would visit jailed militants, take them shoes, a shirt, pyjamas, cigarettes and collect funds to bail them out. We did go for training in the use of guns, but we never used them." 'Guns and Burqa: Women in the Kashmir Conflict', in Rita Manchanda (ed.), *Women, War and Peace in South Asia: Beyond Victimhood to Agency* (New Delhi: Sage, 2001a), p. 52. Shiraz Sidhva witnessed women's political resistance in Srinagar: "Kashmiri women picketed the streets of Srinagar and other towns and villages to voice their agitation about rape and killings by the security forces". See 'Dukhtaran e Millat: Profile of a Militant, Fundamentalist Organisation' in Kamla Bhasin et al (eds.), *Against All Odds: Essays on Women, Religion and Development in India and Pakistan* (New Delhi: Kali for Women 1994), p. 123. Madame Bakhtawar, a member of the JKLF, who was imprisoned for three years told writer Pamela Bhagat: "I have sacrificed my house and my home, my parents, my life for the organisation, for my land." Pamela Bhagat, 'Interviews', in Urvashi Butalia (ed.), *Speaking Peace: Women's Voices from Kashmir* (New Delhi: Kali for Women, 2002), p. 270.

11 Ramachandran 2000, 'Women Lift the Veil'. http://www.atimes.com/ind-pak/DC07Df01.html. Accessed January 17, 2006. See also Kavita Suri, 'Women in the Valley: From Victims to Agents of Change' in W.P.S. Sidhu et al (eds.), *Kashmir: New Voices*, p. 83.

12 Farida Abdulla, 'A Life of Peace and Dignity' in Butalia (ed.), *Speaking Peace*, p. 266.

13 Manchanda, 'Guns and Burqa', p. 52.

14 Personal conversation with Z., Rajouri Kadal, Srinagar, April 22, 2005.

15 Personal conversation with P., Rajouri Kadal, Srinagar, April 22, 2005.

16 Personal interview with Vijayan M.J., Coalition of Civil Society, Amira Kadal, March 12, 2004, Srinagar.

[17] Manchanda, 'Guns and Burqa', p. 44.

[18] Sudha Ramachandran quotes militants belonging to Hizbul Mujahideen, the Hezbollah and al-Jehad who confirmed that "there are no women in militant groups. . . ." Why the exclusion of women? "Because they cannot fight," says an al-Jehad fighter. "Who will look after the home if they go underground?" See Ramachandran, 'Women Lift the Veil.'

[19] Personal interview with C., Habbakadal, Srinagar, March 31, 2004.

[20] Personal interview with Nusrat Andrabi, Rajbagh, Srinagar, March 18, 2004.

[21] 'Kashmir Imprisoned' in Butalia (ed.), *Speaking Peace*, p. 61.

[22] According to MKM President Madam Bakhtawar: "Initially our membership was huge, with people coming voluntarily to join us. There were educated women, doctors, lawyers, who were part of our organisation and supported our cause. . . We supported the families of slain persons financially; arranged marriages of widows; offered monetary help to orphans to continue their studies and even managed the affairs of the city's main cemetery at Eidgah. Public support for the organisation has dwindled because of harassment by security forces and increased governmental pressure." See also Bhagat, 'Interviews', p. 269.

[23] Anjum Zamrood was released in March 2008 after five years of detention in Tihar jail and is the acting chairperson of the MKM. *Greater Kashmir*, March 31, 2008

[24] Personal interview with Yasmeen Raja, Vice President, MKM, Kursoo Rajbagh, Srinagar, October 9, 2004. According to the MKM, there are at least 2000 cases of sexual abuse against women. The organisation is working on 75 cases—a copy of which was provided to me. MKM also provided documentary details of 40 women who were allegedly raped in Kunan Poshpora, Kupwara district, in February 1991, and a cd with details regarding victims of human rights abuse.

[25] Personal interview with Masoodaji, MKM office, Kursoo Rajbagh, Srinagar. October 9, 2004.

[26] Ali Shah Geelani insists on a United Nations supervised plebiscite in Kashmir and justifies Kashmiri resistance in Islamic terms. According to him, "Kashmir is an unresolved issue. It is a situation of military occupation. . . . We do not hate India but question Indian legitimacy to rule Kashmir through force. We are not against India but Indian occupation. . . . We are fighting against occupation and laying down our lives as Muslims. We are fighting tyranny as Muslims, according to Islamic principles. . . . Kashmir is occupied territory. It is up to Indian citizens to put pressure on their government to end occupation of Kashmir." Personal interview with Ali Shah Geelani. Hyderpora, Srinagar. July 8, 2004.

[27] Personal interview with Yasmeen Raja and Masoodaji, Kursoo Rajbagh, Srinagar, October 9, 2004.

[28] Yoginder Sikand, 'The Emergence and Development of the Jama'at-i-Islami of Jammu and Kashmir (1940's–1990), *Modern Asian Studies* 36 (3), 2000, p. 731.

[29] See also Rashida Bhagat, 'Women Get Short Shrift in J&K Polls', *The Hindu Business Line*, September 12, 2002. http://www.blonnet.com/2002/09/12/stories/2002091200040800.htm. Accessed November 15, 2004.

[30] For a fuller discussion see Rita Chowdhari Tremblay, 'Where are Women in Kashmiri Politics?' in Shree Mulay and Jackie Kirk (eds.), *Women Building Peace Between India and Pakistan* (New Delhi: Anthem Press, 2007), especially pp. 112–114 and pp. 127–131.

[31] Personal Interview with J., University of Kashmir, Hazratbal, Srinagar, April 22, 2004.

[32] On February 15, 2001, citizens of Haigam (near Sopore) and adjoining areas blocked the highway to protest against the custodial killing of Jalil Ahmed Shah of Haigam by the Rashtriya Rifles. The military opened fire killing two men and two women. See *Communalism Combat*: 'Wounded Valley', July 2001. http://www.sabrang.com/cc/archive/2001/july01/cover4.htm. Accessed July 18, 2007.

[33] 'Kashmiri Women don't Need Morality Lessons' (*Indian Express*, online edition). Mehbooba Mufti interviewed by Muzammil Jaleel. http://www.kashmirlive.com/kashmirlive/int20010907.html. Accessed February 22, 2006.

[34] 'Kashmir Imprisoned', in Butalia (ed.), *Speaking Peace*, p. 57.

[35] *Voting at the Point of a Gun: Counter-Insurgency and the Farce of Elections in Kashmir: A Report to the People of India* (Bombay: Lokshahi Hakk Sangathana, 1996), p. 24.

[36] 'Kashmir Imprisoned', in Butalia (ed.), op. cit., p. 74.

[37] *Grim Realities*, p. 4.

[38] APDP figure cited in Sumona DasGupta, *Breaking the Silence: Women and Kashmir* (New Delhi: Women in Security, Conflict Management and Peace, 2000), p. 35. It is difficult, if not impossible, to arrive at a definitive figure regarding widows and half-widows. Rita Manchanda cites a figure of 15,000 widows and half-widows. This estimate is corroborated by Urvashi Butalia who cites the same. 'Introduction' in Butalia, op. cit., xii. An independent report (*Grim Realities*, p. 4) cites a similar figure. The figure of 20,000 widows seems a credible estimate.

[39] Muzammil Jaleel, 'Despatches from a War Torn Region', in Butalia (ed.), op. cit., p. 299.

[40] Aasia Jeelani 2002, 'Dardpora—A Village of Pain and Misery'. http://www.geocities.com/kwipd2002/dardpora.html?200412. Accessed November 12, 2004. Assabah Khan 2002, 'Dardpora: Blot on Humanity'. http://www.geocities.com/kwipd2002/dard2.html?200412. Accessed November 12, 2004. Suri, 'Women in the Valley', p. 87. For an account of the travails of widows across Kashmir, see Afsana Rashid, 'Waiting for Justice: Widows and Half-Widows' unpublished monograph, February 10, 2008.

[41] Sarwan Kashani, Idrees Kanth & Gowher Fazli, *The Impact of Violence on the Student Community in Kashmir* (Delhi: Oxford India Trust, 2003). Kashani et al, *The Impact of Violence*, p. 35.

[42] Personal Interview with K., Tengpora, Srinagar, June 29, 2004.

[43] Personal Interview with R, Tengpora, Srinagar, June 29, 2004.

[44] Jaleel, 'Despatches', pp. 301–302.

[45] Bukhari, 'Dying Day by Day'.

[46] Sudha Ramachandran, 'Caught in the Crossfire' in *The Shades of Violence* (WISCOMP, 2003), p. 18. According to Shahzadi, widow of slain JKLF militant, Farooq Ahmed Khan, "Widows of militants are not treated kindly, especially if they are not financially independent." Peerzada Hamid, 'Valley of Dead Flowers', *Tehelka*, July 24, 2004.

[47] Personal Interview with Q., Amirakadal, Srinagar, March 10, 2004.

[48] Sudha Ramachandran writes of Sanaullah War—a farmer in Warpora (a village near the city of Sopore in the north of the Valley) whose death at the hands of the military left his uneducated and unemployed widow dependent upon her neighbour's generosity to feed her five children. See Ramachandran, 'Caught in the Crossfire', pp. 17–18.

[49] Sushobha Barve, 'Kashmir Journeys' in Butalia (ed.), op. cit., p. 253.

[50] Personal Interview with Parveena Ahanger, Batamaloo, Srinagar, March 23, 2004. Simultaneous translation from the Kashmiri by Tahir Ahmed Mir.

[51] See also Parvez Imroz, 'India's Civil Society Has Failed Kashmir', *Communalism Combat*, 10th Anniversary Issue (August–September 2003)). http://www.sabrang.com/cc/archive/2003/aug03/parvaz.html. Accessed January 21, 2007.

[52] 'Censor Board Bans Documentary on Disappeared Kashmiris', *Greater Kashmir*, February 9, 2006. According to the CBFC, "It [the documentary] does not deal with the complex and poignant situation in a comprehensive manner." Ibid.

[53] Ibid. The muzzling of public information through crude censorship has not changed over the years. In 1991, a *Newstrack* video highlighting the difference in perception of reality in Kashmir as opposed to the rest of India was banned. The video documented abuse and torture against civilians by the Indian military and included interviews with Hindus who had stayed on in the Valley and testified to good relations with Muslims. Karan Thapar, executive producer, was told by the censors (the Ministries of Home and External Affairs and the Indian army) that they considered the video unbalanced. Mr. Thapar defended his right to make and distribute the video. "It is the duty of the press to present different views," he said. "Also, in a democracy, how on earth can we persuade six million Kashmiris that their future lies in India, if we ignore their views?" See Derek Brown, 'India Gags Video of Kashmir Torture'. *The Guardian Weekly* (London), November 17, 1991.

[54] Personal Interview with Q., Amirakadal, Srinagar, March 10, 2004.

[55] 'The Twilight Zone of the Half-Widows', *Tehelka*, March 6, 2004.

[56] Lacking alternative means of livelihood, widows are forced into prostitution in order to support their families. Suri, 'Women in the Valley', p. 86.

[57] Bukhari, 'Dying Day by Day'.

[58] Jaleel, 'Despatches', p. 300.

[59] Sheikh Zahoor, 'Impact of Conflict Situation on Children and Women in

Kashmir', *Kashmir Human Rights Site: A Project of the Asian Human Rights Commission.* http://kashmir.ahrchk.net/mainfile.php/articles/45. Accessed January 13, 2004.

60 Ibid.

61 Singh narrated the experience of women from the village of Pazipora who were pursued and raped by soldiers: Recount[ed] 50-year-old Saja: "'They beat me on my head and under my eyes with rifle-butts, but I didn't allow my two daughters to be raped.' But not all women had a Saja to defend them... Twenty-six year old Saba, another victim, sits huddled under in a dingy hut in Pazipora with tears running down her cheeks. 'I want to kill myself,' she cried in a voice choked with emotion. Both her husband and brother-in-law were shot dead by the army shortly before she was raped." Sukhmani Singh, 'Protectors or Predators?' *The Illustrated Weekly of India,* September 30, 1990, p. 34.

62 A similar response was forthcoming in response to the allegation of rape in Haran, a town near Srinagar, on July 20, 1992. See Anuradha Bhasin Jamwal, 'Women in Kashmir Conflict: Victimhood and Beyond' in Shree Mulay and Jackie Kirk (eds.), *Women Building Peace,* p. 98 and p. 109, n. 6.

63 Manchanda, 'Guns and Burqa', p. 73. A number of women were raped in front of their families, their own husbands and their own children. Professor William Wayne Baker, Testimony to the 52nd United Nations Commission on Human Rights. http://www.kashmir-cc.ca/quarterly/kq2-3/SEALEDVA.htm. Accessed November 15, 2004. "Why else", asked a lecturer at the University of Kashmir, "are women raped in front of their families and community?" Ramachandran 'Caught in the Crossfire', p. 19.

64 Personal interview with Lt. Col. V.K. Batra PRO, Ministry of Defence, Badami Bagh, Srinagar, March 13, 2005.

65 Ibid.

66 Conversation with Col. V.X., Station Headquarters, Badami Bagh, Srinagar, April 13, 2005.
   In a moment of rare candour, a senior CRPF officer told a writer: "Who do you think joins the security forces...? Do you think you will be able to pick up the gun and kill? Can you stay away for months from your family, earning just a few thousand rupees, risking your life every day? No, you wouldn't. Only a brute would or someone desperate. We get the worst—the rogues, the thugs, and then we have to play with them. Giving them lead and reining them in. It is not easy." Senior CRPF officer quoted by Sonia Jabbar, 'Blood Soil: Chittisinghpora and After' in *Shades of Violence,* op. cit., p. 64.

67 *Rape in Kashmir: A Crime of War,* (New York, Asia Watch/Physicians for Human Rights, 1993), p. 8. Documented cases of rape indicate official tolerance if not official sanction for rape. "S., about 25, testified that on the night of October 10, 1993, she was in the house that was owned by her father-in-law, who is about 70, and his wife... During the night, there was knocking on the door and three soldiers entered and asked, "Where are the womenfolk?" One soldier kept guard at the door and two of them raped me.

They said, 'We have orders from our officers to rape you'. Two raped me and my sister-in-law. Then they left." Testimony of S. Ibid. pp. 10–11.

"G. stated that three soldiers entered her house and took her husband outside. Only one came into the room. He told me, 'I have come to search you'. I told him women are not searched, but he said, 'I have orders,' and he tore off my clothes and raped me. Testimony of G." Ibid.

68 Singh, 'Protectors or Predators?' p. 35.

69 Testimony of three women of Bihota. July 1, 2001. An FIR (No.59/2001) was lodged at Doda, under Sections 362,452,382,149 RPC (Ranbir Penal Code). No action has been taken against the accused. See *Grim Realities*, p. 62.

70 In Sopore, northern Kashmir, Parveen and her neighbour Rehana were raped by members of the Border Security Force (BSF). "They narrated their tale not with indifference, but with the intended attempt of eschewing all the humiliation they had to go through. 'We want to die', they said, 'We can't live this life of shame'." Jamwal, 'Women in Kashmir Conflict', p. 100.

71 Personal interview with N., ex-militant JKLF. Agence France Press office, Polo View, Srinagar, March 20, 2004.

72 Dewan, et al, *Women's Testimonies: The Green of My Valley is Khaki*, p. 11.

73 Personal interview with O. Gowkadal, Srinagar, March 23, 2004. Simultaneous translation from the Kashmiri by Tahir Ahmed Mir.

74 Ibid.

75 Ibid.

76 Identities withheld.

77 Personal interview with O. Gowkadal, Srinagar, March 23, 2004. Simultaneous translation from the Kashmiri by Tahir Ahmed Mir.

78 Personal interview with F., Srinagar, March 24, 2004. Location withheld in order to protect identity.

79 Anuradha Bhasin Jamwal, "Women in Kashmir Conflict", op. cit.

80 For instance, in Saderkot village in Ganderbal district, "Hanifa, a schoolgirl claimed that her brother, Gulzar Ahmed Bhat, was blasted with explosives by the army because he refused to co-operate in procuring her for one of the officers at the army camp in Saderkot." Manchanda, 'Guns and Burqa', p. 88.

81 The NCW has no jurisdiction over Kashmir.

82 "The case of withholding permission to the office-bearers of NCW to examine the victims in the Valley is . . . [an] example of official apathy towards the victims and its attempts at preventing the unravelling of the truth. If the government has nothing to hide, as it so claims, then it should have no objection to the NCW meeting the victims. NCW Chairperson Mohini Giri said she had failed in her endeavour in the Valley due to the non-cooperation of the state authorities. She said she has enquired about the incidents of alleged rape and other excesses against Kashmiri women, but authorities, including Financial Commissioner Sushma Chowdhry, asserted that no such incidents were taking place in Kashmir." *Greater Kashmir*, August 6, 1997.

83 Jamwal, 'Women in Kashmir Conflict', pp. 96, 109.

[84] For instance, Mehtaba and her two daughters were gang-raped by the military in Kupwara district in 1998. Rape was confirmed by Dr.Bilkees at the district hospital. After initial denials by the state government, Dr.Bilkees was charged with colluding with pro-separatist militants and inciting Mehtaba's mother to make allegations of rape. In the end, the women were discredited and branded as 'known keeps of militants'. Discrepancies in the government's version were pointed out by the senior most district police officer. *Kashmir Times*, July 3, 1998, cited in Manchanda, 'Guns and Burqa', p. 82.

[85] 22 year-old Marium Begum played an instrumental role in the surrender of militants, after which she was disfigured and raped by the latter. Marium's personal tragedy at the hands of militants fitted well into the propaganda machinery of the military which, under the pretext of 'protecting' Marium, made her a virtual prisoner within the military camp at Doda. See Jamwal, 'Women in Kashmir Conflict', 2007, p. 104.

[86] For a fuller discussion on this aspect and documented cases, see Ibid. pp. 98–99.

[87] For more details regarding violence against Pandit women, see Kshama Kaul, 'A Pandit Story', pp. 187–188 in Butalia (ed.), *Speaking Peace*, and Shakti Bhan Khanna, 'Leaving Home', Ibid, pp. 178–182. According to Dr. Khanna, one of Srinagar's female Hindu residents who eventually fled Kashmir: "As a doctor, I have dealt with both Hindu and Muslim women in Srinagar and here (Delhi). I don't want to give any names but there are a number of Kashmiri Hindu (Pandit) women who have been sexually assaulted and violated. . . . Many of them come to me for help; sometimes they need abortions. I remember a very beautiful young woman who used to teach at a college: the militants sent a message to her husband one day that she should come to a particular place between this and this time, and that they would let her go afterwards. The husband just put her on a plane to Delhi the same day. . . . I receive[d] her at the airport."

[88] Muslim women are specific targets of an Islamist militancy that perceives Kashmir's struggle in social rather than political terms. The battle to advance a regressive and obscurantist Islamist agenda has shifted to Kashmir's rural hinterlands.

[89] Shahnaz Kouser was abducted by militants after which she was raped, tortured and drugged and forced to work for them for six months. See Jamwal, 'Women in Kashmir Conflict', p. 98.

[90] *Rape in Kashmir: A Crime of War*, Asia Watch and Human Rights Watch (New York: 1993), p. 16. In August 2004, a 'divisional commander' of the militant group Harkatul Mujahideen (HUM) Barkat Ali, barged into the house of one Mohammed Din Sheikh at Dewari in Kashmir's Doda district and kidnapped him daughter, Tahira Bano. They were taken to a remote place Behar Nallah (Dhar) where the militants forcibly conducted the *nikah* (marriage) of Tahira with Barkat Ali. See 'J&K Rebels Force Teen Girl to Wed Chief', *The Asian Age*, August 28, 2004.

[91] Sudha Ramachandran has documented the case of Najma, a resident of

Srinagar, who visited a BSF camp to secure the release of her husband and
was shot dead by militants on the assumption that she was an informer. See
Ramachandran, 'Caught in the Crossfire', p. 19. In December 2002, three
women in the hamlet of Hasiyot, Thanamandi, in Kashmir's Rajouri District
were killed on grounds that they were informants. Praveen Swami, 'Through
the Valley of the Shadow of Death'. http://www.atimes.com/atimes/
South_Asia/EAD9Df02.html. Accessed November 16, 2004.

92 Manchanda, 'Guns and Burqa', p. 87.

93 Shahnaz Kouser was rescued by the police after handing over one of the
militants to them, after which she worked with the Intelligence Bureau
where she was subject to the same treatment she had suffered under the
militants. For a fuller description of Shahnaz's ordeal, see Jamwal, 'Women
in Kashmir Conflict', 2007, pp. 98–99.

94 Ibid. p. 95 and p. 106.

95 Afsana Rashid. 'Honour Need not be Associated with Rape'. *The Kashmir
Times*, January 20, 2006. http://www.kashmirtimes.com/news5.htm.
Accessed January 20, 2006.

96 Kashani et al, *The Impact of Violence*, p. 36.

97 In 1991, the Jammu and Kashmir Student Liberation Front (JKSLF) parted
ways from its parent body, the JKLF, to morph into the Ikhwan-ul-Muslimeen
(Muslim Brotherhood). See Harinder Baweja, 'A Subtle Change in Mood',
India Today, March 31, 1991. In a presentation during a seminar on Kashmir
in New Delhi, a young student from Kashmir noted that, "In this armed
conflict . . . masculine power emerged as all important, men became even
more dominating and commanding than usual and [gender] discrimination
. . . further heightened." DasGupta, *Breaking the Silence*, p. 27.

98 Personal interview with Dr.Hameeda Bano, University of Kashmir, Hazratbal
Campus, Srinagar, June 29, 2004.

99 Sidhva 'Dukhtaran e Millat', p. 124.

100 Neerja Mattoo, 'The Story of a Women's College in Kashmir', in Butalia
(ed.), op. cit., p. 168.

101 Sidhva, 'Dukhtaran e Millat', p. 128; Dewan, et al, *Women's Testimonies*,
p. 19; Manchanda, 'Guns and Burqa', pp. 57–60. A stinging riposte to the
imposition of a dress code for women in *Al Safa*, a Srinagar daily, symbolised
women's resistance to the burqa: "During the struggle for freedom we have
witnessed things which have no bearing on the movement. One aspect of
this [struggle for freedom] which needs to be focused upon is the movement
for the imposition of the burqa. . . Burqa is a symbol which makes the
woman feel inferior. . . . This move to impose burqa is a madness which has
consumed young men and girls. It cannot be successful. . . My brothers, you
who are compelling me to wear the burqa on the threat of death, who want
me to be faceless. . . . If I am actually murdered I will call these Islamic
fanatics my murderers. . . . If I am made a target of acid and poisonous
colour in the name of Islam, I will give up this kind of Islam and become a
Christian but I will never accept to become a *kala bhoot* (black demon) and

live with a sense of inferiority." See 'Kashmir Imprisoned' in Butalia (ed.), op. cit., p. 80.

[102] Personal interview with H. Hazratbal, Srinagar, October 5, 2004.

[103] Grateful thanks to Feizal Mir for this point. Personal conversation with Feizal Mir, University of Kashmir, Hazratbal, June 27, 2004.

[104] The irony of being a (Muslim) woman and witness to crude hostility from Muslim men—who were ostensibly struggling for justice and democracy in Kashmir—for criticising patriarchal dominance was bitter. Among other epithets, I was branded an Indian/Hindu-US-Zionist agent, shouted down and threatened. I was advised to keep away from the campus for a few days and not move around alone. Informal discussion with students, University of Kashmir, Hazratbal, Srinagar. 13 June 2004.

[105] Personal interview with Dr.Hameeda Bano, University of Kashmir, Hazratbal, Srinagar.

[106] Group discussion with students, Govt. College for Women, Srinagar, March 23, 2004.

[107] Personal interview with W., Government College for Women, March 23, 2004, Srinagar.

[108] Bhagat, 'Interviews', p. 291.

[109] Dewan et al, *Women's Testimonies*, p. 15. Militant diktats regarding women's reproductive choices are not limited to Srinagar. In Sopore, activists of the Hizbul Mujahideen decry contraception as an un-Islamic practice. According to Dr. Ayesha Haider, members of the Banat-ul-Islam, the Jamaat e Islami's women's wing, would tell women they were life-givers and should not kill their unborn children. Shazia, a 24-year-old woman from Srinagar could not afford to have a fifth child. Fearful of inviting the wrath of militants she undertook a ten-hour bus journey to in order to terminate her pregnancy. Abdul Wani, Jamat-e-Islami activist, Dr. Ayesha Haider in a government hospital, and Shazia quoted in Ramachandran 2003d), 'Paradise on Earth— But Not for Women', in *Shades of Violence*, pp. 46–47. Names changed in order to protect identity.

[110] Das Gupta, *Breaking the Silence*, p. 20.

[111] Ibid. p. 28.

[112] *Dropout Rate of Schoolgoing Children in Kashmir*

Year	Class	Boys (%)	Girls (%)
1990–1991	1–5	40	45
	6–8	20	53
1996–1997	1–5	37	43
	6–8	17	52

Source: Mumtaz Soz, Director of Education, Jammu and Kashmir State Government, Srinagar, January 1999 (Reproduced from Manchanda 2001, 'Guns and Burqa', p. 72).

[113] In the district education office of Kupwara, Apu Esthose Suresh, a researcher from Delhi, personally scrutinised bundles of complaints forwarded by the

heads of girls' schools about the physical frisking and other forms of humiliation suffered by Kashmiri girls at the hands of the security forces, particularly the Rashtriya Rifles (RR) camped in the premises of rural schools. According to Suresh, "This is not a one-off incident. Kashmiri society being conservative, no one wants to face social ostracism; hence many such cases go unregistered. As such incidents get reported in the local media, the sense of insecurity of the parents has increased. As a direct consequence, the drop-out rate of girls in the last few years reveals an upward trend." 'Barbed Wire Mentality: Indian troops pose a serious threat to the inherent right to life of the child by bringing the child in the line of direct hostilities.' *The Daily Etalaat* (Srinagar) http://etalaat.net/english/index.php?option=com_content&task=view&id=3422&Itemid=2. Accessed January 23, 2008.

"A news report was published in 2006 regarding another incident in Singpura where men from II Rashtriya Rifles tried to molest a ninth class student on her way back home from the school, which is just three km away. Later, not only did the girl opt out of school, but so did many of her classmates. Many others, including her teachers, are yet to recover from that trauma. . . . From the available documents there are about 20 schools occupied by the RR alone, out of which 14 are either primary or middle schools. The emotional impact of these incidents is far-reaching. In a study conducted with 536 respondents with a proportional representation from different parts of the Valley, it was found that 40 per cent of children in the age group of 4–18 years suffer from post–traumatic stress disorders, fear psychosis and panic. Ibid.

[114] A women's team that visited Kashmir noted that in every area they visited, girls complained that they were being compelled to give up education. The most oft cited reason was widespread sexual harassment by military forces. *Wounded Valley. . . Shattered Souls*, p. 11. Mehjabeen, a 20-year-old college student who discontinued her studies, told a women's fact-finding commission that it was unsafe to go to college because girls are molested in broad daylight. According to Mehjabeen: On an average, girls are getting married much earlier because of the fear of getting raped and not being accepted for marriage thereafter. Earlier, girls in Kashmir used to get married at an average age of 22 to 25 years. The girls normally studied at least till graduation. However, the situation has now undergone change. The girls do not opt for higher studies but prefer to get married earlier. Ibid. pp. 9–10.This trend was corroborated by a student in Mohanpura. It is virtually impossible for women to get married after rape or sexual abuse. Uma Chakravarti, 'A Kashmir Diary: Seven Days in an Armed "Paradise"', in Butalia (ed.), op. cit., p. 115.

[115] Personal interview with N., ex-militant JKLF. Agence France Press office, Polo View, Srinagar, March 20, 2004.

[116] Bukhari, 'Dying Day by Day.'

[117] DasGupta 2000, p. 39.

[118] Interview with I. at Lal Chowk, Srinagar, March 14, 2004.

[119] Group discussion with students at Government College for Women, Srinagar, March 22, 2004.

[120] A woman told Sudha Ramachandran. "We tie these strips of cloth when we go to the wayside shrines to pray and make a wish. Of course, most of the time we are asking for peace of mind." Ramachandran, 'Scarred Psyche' in *Shades of Violence*, p. 27.

[121] Noorani, 'Contours of Militancy', *Frontline*, September 20–October 13, 2000. http://www.flonnet.com/fl1720/17200800.htm. Accessed November 12, 2004.

[122] Sufi missionaries from Central Asia and Persia played an important part in fostering a non-orthodox Kashmiri Islamic practice rooted in regional traditions.

[123] Sikand, 'The Emergence and Development of the Jama'at-i-Islami', p. 750.

[124] Noorani, 'Contours of Militancy'.

[125] Sidhva, 'Dukhtaran e Millat', p. 131. There exists an enduring tension between the reformist impulse of the JI that is confined to literate middle and lower-middle class Muslims, and Kashmir's peasants and workers who remain loyal to its Sufi traditions. Upon being asked what Kashmiriyat (a historically determined understanding of Kashmiri cultural identity that transcends religion) meant to her, Asiya's response was categorical: "Kashmiriyat is a rubbish slogan. I believe only in Islam. Kashmiriyat is un-Islamic. It is Indianised culture." Asiya Andrabi quoted in Ramachandran (2003b), 'I Believe in Armed Struggle Only' in *Shades of Violence*, p. 34.

[126] Sidhva, 'Dukhtaran-e Millat', pp. 127–128.

[127] "Kashmiri women have always been an active component of the society. Much of their social, educational and professional growth has seen a steady increase over the years. Barring the elite and clergy . . . within the trader and artisan class there exist[s] a unique form of gender equity, born of a complementary relation between the men and women as they pursued their family trade. Amongst the fisherfolk, women took care of selling the catch while men procured it; in the baker community males baked the goods and women were responsible for selling. . . In rural areas, women have always been counted as sturdy workers tending farms, cultivating rice, and raising cattle." Ather Zia, 'Kashmiri Women: Concerns, Milestones & Solutions'. http://www.kashmiraffairs.org/Zia_Ather_Kashmiri_women.html. Accessed February 28, 2007.

[128] At a seminar on women in Kashmir in New Delhi, Shyamala Mufti described the condition of elite Muslim women in Kashmir prior to 1947: "Before 1947 the hold of the orthodox ulema [clergy] was strong, purdah was strictly observed in upper class and middle class families. . . . Changes in the condition of women started appearing in the post-1947 period, and by the 1960's a considerable number of women had come out of purdah. School and college education became a routine matter and women entered new professions—as teachers, lecturers, doctors, lawyers, as well as the service sector." See DasGupta, *Breaking the Silence*, pp. 21–22.

[129] Personal interview with Asiya Andrabi, Khanyar, Srinagar, October 8, 2004.

130 Ibid.

131 Group discussion with students at Government College for Women, Srinagar, March 22, 2004.

132 Bashir Ahmed Dabla, Sandeep K. Nayak and Khurshidul Islam (eds.), *Gender Discrimination in the Kashmir Valley: A Survey of Budgam and Baramulla Districts* (New Delhi: Gyan Publishing House, 2000), p. 35.

133 "For those taking this course, life might be short, but it is sweet. Recruits have access to luxuries unavailable to common folk, such as staying in houseboats and five-star hotels and consorting with young women, themselves orphans with no prospects of marriage and fed up with commonplace, increasingly burdensome lives." Wajahat Habibullah, 'The Political Economy of the Kashmir Conflict: Opportunities for Economic Peace-building and for U.S. Policy' (Washington D.C.: United States Institute of Peace, 2004), p. 8.

134 Personal Interview with Y., Lal Chowk, Srinagar, October 7, 2004.

135 As a student told Victoria Schofield: "The lady next door was approached one night by militants who asked for money. . . In the old days, she would have asked them in and given them food. This time she refused and shut the door in their face. So they pushed the door in and shot her." Schofield, *Kashmir in Conflict*, p. 173.

136 Luke Harding, 'Valley of Vanishing Women', *The Guardian* (London), September 4, 2001. http://www.guardian.co.uk/kashmir/Story/ 0,2763,546762,00.html. Accessed November 15, 2004.

137 David Orr, 'Fears of Acid Attacks Rife in Kashmir', *The Irish Times,* September 10, 2001. http://www.ireland.com/newspaper/front/2001/0910/ fro3.htm. Accessed November 15, 2004.

138 "The tailors in Srinagar", reported Luke Harding, "have rarely been so busy. . . . Over the past three weeks, sales of black cloth have shot up dramatically." BBC, 'Patrols Against Kashmir Acid Attacks', August 15, 2001. http://news.bbc.co.uk/2/hi/south_asia/1487395.stm. Accessed November 15, 2004.

139 Swami, 'Through the Valley of the Shadow of Death.'

140 Personal conversation with Sohail Ahmed, PhD research student from Srinagar. New Delhi, February 2, 2008.

141 Personal interview with E., JKLF office, Maisooma, April 2, 2004, Srinagar.

142 Marysia Zalewski, 'Well, What's the Feminist Perspective on Bosnia?' *International Affairs* 71(2): 339–356 (1995), p. 348.

143 They waved banners that read: "Indian army take our flesh, Indian army rape us." See Nitin Gokhale, 'Look What the Armed Forces Have Reduced Manipuri Women to', *Tehelka*, July 31, 2004. The women shouted: "We are Manorama's mothers." See Debabrata Roy Laifungbam, 'Manipur's Mothers', *Tehelka*, August 7, 2004.

144 Showkat Motta, 'Shabnam Becoming Manipur's Manorama for Kashmir', *Greater Kashmir*, November 11, 2004.

5 Conclusion

> If you hit a note with power, you cannot sustain it. Therefore you are not strong. It's like Israel. I'm sure it has the capacity to win a war against nearly all Arab states that surround it. But the Palestinian problem is inside, and a powerful army is no use there. So Israel is powerful, but it is not strong.
>
> *Daniel Barenboim*[1]

One of the most significant developments towards the end of the twentieth century was the changed perception regarding military 'power'. At a systemic (international) level, state military power is no longer synonymous with, or the sole determinant of, state power. The demise of the Cold War exposed the shaky foundations of Soviet 'power' built on an unsustainable and brittle military capacity. While the decline of the erstwhile Soviet Union paralleled the emergence of the United States as the pre-eminent military 'power' in the world, the waning influence of a militarily 'powerful' United States in Iraq and Afghanistan symbolises the limits of military power in the contemporary world.

On the other hand, the diminishing effectiveness of state consolidation through military means at a 'national' level is no less significant. The replacement of civil governance with militarily-backed central rule by states across the world—legitimised and affirmed as a measure and function of 'sovereignty'—precipitated endless cycles of state and societal violence that served to undermine rather than uphold the legitimacy and integrity of the state. Mary Kaldor notes the limits of state military power in the domestic/national context: "Russia cannot control Chechnya. Israel cannot control the Palestinian territories. India cannot control Kashmir" (2005).

These two seemingly disparate strands of militarisation in

the context of India are not mutually exclusive, but interlinked. Both are rooted in a cosmology of 'nation' and 'national' power that endorses the exercise of coercive, centralised force in domestic and foreign affairs. Paradoxically, however, military and nuclear consolidation without, and political consolidation through military means within, has not translated into 'security' or strategic advantage for the Indian state, nor has it eliminated domestic challenges to the latter. Fortified by military and nuclear power, the Indian state *seems* unassailable; yet, as the tragedy of Kashmir so vividly demonstrates, an extraordinarily 'powerful' state backed by the world's fourth largest military, can hold on to Kashmir only through brute force, even as its formidable 'power' is spectacularly unsuccessful in eliminating what Daniel Barenboim appropriately terms 'the problem inside'. Before summing up the limits and dangers of both dimensions of militarisation in India, I underline the significance of analysing the same within a *single* historical frame.

A historical analysis of the militarisation of the Indian state illustrates that its nuclear consolidation during the 1947–1962 period did not derive from normative IR perceptions of 'security' in an 'anarchic world, but from ideas of post-colonial identity and secular modernity. Even though the post-1962 military and nuclear build-up of the Indian state was informed by realist IR discourse, it was shaped more by aspirations to 'power' and international status than by identifiable external (military) threats to the state. On the other hand, a historical analysis of militarisation's secondary[2] dimension, namely, its increasing influence in the political life of the nation-state, reveals India's disastrous legacy of nation-state building through military means. India's domestic crisis of militarisation does not approximate with its classic variant namely, military dictatorship and/or rule by a military junta, as is the case with Latin America or Africa. Rather, militarisation in India represents the dark underside of democracy where a crisis of state legitimacy prompts state elites to use the military for domestic repression, identify political opponents as 'the other,' and appropriate both measures within a hegemonic narrative of 'the nation'.

In sum, a historical analysis of militarisation in India highlights that the crisis of state legitimacy which underwrites military (and nuclear) power projection in the international realm is the same that precipitates political consolidation through military means in the domestic arena. More specifically, the state that edges India close to nuclear war *over* Kashmir is the same state that wages war *in* Kashmir. Both dimensions of militarisation are rooted in a profoundly undemocratic political order that views the state as a centralised governing institution with little regard, or respect, for citizens or social groups existing within it. For precisely this reason, India's external and domestic crises of militarisation mandate a re-imagining of the Indian state. The argument here is not against the modern state as such, but against the centralised, unitary, realpolitik version of the state that contains within it the seeds of militarisation and war. Before proceeding with the argument, it is useful to review the historical legacy that necessitates such a re-imagining.

Illusions of 'power'

India's first three wars with Pakistan (1947, 1965 and 1971) and her 1962 war with China originated in competing claims to territory, rather than from (western) notions of an explicit military threat to the political identity or independence of the state. The 'insecurities' of the Indian state, in other words, are historically rather than militarily determined. The historical legacy of disputed borders that is at the heart of the militarisation of the Indian state cannot be resolved through military means. This is why the acquisition of the instruments of 'security' (i.e., arms and weapons of mass destruction) has not 'secured' the state, but been transformed into a source of *insecurity* for Indian *and* South Asian citizens.

This militarisation also symbolises the imitation and replication of western ideas of military 'power' that have shaped and defined post-independence elite interests. Since 1962, these interests centred on the Indian state's ambition for recognition as a major 'power' in the subcontinent based on perceived notions of India's 'rightful' place in the world. Accordingly, even though the decision for the 1998 Pokharan II nuclear tests was taken by a Hindu nationalist government, the militarisation of the Indian state cannot be attributed *entirely* to the rise of right-wing Hindu nationalism. Much before the fateful summer of 1998, the Indian state chose to replicate, rather than deviate from, a mode of global 'power' politics that Jawaharlal Nehru had once roundly condemned. Hindu nationalism merely imparted a grotesque twist to imperial and imperious constructs of state, nation and political power that have dominated the Indian political spectrum since 1962.

India's nuclear folly, symbolised by her acquisition of the ultimate marker of state 'power,' and 'security' failed to translate into strategic advantage[3] for the state, nor did it place India on par with China, or direct world attention towards her supposed security concerns regarding the latter.[4] In general, the attempt by the Indian state to gain international prestige by acquiring the discredited and outdated symbols of 'power' was at best unsuccessful, and at worst, a failure. As Itty Abraham observes:

> International ideas about nuclear power have come full circle.
> . . . A country acquires neither international respect nor prestige
> by developing, or continuing to hold nuclear weapons. . . .
> International public opinion . . . is now where India was nearly
> half a century ago. But India has moved on from its once lofty,
> idealistic standpoint. India has demanded its right to become a
> nuclear power just when the atomic age has come to an end, and
> thus remains an outsider, a spoiler, but for reasons completely
> opposed to its original purpose (1999, 166).

Compelling as all these arguments are, the principal argument against militarisation is the increased insecurity of citizens. The nuclear imaginary that has insecured Indian and South Asian citizens, is underpinned by congealed and hierarchical constructs of state and nation that erode and undermine the state's credibility as a democracy and raise crucial questions regarding the role of the military within it.

Democracy, militarisation and the Indian state

> The government has created political problems by its . . . policies.
> When people have protested, the government has sought to block
> all channels of democratic dissent. When people have had the
> courage to organise and challenge this injustice, the government

has tried to put down their spirit of revolt by brute, military force. And like every other government [that] has tried to solve a political problem by military force, the Indian government too, has failed. It has only succeeded in alienating more and more people from itself and its armed forces—whether in Nagaland, Mizoram or in Punjab (Haksar 1985, 15).

Kashmir exemplifies the gravity of a crisis that flows from using the military as an instrument of political power and domestic repression.

In the name of fighting secessionist militants, those responsible for the governance of this great country are themselves hitting at the very foundations of our democratic republic. . . . A republic does not last by enforced submission of its people at gunpoint. It has just the opposite effect (Bonner 1994, 249).

Notwithstanding its own specificities, Kashmir is part of a larger crisis of the Indian state that is neither incidental nor transient, but a symptom of centralised tyranny whose collective discontents are negotiated through military means. This crisis has crucial implications not just for citizens, but also for the military. When the latter battles citizens in Kashmir or, for that matter, in Manipur, Mizoram, Assam or Nagaland, it raises serious questions regarding the legality and morality of the state. The violation of citizens' civil and human rights by an institution that is meant to protect citizens underlines the crisis:

When the army is deployed to deal with a situation in which the country's own people are involved, the question arises—who is the enemy? Can a citizen of a country be treated as an enemy to be destroyed by its own armies? (Haksar 1985, 17).

The use of the military as a proxy for civil governance represents political failure on the part of the state, exacerbated by legislative sanction for Indian soldiers to kill citizens. The fundamental question raised by the crisis is this: is a state that *legalises* violence against citizens a legitimate[5] instrument of governance? The transformation of an important institution of the state into a source of violence and insecurity for citizens highlights the paradox of a democracy that ('legally') divests citizens' of their rights of citizenship. Despite a formal civil-military separation, the military has come to play a direct role in domestic affairs of the state—a trend that threatens democracy in India, raises questions regarding the apolitical nature of the military, tarnishes its own professional integrity and, indeed, the very principles on which the military is based. A military, and by extension, a state that uses terror, torture and rape as operative tactics against citizens is at best repressive and at worst illegitimate. 'Law and order' cannot be imposed at the cost of the violation of citizens' liberty, dignity or physical and sexual integrity. It therefore follows that the Indian state's domestic crisis of militarisation cannot be eliminated unless the fundamental distinction between the role of the state and the function of the military is maintained. The gender dimensions of militarisation in Kashmir demonstrate the compelling need to maintain this distinction.

This crisis of militarisation is inextricable from the military and nuclear rivalry between Indian and Pakistan. This inter-state impasse, with its genesis in the division of Kashmir, effectively means that state attempts to secure 'the nation' (on either side) can only be made at the cost of increased insecurity for Kashmir's divided citizenry. For precisely this reason, it is imperative to re-imagine India in ways that can complement, rather than contradict, the security *and* aspirations of Kashmiri citizens on both sides of the LOC.

Re-imagining India by re-imagining Kashmir

The history of the modern (Indian) state does not correspond with its normative 'realist' understanding as an unproblematic *unitary* given. The emergence of the state in India was not a politically neutral event; it was born of violence, and violence continues to dominate its society.[6] Its relevance here, however, relates to the political *legacy* of this violence. The division of Kashmir, achieved militarily in 1948, affirms the territorial sovereignty of India (and Pakistan), but fragments and divides family, community and society in Kashmir. Kashmir, in other words, confounds the inside/outside dichotomy of the normative, territorial, Westphalian state. A 'border' that is supposed to demarcate the inside (citizen) from the outside (alien) in Kashmir is, in effect, the *source* of the problem for the citizens and community it divides. A vignette in a national daily captured the accumulated history of pain underpinning the stately 'Line-of-Control' dividing Kashmir, India and Pakistan:

> Thousands of people kept apart for nearly a generation by the heavily fortified frontline between India[n] and Pakistan-occupied Kashmir saw each other across a raging river . . . in the biggest family reunion since a ceasefire was declared two months ago. Weeping and wailing men, women and children lined up along opposite banks of the Neelum river that divides this corner of Kashmir between India and Pakistan. . . . They were not able to cross to embrace each other, and could barely make themselves heard over the fast-rushing waters. But they were close enough to throw letters weighted with stones across the twenty-metre-wide river to family members and friends. . . . From the Pakistani side, Hajra Bibi, 26, held her one-year-old son up for her mother, on the opposite bank, to see for the first time. 'My mother is standing over there on the other side and I haven't seen her in fourteen years,' Bibi said between sobs. Across the bank, three men held Bibi's mother back as she tried to jump into the dangerous icy waters and forge her way across to her daughter and grandson. The highly emotional scene encapsulates the despair of the 56-year-old division of Kashmir. . . . The cold, persistent rain barely dampened their enthusiasm. About 1,500 people converged at the water's edge on the Indian side. Some 600 people gathered on the Pakistani side. . . . Mohammed Karim, 50, hurled a coconut from the Pakistani side to his brother on the Indian bank. Mohammed Majid nearly fell into the water, but managed to catch the gift. 'This was only a coconut, but its more than the whole world to me, because I have seen my brother after fourteen years,' Mohammed Karim said. . . . A day will come when we will speak with each other, close-up (*The Asian Age* 2004)[7]

Kashmir is not the only space where state claims to territorial 'sovereignty' mask the history that precedes these claims. Sankaran Krishna describes a similar predicament on the eastern frontier of the Indian nation-state:

Hoseb Ali, a resident of Nabinnagar village in Nadia (a district in West Bengal, India), sat in his courtyard, lit a bidi and gently tossed the matchstick away. The matchstick, still smouldering, landed in Bangladesh. 'Uncle, come over, I have something to tell you,' he shouted. Hoseb Ali was calling his maternal uncle, Emdadul, to discuss the up-coming village-level administrative elections being held in the state of West Bengal. They were neighbours, but it so happened that the international boundary between India and Bangladesh cut across their courtyard, rendering them citizens of different countries (1996, 205).

The division of the Kashmiris between the 'independent' and 'sovereign' states of India and Pakistan (or indeed, as the example of Hoseb Ali illustrates, the division of the Bengalis between India and Bangladesh) indicates exactly why the post-colonial nation can never fit within the borders of the post-colonial state. 'National' frontiers in Kashmir are the root of an 'insecurity' defined not so much by an 'anarchic' world of rival states, but by the longings and imaginings of a sub-national community divided by militarised and nuclearised frontiers, and competing nationalisms. And it is precisely *because* these longings do not correspond with the 'national' narrative of the unitary nation-state that the latter seeks to submerge or eliminate the former. The concept of a unitary nation-state disregards India's plurality and diversity even as it places great emphasis on the doctrine of centralisation through repression.[8] The collective discontents of centralised domination and coercion are treated as a 'law and order problem' and negotiated through military means. A wide range of citizens are deemed (by the state) to be beyond the pale of 'the nation' and undeserving of civil and political rights. The violent pacification of ethnic minorities that a unitary state entails *objectifies* entire communities and the violence done to them, even as the compulsions of power that underpin this violence remain insulated from democratic scrutiny. In this political imaginary, 'the nation' can only be forged through the rituals of war.

A 'national' narrative that normalises violence as an inevitable and integral part of producing a nation cannot be the foundation for as diverse and plural a society as India; it can only culminate in a "national cul-de-sac" (Krishna 1992, 859) whose discontents have been documented in depressing detail by civil and human rights groups. Indian political elites must discard their futile pursuit of a unitary nation and national citizen and re-imagine India in ways that reflect her own historical, cultural and political realities. In other words, the Indian state must accommodate and absorb alternative affiliations and identities accumulated and sustained through history, instead of seeking to destroy or discredit them.

Six decades of coercive nation-state building and four wars have prolonged, but not effaced, the imaginings of Kashmiris on both sides of the Line-of-Control. It is these imaginings, not singular constructs of state and nation, that must form the basis of a new political imaginary that steers the Indian state away from its violent and tragic impasse in Kashmir. This is to suggest that the 'national' obsession with borders and boundaries being played out in blood in Kashmir must end, an obsession involving not just citizens but also soldiers. Amidst the icy peaks of Siachen, at a height of 22,000 feet, Indian soldiers guard the frontiers of 'the nation' in what is acknowledged to be the world's highest battleground; one in two soldiers posted to Siachen will die.[9] In order to re-imagine and work its way out of this impasse, the Indian state must relinquish its pursuit of the script of state and nation that is at the heart of the impasse. This script

> . . . is the story of the making of the nation. . . . The master narrative of Europe becomes the . . . recipe for the unsuccessful production of the nation-state from recalcitrant peoples, religions, regions, tribes, languages and other rubrics of identity. . . . This modulation and dissemination of reality is central to the emergence of post-colonial nations and their conceptualisations of the past and desired future. It is . . . the key step in the normalisation of violence that accompanies the making of the nation (Krishna 2001, 45).

As India herself, rather than Europe, becomes the basis for scripting a new imaginary, 'the nation' can be 'unified' by the modern concept of citizenship *and* a *plural* ethos and imaginary— a defining characteristic of India herself. By renouncing its ill-fated imitation of the unitary nation-state, India can embark on an alternative future where the state does not engage in imprinting the 'national' idea through violence and war, but embodies and reflects the energies and achievements of a democratic, multinational and multi-cultural society.

A plural concept of nation and identity is premised on a commitment to nurturing multiple communities and identities, where no one community or identity is privileged over the other. The articulation and assertion of Kashmiri cultural identity, rather than evoking a disciplining response, should be accommodated and absorbed within a non-hierarchical, egalitarian vision of the nation-state. This re-imagining would also, necessarily, reject normative, abstract prescriptions for nation-state building that legitimise and objectify what can only be termed "cycles of violence and murder" (Krishna 1999, 859) on a grand scale. Such an imaginary would also reject Mohammed Ayoob's prescription for nation-state building where, according to him, "Third World state-makers need . . . a relatively free hand [sic] to persuade, cajole and coerce the disparate population under their nominal rule to accept the legitimacy of [the] state" (1996, 73). Kashmir is one among several regions and communities where, instead of cohering 'the nation,' the long, 'free' hand of the state has proved extraordinarily divisive and has ended up generating its own worst nightmare—separatism and/or demands for secession.

Veena and Sunita—two Pandit sisters from Pulwama, south Kashmir—vindicate the need for a non-'national' vision of the Indian state:

> We would like to live in India if Kashmir goes to Pakistan. . . We cannot identify with a religious state. However, if independence is an option then we would like to go with Kashmir. If there is a choice between India and independent Kashmir, *we go with Kashmir because we are Kashmiris* (Veena and Sunita, emphasis added).[10]

Veena and Sunita's views illustrate that the modern Indian state has neither diluted nor erased citizens' identification with, and allegiance to, (Kashmiri) cultural identity. This is not a failure of the state as such but an indication that the modern concept of citizenship must accommodate parallel cultural and ethnic affiliations that do not fit narrow and exclusivist constructs of nation and/or national citizen. As Hindus of Kashmir, Veena and Sunita share a cultural affinity with India, yet they would choose Kashmir, not India, in the event of a choice between both. Their views illustrate why any new construct of the Indian nation-state must coexist with, rather than eliminate, forms of self-identity and community that long predate its short and rather violent 'national' history. A decentralised, *democratic* federation of India is the best safeguard against state tyranny and its ill-fated attempt to produce 'nation' and 'national' citizen. *Substantive* (not merely formal) democracy is the only possible future for a people who have paid so dear a price struggling for it. Democracy in Kashmir would mean that its formal, participatory dimensions—involving elections at the local and state level—are complemented and augmented by its substantive dimensions. It would be synonymous with the restoration of *full* citizenship rights for Kashmiris— namely, freeing Kashmiri civilians from violence and harassment from the police and the military, the revocation of repressive legislation, the end of unlawful killings, arbitrary searches and detentions, the restoration of Kashmir's judiciary, the protection of civil rights, including the right to freedom of speech and assembly, freedom for Kashmir's citizens to travel within and beyond state borders, the promotion of a free press, and last, but certainly not least, the initiation of a process of public accountability for Kashmir's human rights tragedy.

Important and urgent as democracy, decentralisation and pluralism are, the crises of militarisation in and over Kashmir are inter-linked. The problem that appears to be 'inside' is, in effect, inextricable from the 'outside'. The 'Line-of-Control' that divides Kashmir, as well as India and Pakistan, contradicts rather than conforms to the inside/outside, domestic/foreign, citizen/alien antinomies. The new imaginary shall acknowledge the existence of civil community beyond national borders, and the fact that the territorial border dividing Kashmir is as much a source of militarisation as the construct of 'the nation' within. Kashmiri longings—epitomised by Hajra Bibi and Mohammed Karim and indeed, by Veena and Sunita—connote symbolic defeat for the present status quo and plead for an imagination that sheds obsolete and hierarchal forms of state and nation and thinks of reconciliation, justice and accommodation.[11] Kashmir calls for an end to a tragic impasse that is the source of violence, division, collective pain and a ruinous military and nuclear rivalry.

Outside as inside: bridging the inside/outside dichotomy

A new political imaginary must necessarily move beyond 'national'/constitutional legalese, and a conservative geo-politics that has imprisoned a people's imagination within the bordered, militarised and nuclearised version of the nation-state. A Kashmir-centric imaginary would mandate that India (and Pakistan) relinquish a six-decade long legacy of competing nationalisms fortified by military and nuclear 'power' that have proved to be politically divisive, economically ruinous and ethically barren. As the entity primarily responsible for the crisis in Kashmir, India must accept that the present status quo is politically untenable and morally indefensible; it must also respect the principle that Kashmiris are the ultimate and final arbiters of their political destiny. Taking both as a point of departure, the Indian state should envision a democratic and non-national vision for Kashmir based on recognition and respect for Kashmiri identity, and Kashmiris' desire to chart a political future free from central control and dominance. This is not to formulate a 'solution' to the crisis (itself an ongoing debate and not the focus of this study) but to emphasise its foundational basis, namely, the compelling need for India (and Pakistan) to envision a future based on *Kashmiri* aspiration rather than territorial obsession. By bridging a divided and militarised LOC—as desired by Kashmiris—and, by extension, restoring Kashmir's territorial integrity, cultural contiguity and historical eminence as the point of confluence for South Asia's three great cultural and religious traditions, can the great and grievous chasm between India and Pakistan be bridged. A restored Kashmir can, in turn, restore a subcontinent divided by war, militarised nationalism and nuclear weapons. In Eqbal Ahmed's eloquent words:

> To become prosperous and normal peoples, we must make peace where there is hostility. . . . Kashmir is the finest place to start, and not merely because it is the core of the Indo-Pakistan conflict.

Our histories, cultures and religions have converged in Kashmir.
Our rivers begin there, mountains meet there, and our dreams
rest there (1996, 24).

Once the Kashmiris secure political autonomy, justice and the
dignity they so richly deserve, India and Pakistan can emerge
from their mutual abyss of violence to chart a new future—not as
rival states or 'enemies' that need to 'secure' themselves from each
other by military and nuclear means, but as modern states with
interlinked cultures and communities. Past and future exist in
close proximity; the mere possibility of an alternative future for
Kashmir rendered ever more poignant by hopes and dreams for
its fulfilment. Agha Shahid Ali captures Kashmir's frail hope and
deep longing with eloquence: "What is the blessed word? . . .
One day the Kashmiris will pronounce that word truly for the
first time." (2000, 5)

And if the Kashmiris do pronounce that word for the first
time, India and Pakistan will overcome the principal source of
militarisation in South Asia and conclusively disprove the inside/
outside antinomy.

Tum aao gulshan-e-Lahore se chaman bar dosh
Hum aaen subh-e-Banaras ke roshni lekar
Himalaya ki hawaaon ki taazgi lekar
Aur uske baad ye poochhen ke kaun dushman hai?

You bring us flowers from the gardens of Lahore
We bring you light from the dawns of Benares
Freshness of the Himalayan breeze
And thereafter we ask each other:
Who is the enemy?

Ali Sardar Jafri, 1965.

Notes

1 Daniel Barenboim, Conductor, Berlin Staatskapelle interviewed by Sholto Byrnes. Sholto Byrnes, 'The Maestro', *The Independent* (London), January 8, 2006.

2 See Bowman, *Militarisation, Democracy and Development*, p. 19.

3 Unable to take advantage of its conventional military superiority and mindful of the new nuclear parity with Pakistan, the Indian state had little room for manoeuvre during the 1999 military conflict with Pakistan at the Kargil heights in Kashmir.

4 "There was not much success in getting recognition for India as being in the same league as China, or for its grumble that inadequate attention is internationally paid to the dangers India is supposed to face from China . . . China could stand well above India's little grumbles, gently admonishing it for its criticism of China, and placing itself in the position of being a subcontinental peace-maker." Amartya Sen, *The Argumentative Indian*, pp. 265–266.

5 "If the state itself becomes[s] a source of insecurity for its citizens . . . does it not thereby undermine the prime justification for its existence?" Barry Buzan, *People, States, Fear*, op. cit., p. 21.

6 Sumanta Banerjee, 'The Politics of Violence in the Indian State and Society', in Kumar Rupesinghe and Khawar Mumtaz (eds.), *Internal Conflicts in South Asia* (London: Sage, 1996), p. 81.

7 Roshan Mughal, 'River of Emotion Bursts on LoC', *The Asian Age*, January 22, 2004.

8 Banerjee, 'the Politics of Violence', p. 94.

9 Sankaran Krishna, 'Mapping the Body Politic in India', in Michael J. Shapiro and Hayward R. Alker (eds.), *Challenging Boundaries: Global Flows, Territorial Identities* (Minneapolis; London: University of Minnesota Press 1996), p. 200.

10 Personal interview with Veena and Sunita, Barbarshah, Srinagar, July 7, 2004.

11 Ranabir Samaddar, 'Crossed Lines in Kashmir', *Security Dialogue*, 32 (1), 2000, p. 70.

Select Bibliography

Press and Media Reports

Amnesty International Press Release UA 108/91. 1991. London: Amnesty International.

BBC. 2001. Patrols Against Kashmir Acid Attacks, August 15. http://news.bbc.co.uk/2/hi/south_asia/1487395.stm. Accessed November 15, 2004.

"Bid for National Stand on Kashmir". 1990. *The Hindu*, February 11.

"Censor Board Bans Documentary on Disappeared Kashmiris". 2006. *Greater Kashmir*, February 9.

"Change in Kashmir". 1989. *The Hindustan Times*, December 26.

"Farooq Takes Tough Stand on MUF". 1987. *The Indian Express*, April 4.

"India Gags Video of Kashmir Torture". 1991. *The Guardian Weekly*, London, November 17.

"India Withdraws Patronage to EU Visits in J&K". 2004. *The Times of India*, August 21.

"Kashmiri Engineer Completes 12 Years in Delhi Jail". 2008. *Greater Kashmir*, May 24.

"Kashmir: Nursing a Shattered Dream". 1993. *The Hindustan Times*, August 22.

"Kashmir Valley: Militant Siege". 1990. *India Today*, January 31.

Keeping the Kashmir Cauldron Boiling. 2001. *The Tribune*, October 24. http://www.tribuneindia.com/2001/20011024/j&k.htm#1. Accessed June 27, 2006.

"More Kashmiri Women Turning Militant". 1990. *The Hindu*, September 3.

"Moves on Kashmir". 1991. *The Times of India*, November 15.

Press Statement on Return of Delegation of IKV and Lawyers Without Borders. 2004. Interchurch Peace Council and Lawyers Without Borders, The Netherlands.

"Security Forces Foiling Plans of Militants". 1990. *The Hindu*, September 14.

Summary Report (Recommendations) of the Ad Hoc Delegation of the

European Parliament to Kashmir. 2004. December 8–11, 2003 and June 20–24, 2004.

"Till Freedom Come". 1995. *Outlook*, October 8.

"The Need for a Political Approach". 1991. *The Hindu*, July 26.

"They are on the Run": Interview With Director General of Police, Jammu and Kashmir. 1989. *Frontline*, April 15–28.

"Tight Security for Kashmir Bandh". 1990. *The Hindu*, February 11.

"Trauma in Prison: Surreal Story of KU PhD Aspirant". 2008. *Kashmir Times*, Online edition, April 24.

"Unambiguous Signals". 1991. *The Indian Express*, November 15.

"Valley Where Normality is Enforced". 1990. *The Hindu*, September 8.

Human Rights Reports

Arms and Abuses in Kashmir. 1994. New York: Human Rights Watch.

Behind the Kashmir Conflict: Abuses by Indian Security Forces and Militant Groups Continue. 1999. New York: Human Rights Watch.

Blood in the Valley: Kashmir—Behind the Propaganda Curtain: A Report to the People of India. 1995. Bombay: Lokshahi Hakk Sangathana.

Everyone Lives in Fear: Patterns of Impunity in Jammu and Kashmir, Vol. 18, No. 11(C). September 2006. New York: Human Rights Watch. http://www.hrw.org/reports/2006/india0906/. Accessed November 23, 2007

Grim Realities: Of Life, Death and Survival in Jammu and Kashmir. 2001. New Delhi: Andhra Pradesh Civil Liberties Committee, Human Rights Forum, Organisation for Protection of Democratic Rights, People's Democratic Forum, People's Union for Democratic Rights.

India: Briefing on the Armed Forces (Special Powers) Act, 1958. 2005. Amnesty International. http://web.amnesty.org/library/print/ ENGASA200252005. Accessed May 30, 2005.

India's Secret Army in Kashmir: New Patterns of Abuse Emerge in the Conflict. 1996. New York; London: Human Rights Watch.

No End in Sight: Human Rights Violations in Assam. 1993. New York: Asia Watch.

Rape and Ill-Treatment of Women. 1991. London: Amnesty International.

Rape in Kashmir: A Crime of War. 1993. New York: Asia Watch and Human Rights Watch.

Undeclared War on Kashmir. 1991. Bombay: Andhra Pradesh Civil Liberties Committee, Committee for Protection of Democratic Rights, Lok Shahi Hakk Sangathana, Organisation for Protection of Democratic Rights.

The Crackdown in Kashmir: Torture of Detainees and Assaults on the Medical Community. 1993. New York: Asia Watch and Physicians For Human Rights.

The Human Rights Crisis in Kashmir: A Pattern of Impunity. 1993. New York: Asia Watch and Human Rights Watch.

Women and War, International Committee of the Red Cross Special Brochure. 1995. Geneva: International Committee of the Red Cross.

Women's Human Rights World Report, 2002: Events of 2001. 2002. New York: Human Rights Watch (Women's Rights Division).

Wounded Valley ... Shattered Souls: Women's Fact Finding Commission Probing Army Atrocities on Women and Children in Kashmir. 1997. Bombay: The Indian People's Tribunal on Environment And Human Rights.

Books and Articles

Abdulla, Farida. 2002. "A Life of Peace and Dignity", in *Speaking Peace: Women's Voices From Kashmir,* edited by U. Butalia. New Delhi: Kali for Women.

Abraham, Itty. 1999. *The Making of the Indian Atomic Bomb: Science, Secrecy and the Postcolonial State,* Hyderabad: Orient Longman.

Ahmed, Aijaz. 2001. "The Hindutva Weapon", in *Out of the Nuclear Shadow,* edited by S. Kothari and Z. Mian, New Delhi: Lokayan and Rainbow Publishers.

Ahmed, Eqbal. 1996. "A Kashmiri Solution for Kashmir", *Himal South Asia,* 9 (8).

Ahmed, Junaid. *Putting Kashmir on the Agenda.* Znet 2002 (March 24, 2002). http://www.zmag.org/content/SouthAsia/junaid_ahmad_kashmir.cfm Accessed July 17, 2006.

Ahmed, Imtiyaz. 2008. "Giving Flowers is Pointless", *Rising Kashmir,* April 26.

Alba, Victor. 1962. "The Stages of Militarism in Latin America", in *The Role of the Military in Underdeveloped Countries,* edited by J.J. Johnson. Princeton: Princeton University Press.

Albanese, Patricia. 2001. "Nationalism, War and the Archaisation of Gender Relations in the Balkans", *Violence Against Women,* 7 (9): 999–1023.

Albrecht, Ulrike, and Mary Kaldor. 1979. "Introduction", in *The World Military Order: The Impact of Military Technology on the Third World,* edited by U. Albrecht and M. Kaldor. London, Basingstoke: Macmillan.

Alcoff, Linda. 1995. "The Problem of Speaking for Others", in *Who Can Speak? Authority And Critical Identity,* edited by J. Roof and R. Wiegman. Urbana: University of Illinois Press.

Ali, Agha Shahid. 2000. *The Country Without a Post Office: Poems 1991– 1995,* Delhi: Ravi Dayal.

Ali, S. Mahmud. 1993. *The Fearful State: Power, People and Internal War in South Asia,* London: Zed Books.

Ananth, Krishna V. 2003. "The Politics of the Bomb: Some Observations on the Political Discourse in India in the Context of Pokharan II", in *Prisoners of the Nuclear Dream*, edited by M.V. Ramana and C.R. Reddy. Hyderabad: Orient Longman.

Ashiq, Peerzada. 2004. "Death is Still a Livelihood in Kashmir", *Tehelka*, June 26.

———. 2004a. "Forget Abu Ghraib, Look Whats Happening in the Prisons of Kashmir', *Tehelka*, June 5.

———. 2004b. "The Twilight Zone of the Half-Widows", *Tehelka*, March 6.

Ayoob, Mohammed. 1994. "Security in the Third World: Searching for the Core Variable", in *Seeking Security and Development: The Impact of Military Spending and Arms Transfers*, edited by N.A. Graham, Colorado and London: Lynne Rienner.

———. 1995. *The Third World Security Predicament: State-making, Regional Conflict and the International System*, Boulder: Lynne Rienner.

———. 1996. "State-Making, State-Breaking and State Failure: Explaining the Roots of 'Third World' Insecurity", in *Between Development and Destruction: An Enquiry into the Causes of Conflict in Post-Colonial States*, edited by L.V.D. Goor, K. Rupesinghe and P. Sciarone, London: Macmillan.

Azar, Edward E, and Chungin Moon. 1988. "Rethinking Third World National Security", in *National Security in the Third World*, edited by E.E. Azar and C. Moon. Aldershot: Edward Elgar Publishing Limited.

———. 1988b. "Towards an Alternative Conceptualisation", in *National Security in the Third World*, edited by E.E. Azar and C. Moon. Aldershot: Edward Elgar Publishing Limited.

Balachandran, G. 1996. "Religion and Nationalism in Modern India", in *Unravelling the Nation: Sectarian Conflict and India's Secular Identity*, edited by K. Basu and S. Subrahmanyam. New Delhi: Penguin.

Banerjee, Sumanta. 1996. "The Politics of Violence in the Indian State and Society", in *Internal Conflicts In South Asia*, edited by K. Rupesinghe and K. Mumtaz. London: Sage.

Bardhan, Pranab. 1989. *The Political Economy of Development in India*, New Delhi: Oxford University Press.

Baruah, Sanjib Kumar. 1999. *India Against Itself: Assam and the Politics of Nationality*, Philadelphia: University of Pennsylvania Press.

Berghahn, Volker R. 1981. *Militarism: The History of an International Debate 1861–1979*, Warwickshire: Berg Publishers.

Bhagat, Pamela. 2002. Interviews, in *Speaking Peace: Women's Voices From Kashmir*, edited by U. Butalia. New Delhi: Kali For Women.

Blanchard, Eric. 2003. "Gender, International Relations and Security", *Signs: Journal of Women in Culture and Society*, 28 (3).

Blank, Jonah. 1999. "Kashmir: Fundamentalism Takes Root", *Foreign Affairs*, 78 (6).

Bonner, Arthur. 1994. "The Culture of Caste", in *Democracy in India: A Hollow Shell*, edited by A. Bonner, Washington D.C.: The American University Press.

Bose, Sumantra. 1997. *The Challenge In Kashmir: Democracy, Self-Determination and a Just Peace*, New Delhi: Sage.

———. 1998. "Hindu Nationalism and the Crisis of the Indian State", in *Nationalism, Democracy and Development: State and Politics in India*, edited by S. Bose and A. Jalal, New Delhi: Oxford University Press.

———. 2000. "Kashmir, 1990–2000: Reflections on Individual Voices in a Dirty War", *Development* 43 (3): 99–102.

———. 2003. *Kashmir: Roots of Conflict, Paths to Peace*, New Delhi: Vistaar Publications.

Bose, Tapan, Dinesh Mohan, Gautam Navlakha, and Sumanta Banerjee. 1990. *India's Kashmir War*, New Delhi: Committee for Initiative on Kashmir.

Bowman, Kirk. 2002. *Militarisation, Democracy and Development: Perils of Praetorianism in Latin America*, Pennsylvania: The Pennsylvania State University Press.

Bracken, Paul. 1999. *Fire in the East: The Rise of Asian Military Power and the Second Nuclear Age*, New York: HarperCollins.

Brass, Paul. 1994. *The Politics of India Since Independence*, The New Cambridge History of India IV: 1, New Delhi: Cambridge University Press.

———. 2006. "Nirvana is Tomorrow", *Outlook*, August 21.

Bukhari, Fayaz. 2002. "Dying Day by Day: Taking Stock of Mental and Social Health In Kashmir", *Himal South Asia* (November). http://www.himalmag.com/2002/november/report.htm. Accessed November 15, 2004.

Bukhari, Shujaat. 2004. "105-year-old School in Srinagar Burnt Down", *The Hindu*, July 6.

———. 2006. "Threat of Physical Violence Looms in Kashmir", *The Hindu*, December 25.

Butalia, Urvashi. 2002. "Introduction", in *Speaking Peace: Women's Voices From Kashmir*, edited by U. Butalia, New Delhi: Kali for Women.

Buzan, Barry. 1983. *People, States, Fear: The National Security Problem in International Relations*, Sussex: Wheatsheaf Books.

———. 1988. "People, States, Fear: The National Security Problem in the Third World", in *National Security in the Third World: The Management of Internal and External Threats*, edited by E.E. Azar and C. Moon, Aldershot: Edward Elgar Publishing Limited.

Byrnes, Sholto. 2006. "The Maestro", *The Independent*, London, January 8.

Chakravarti, Uma. 2002. "A Kashmir Diary: Seven Days in an Armed 'Paradise'", in *Speaking Peace: Women's Voices From Kashmir*, edited by U. Butalia, New Delhi: Kali for Women.

Chengappa, Raj. 2000. *Weapons of Peace: The Secret Story of India's Quest to be a Nuclear Power*, New Delhi: HarperCollins Publishers.

Chenoy, Anuradha M. 2002. *Militarism and Women in South Asia*, New Delhi: Kali for Women.

Chinkin, Christine. 1994. "Rape and Sexual Abuse of Women in International Law", *European Journal of International Law*, 5 (3): 326–341.

Chopra, Mannika. 2002. "Women Leaders Wanted in Kashmir", Available from http://www.freeindiamedia.com/women/ 13_aug_women.htm. Accessed November 15, 2004.

Clad, James. 1990. "Valley of Violence: The Deep Chasm Between Kashmiri Muslims and India", *Far Eastern Economic Review*, May 24.

Clad, James, and Salamat Ali. 1990. "Will Words Lead to War?" *Far Eastern Economic Review*, April 26.

Cockburn, Cynthia. 1998. *The Space Between Us: Negotiating Gender and National Identities In Conflict*. London: Zed Books.

————. 2001. "The Gendered Dynamics of Armed Violence and Political Conflict", in *Victims, Perpetrators or Actors? Gender, Armed Conflict and Political Violence*, edited by C.O.N. Moser and F.C. Clark, New Delhi: Kali for Women.

Cohen, Stephen. 1976. "The Military", in *Indira Gandhi's India: A Political System Reappraised*, edited by H.C. Hart, Colorado: Westview Press.

————. 1990. "The Indian Military and Indian Democracy", in *India's Democracy: An Analysis Of Changing State-Society Relations*, edited by A. Kohli, Princeton: Princeton University Press.

————. 2001. *India: Emerging Power*, Washington, D.C.: Brookings Institution Press.

Cohn, Carol. 1993. "War, Wimps and Women: Talking Gender and Thinking War", in *Gendering War Talk*, edited by M. Cooke and A. Woollacott, Princeton: Princeton University Press.

Connell, R.W. 1990. "The State, Gender and Sexual Politics", *Theory and Society*, 19: 507–544.

Cooke, Miriam. 1996. *Women and the War Story*, Berkeley: University of California Press.

Cooke, Miriam, and Roshni Rustomji-Kearns, 1994. "Introduction", in *Blood Into Ink: South Asian and Middle Eastern Women Write War*, edited by M. Cooke and R. Rustomji-Kearns, Colorado: Westview Press.

Corbridge, Stuart, and John Harriss. 2000. *Reinventing India: Liberalisation, Hindu Nationalism and Popular Democracy*, Cambridge: Polity.

Committee for the Protection of Democratic Rights. 1991. "War and Our Civil Liberties", in *Expanding Governmental Lawlessness and Organised Struggles: Violation of Democratic Rights of the Minorities, Women, Slum Dwellers, Press and Some Other Violations*, edited by A.R. Desai, Bombay: Popular Prakashan. Original edition, 1987.

Cranna, Michael, ed. 1994. *The True Cost of Conflict*, London: Earthscan Publications.

Crossette, Barbara. 1991. "India Moves Against the Rebels", *The New York Times*, April 7.

Das, Runa. 2003. "Engendering Post-Colonial Nuclear Policies through the Lens of Hindutva: Rethinking the Security Paradigm of India", *Comparative Studies of South Asia, Africa and the Middle East XXII (1&2)*.

Dasgupta, Chandrashekhar. 2005. "Jammu and Kashmir in the Indian Union: The Politics of Autonomy", in *Prospects for Peace in South Asia*, edited by R. Dossani and H.S. Rowen, Stanford: Stanford University Press.

DasGupta, Sumona. 2000. "Breaking the Silence: Women and Kashmir", New Delhi: Women in Security, Conflict Management And Peace (WISCOMP).

Deng, Francis M. 1996. "Anatomy of Conflicts in Africa", in *Between Development and Destruction: An Enquiry into the Causes of Conflict in Post-Colonial States*, edited by L.V.D. Goor, K. Rupesinghe and P. Sciarone, London & New York: Macmillan.

Dewan, Ritu, Sheba Chhachhi, Gouri Choudhry, and Manimala. 1994. *The Green of My Valley is Khaki: Women's Testimonies from Kashmir*, New Delhi: Women's Initiative.

Dixit, Aabha. 1996. "Status Quo: Maintaining Nuclear Ambiguity", in *India and the Bomb: Public Opinion and Nuclear Options*, edited by D. Cortright and A. Mattoo, Notre Dame: University of Notre Dame Press.

Egan, Carlos. 1988. "National Security Regimes and Human Rights Abuse: Argentina's Dirty Wars", in *National Security in the Third World: The Management of Internal and External Threats*, edited by E.E. Azar and C. Moon, Aldershot: Edward Elgar Publishing Limited.

Eide, Asbjorn, and Marek Thee. 1980. "Introduction", in *Problems of Contemporary Militarism*, edited by A. Eide and M. Thee, London: Croom-Helm.

Elshtain, Jean Bethke, and Shiela Tobias. 1990. "Preface", in *Women, Militarism And War: Essays in History, Politics and Social Theory*, edited by J.B. Elshtain and S. Tobias, Maryland: Rowman and Littlefield.

Enloe, Cynthia. 1983. *Does Khaki Become You?: The Militarisation of Women's Lives*, London: Pluto.

Falk, Richard. 1977. Militarisation and Human Rights. *Bulletin of Peace Proposals*, 8 (3).

———. 1980. "Militarisation and Human Rights in the Third World", in *Problems Of Contemporary Militarism*, edited by A. Eide and M. Thee, London: Croom-Helm.

Ferguson, James P. 1961. *Kashmir: An Historical Introduction*, London: Centaur Press.

Ganguly, Sumit. 1997. *Kashmir: Portents of War, Hopes for Peace*, Cambridge & New York: Woodrow Wilson Centre Press and Cambridge University Press.

Geyer, Michael. 1989. "The Militarisation of Europe 1914–1945", in *The Militarisation of the Western World*, edited by J.R. Gillis, New Brunswick: Rutgers University Press.

Giddens, Anthony. 1985. *The Nation-State and Violence: A Contemporary Critique of Historical Materialism Vol. 2*, London: Polity.

Gillis, John. "Introduction", in *Militarisation of the Western World*, edited by J. Gillis, New Brunswick: Rutgers University Press.

Gokhale, Nitin. 2004. "Look What the Armed Forces Have Reduced Manipuri Women to", *Tehelka*, July 31.

Gossman, Patricia. 2000. "India's Secret Armies", in *Death Squads in Global Perspective*, edited by B.B. Campbell and A.D. Brenner, London: Macmillan.

Grant, Rebecca, and Kathleen Newland, 1991. "Introduction", in *Gender and International Relations*, edited by R. Grant and K. Newland, Milton Keynes: Open Press.

Gupta, Prakrit. 2005. "Kashmir Women Take Up Arms for Self-Protection", *Middle East Times* (23 September). http://www.metimes.com/storyview.php?StoryID=20050923-083928-8729r. Accessed February 22, 2006.

Gupta, Shekhar. 1990. "Kashmir Valley: Militant Siege", *India Today*, January 31.

Gupta, Smita. 1990. "Storm Over Srinagar", *The Independent*, February 17.

Habibullah, Wajahat. 2004. "The Political Economy of the Kashmir Conflict: Opportunities for Economic Peacebuilding and for U.S. Policy, Washington D.C.: United States Institute of Peace.

Haksar, Nandita. 1985. "A Case Study", *Seminar*, 308 (Using the Army).

Hamid, Peerzada A. 2004. "Valley of Dead Flowers", *Tehelka*, July 24.

———. "Deathly News, What Else?", *Tehelka*, July 21, 2007.

Hammer, Rhonda. 2003. "Militarism and Family Terrorism: A Critical

Feminist Perspective", *The Review of Education, Pedagogy and Cultural Studies*, 25: 231–256.

Haraway, Donna. 1988. "Situated Knowledges: The Science Question in Feminism and the Privilege of Partial Perspective", *Feminist Studies*, 14 (3): 588–607.

Hasan, Zoya. 1991. "Changing Orientation of the State and the Emergence of Majoritarianism in the 1980s", in *Communalism in India: History, Politics and Culture*, edited by K.N. Panikkar, Delhi: Manohar Books.

Imroz, Parvez. 2003. "The Informative Missive: A Monthly Newsletter of the Public Commission on Human Rights", Srinagar, September 19.

Jabbar, Sonia. 2003. "Blood Soil: Chittisinghpora and After", in *The Shades of Violence: Women and Kashmir*, Women in Security, Conflict Management and Peace.

Jacobs, Susie M, Ruth Jacobson and Jennifer Marchbank, eds., States of Conflict", in *States of Conflict: Gender, Violence and Resistance*, edited by S.M. Jacobs, R. Jacobson and J. Marchbank, London: Zed Books.

Jafri, Ali Sardar. *Kaun Dushman Hai?* (Who is the Enemy?) 1965. Available from http://dcubed.blogspot.com/2006/02/we-can-ask-one-another.html. Accessed October 22, 2006.

Jalal, Ayesha. 1995. *Democracy and Authoritarianism in South Asia: A Comparative and Historical Perspective*, Cambridge: Cambridge University Press.

Jaleel, Muzammil. "Kashmiri Women Don't Need Morality Lessons", *Indian Express* (online edition), Mehbooba Mufti interviewed by Muzammil Jaleel. http://www.kashmirlive.com/kashmirlive/int20010907.html. Accessed February 22, 2006.

———. 2002. Despatches from a War Torn Region", in *Speaking Peace: Women's Voices From Kashmir*, edited by U. Butalia, New Delhi: Kali for Women.

Jamwal, Anuradha Bhasin. 2007. "Women in Kashmir Conflict: Victimhood and Beyond", in *Women Building Peace Between India and Pakistan*, edited by S. Mulay and J. Kirk, New Delhi: Anthem Press.

Jaudel, Etienne. 1993. *Violations of Human Rights Committed by the Indian Security Forces in Jammu And Kashmir*, Paris: Federation Internationale Des Ligues Des Droits De L'Homme (FIDH).

Jeffrey, Robin. 1986. *What's Happening to India? Punjab, Ethnic Conflict, Mrs.Gandhi's Death and the Test For Federalism*, Macmillan: London.

Jha, Padmanand. 1995. "Carving Up the Valley", *Outlook*. http://www.outlookindia.com/full.asp?fodname=19951018&fname=COVER+STORY&sid=3. Accessed November 12, 2004.

Joshi, Arun. 1990. "BJP-JD Rift over Kashmir", *The Hindustan Times*, September 8.

Judd, Terry. 2006. "For the Women of Iraq, the War is Just Beginning", *The Independent*.

Kagal, Ayesha. 1990. "Accidental Terrorist", *The Times of India*, April 29.

Kaldor, Mary. 1978. "The Military in Third World Development", in *Disarmament and World Development*, edited by R. Jolly, Oxford: Pergamon.

————. 1982. *The Baroque Arsenal*, London: Andre Deutsche Limited.

————. 1990. "After the Cold War", *New Left Review*, I/180 (March–April): 25–37.

————. 2001. *New and Old Wars: Organised Violence in a Global Era*, Cambridge: Polity.

————. 2005. "We Have to Think about the Security of Individuals Rather than the Protection of States", *Boston Review* (March/April). http://www.bostonreview.net/BR30.1/kaldor.html. Accessed September 23, 2005.

Kannabiran, K.G. 1990. "The Slow Burn", *The Illustrated Weekly of India*, July 1.

Karat, Prakash. 1998. "A Lethal Link", *Frontline*, June 19.

Kashani, Sarwar, Idrees Kanth and Gowher Fazli. 2003. *The Impact of Violence on the Student Community in Kashmir*, New Delhi: Oxfam India Trust: The Violence Mitigation and Amelioration Project.

"Kashmir Imprisoned", Committee for Initiative on Kashmir. 2002. In *Speaking Peace: Women's Voices From Kashmir*, edited by U. Butalia, New Delhi: Kali for Women.

Kaur, Inpreet. 2006. "Warring over Peace in Kashmir", in *Kashmir: New Voices, New Approaches*, edited by W.P.S. Sidhu, B. Asif and C. Samii, Boulder: Lynne Rienner.

Kelly, Liz. 2000. "Wars Against Women: Sexual Violence, Sexual Politics and the Militarised State", in *States of Conflict: Gender, Violence and Resistance*, edited by S.M. Jacobs, R. Jacobson and J. Marchbank, London: Zed Books.

Keppley Mahmood, Cynthia. 1989. "Sikh Rebellion and the Hindu Concept of Order", *Asian Survey*, XXIX (3).

————. 2000. "Trials by Fire: Dynamics of Terror in Punjab and Kashmir", in *Death Squad: The Anthropology of State Terror*, edited by J.A. Sluka, Philadelphia: University of Pennsylvania Press.

Kesic, Vesna. 2000. "From Reverence to Rape: An Anthropology of Ethnic and Genderised Violence", in *Frontline Feminisms: Women, War and Resistance*, edited by M.R. Waller and J. Rycenga, New York: Garland Publishing Inc.

Khalidi, Omar. 1995. *Indian Muslims Since Independence*, New Delhi: Vikas.

Khanna, Shakti Bhan. 2002. "Leaving Home", in *Speaking Peace: Women's Voices From Kashmir*, edited by U. Butalia, New Delhi: Kali for Women.

Khayal, Ghulam Nabi. 1989. "The Troubled Valley", *The Illustrated Weekly of India*, September 17.

Klare, Micheal T. 1980. "Militarism: The Issues Today", in *Problems of Contemporary Militarism*, edited by A. Eide and M. Thee, London: Croom-Helm.

———. 1989. "East-West versus North-South: Dominant and Subordinate Themes in U.S. Military Strategy since 1945", in *Militarisation of the Western World*, edited by J. Gillis, New Brunswick: Rutgers University Press.

Kochanek, Stanley. 1980. "India's Changing Role in the United Nations", *Pacific Affairs*, 53 (1): 48–68.

Kohli, Atul, ed. 1990. *India's Democracy: An Analysis of Changing State-Society Relations*, Princeton: Princeton University Press.

———. 1998. "Can Democracies Accommodate Ethnic Nationalism? The Rise and Decline of Self-Determination Movements in India", in *Community Conflicts and the State in India*, edited by A. Basu and A. Kohli, New Delhi: Oxford University Press.

Kothari, Rajni. 1989. *State Against Democracy: In Search of Humane Governance*, New York: New Horizons Press.

Koul, Sudha. 2002. *The Tiger Ladies: A Memoir of Kashmir*, London: Review Books.

Krause, Keith. 1996. "Armaments and Conflict: The Causes and Consequences of Military Development", in *Between Development and Destruction*, edited by L.V.D. Goor, K. Rupesinghe and P. Sciarone, London & New York: Macmillan.

Krishna, Sankaran. 1992. "Oppressive Pasts and Desired Futures: Re-imagining India", *Futures* (November).

———. 1996. "Mapping the Body Politic in India", in *Challenging Boundaries: Global Flows, Territorial Identities*, edited by M.J. Shapiro and H.R. Alker, Minneapolis: University of Minnesota Press.

———. 1999. *Postcolonial Insecurities: India, Sri Lanka and the Question of Nationhood*, Minneapolis: University of Minnesota Press.

———. 2001. "Mimetic History: Narrating India through Foreign Policy", in *Handcuffed to History: Narratives, Pathologies and Violence In South Asia*, edited by S.P. Udayakumar, London: Praeger.

Kumar, Krishna, ed. 2001. *Women and Civil War: Impact, Organisations and Action*, Boulder: Lynne Rienner.

Kundu, Apurba. 1998. *Militarism in India: The Army and Civil Society in*

Consensus, London & New York: Tauris Academic Studies.

Laifungbam, Debabrata Roy. 2004. "Manipur's Mothers", *Tehelka*, August 7.

Lamb, Alastair. 1991. *Kashmir: A Disputed Legacy 1846–1990*, Karachi: Oxford University Press.

Leibknecht, Karl. 1973. *Militarism and Anti-Militarism*, Cambridge: Rivers Press. Original edition 1907.

Leonardo, Micaela di. 1985 (Fall). "Morals, Mothers and Militarism: Anti-Militarism and Feminist Theory", *Feminist Studies*, 11 (3).

Louscher, David J and J Sperling. 1994. "Arms Transfers and the Structure of International Power", in *Seeking Security and Development: The Impact of Military Spending and Arms Transfers*, edited by N.A. Graham, Boulder: Lynne Rienner.

Luckham, Robin. 1979. "Militarism: Force, Class and International Conflict", in *The World Military Order: The Impact of Military Technology on the Third World*, edited by M. Kaldor and A. Eide, London: Macmillan.

MacKinnon, Catharine A. 1993. "Crimes of War, Crimes of Peace", in *On Human Rights*, edited by S. Shute and S.L. Hurley, New York: Basic Books.

Malik, Yasin. 1994. *Our Real Crime*, Srinagar: Jammu and Kashmir Liberation Front.

Manchanda, Rita. 1990. "Facts and Propaganda", *Far Eastern Economic Review*, July 19.

———. 1999. Kashmir's Worst-Off Half. *Himal South Asia*, 12 (4): May.

———. 2001. "Guns and Burqa: Women in the Kashmir Conflict", in *Women, War and Peace in South Asia: Beyond Victimhood to Agency*, edited by R. Manchanda, New Delhi: Sage.

Mann, Michael. 1987. "The Roots and Contradictions of Modern Militarism", *New Left Review*, I/162 (March–April 1987).

Mansfield, Edward D and Jack Snyder. 2002. "Democratic Transitions, Institutional Strength and War", *International Organisation*, 56 (2): 298–99.

Mattoo, Amitabh. 1993. "A Community in Exile", *The Independent*, June 17.

Mattoo, Neerja. 2002. "The Story of a Women's College in Kashmir", in *Speaking Peace: Women's Voices From Kashmir*, edited by U. Butalia, New Delhi: Kali for Women.

Mc Laurin, R.D. 1988. "Managing National Security: The American Experience and Lessons for the Third World", in *National Security in the Third World: The Management of Internal and External Threats*, edited by E.E. Azar and C. Moon, Aldershot: Edward Elgar Publishing Limited.

Mehta, Ved. 1978. *The New India*, Harmondsworth: Penguin.

Mishra, Pankaj. 2000. "Death in Kashmir", *The New York Review of Books*, 47 (14).

———. 2000a. "Kashmir: The Unending War", *The New York Review of Books*, 47 (16).

Mladjenovic, Lepa and Donna M Hughes. 2000. "Feminist Resistance to War and Violence in Serbia", in *Frontline Feminisms: Women, War and Resistance*, edited by Marguerite R. Waller and Jennifer Rycenga, New York: Garland Publishing Inc.

Mohanty, Chandra Talpade. 1991. "Under Western Eyes: Feminist Scholarship and Colonial Discourses", in *Third World Women and the Politics of Feminism*, edited by C.T. Mohanty, A. Russo and L. Torres, Bloomington: Indiana University Press.

Moser, Caroline O.N. 2001. "The Gendered Continuum of Violence and Conflict: An Operational Framework", in *Victims, Perpetrators or Actors*, edited by C.O.N. Moser and F.C. Clark, New Delhi: Kali for Women.

Motta, Showkat. 2004. "Shabnam Becoming Manipur's Manorama for Kashmir", *Greater Kashmir*, November 11.

Mughal, Roshan. 2004. "River of Emotion Bursts on LoC", *The Asian Age*, January 22.

Navakha, Gautam. 2004. "Limits and Scope of Dialogue", *Spotlight*, 23 (39). http://www.nepalnews.com/contents/englishweekly/spotlight/2004/apr/apr16/viewpoint.htm. Accessed January 22, 2007.

Navlakha, Gautam. 2000. "Downsizing 'National' Security", *Economic and Political Weekly*, May 13.

Noorani, A.G. 1964. *The Kashmir Question*, Bombay: Manaktalas.

Noorani, A.G. 2000. Jammu And Kashmir: Contours Of Militancy", *Frontline*, September 20–October 13. http://www.flonnet.com/fl1720/17200800.htm. Accessed November 12, 2004.

Nordstrom, Carolyn, and Jo Ann Martin. 1992. "Introduction", in *Paths to Domination, Resistance and Terror*, edited by C. Nordstrom and J.A. Martin, Berkeley: University of California Press.

Oberg, Jan. 1980. "The New International Military Order: A Threat to Human Security", in *Problems of Contemporary Militarism*, edited by A. Eide and M. Thee, London: Croom-Helm.

Oberoi, Surinder Singh. 1997. "Kashmir is Bleeding", *Bulletin of the Atomic Scientists* 53 (2). http://www.mtholyoke.edu/acad/intrel/crisis/bul.htm. Accessed November 7, 2005.

———. 2001. "Fear And Loathing in Kashmir", *The Washington Quarterly*, 24 (2): 195–99.

———. 2004. "Ethnic Separatism and Insurgency in Kashmir", in *Religious Radicalism and Security in South Asia*, edited by S.P. Limaye, M. Malik and R. Wirsing, Honolulu: Asia-Pacific Center for Security Studies.

Pauker, Guy J. 1958. "Southeast Asia as a Problem Area in the Next Decade", *World Politics*, 11 (April).

Pearce, Jenny. 2006. "Bringing Violence 'Back Home': Gender Socialisation and the Transmission of Violence through Time and Space", in *Global Civil Society*, edited by H.K. Anheier, M. Kaldor and M. Glasius, London: Sage.

Peer, Basharat. 2005. "It Could be Follow-on for Mufti", *Tehelka*, October 8.

Perkovich, George. 2000. *India's Nuclear Bomb: The Impact on Global Proliferation*, New Delhi: Oxford University Press, Original edition, 1999.

———. 2002. "What Makes the Indian Bomb Tick?" in *Nuclear India in the Twenty-first Century*, edited by D.R. SarDesai and R.G.C. Thomas, New York: Palgrave.

———. 2003. "Is India a Major Power?" *The Washington Quarterly*, 27 (1): 129–144.

Peterson, V. Spike 1992. *Gendered States: Feminist (Re)Visions of International Relations Theory*, Boulder: Lynne Rienner.

Prashad, Vijay. 2003. *Namaste Sharon: Hindutva and Sharonism Under US Hegemony*, New Delhi: Leftword Books.

PUDR. 1986. "Disturbed Areas—The Roots of Repression in Nagaland, Mizoram and Andhra Pradesh", in *Violation of Democratic Rights in India*, edited by A.R. Desai, Bombay: Sangam Books.

———. 1991. "A Citizen's Guide to Rajiv Gandhi's India", in *Expanding Governmental Lawlessness and Organised Struggles: Violation of Democratic Rights of the Minorities, Women, Slum Dwellers, Press and Some Other Violations*, edited by A.R. Desai, Bombay: Popular Prakashan. Original edition, 1987.

Pye, Lucien. 1962. "Armies in the Process of Political Modernisation", in *The Role of the Military in Underdeveloped Countries*, edited by J.J. Johnson, Princeton: Princeton University Press.

Quraishi, Humra. 2002. "Carrying the Cross", *The Times of India*, September 24.

Ram, N. 1999. *Riding the Nuclear Tiger*, Delhi: Leftword Books.

Ramachandran, Sudha. 2002. "Women Lift the Veil on Kashmir", *Asia Times Online*, (7 March). http://www.atimes.com/ind–pak/DC07Df01.html. Accessed January 17, 2006.

————. 2003. *The Shades of Violence: Women and Kashmir*, New Delhi: Women in Security, Conflict Management and Peace.

Ramana, M.V. 2003. "La Trahison Des Clercs: Scientists and India's Nuclear Bomb", in *Prisoners of the Nuclear Dream*, edited by M.V. Ramana and C.R. Reddy, Hyderabad: Orient Longman.

Ramdas, L. 2003. "Nuclear Weapons and National Security", in *Prisoners of the Nuclear Dream*, edited by M.V. Ramana and C.R. Reddy, Hyderabad: Orient Longman.

Randle, Michael. 1980. *Militarism and Repression.* Boston, Massachussetts: International Seminars on Training for Nonviolent Action.

Regan, Patrick. 1994. *Organising Societies for War: The Process and Consequences of Societal Militarisation,* Westport, Connecticut: Praeger.

Regehr, Ernest. 1980. "What is Militarism?" in *Problems of Contemporary Militarism*, edited by A. Eide and M. Thee, London: Croom-Helm.

Roy, Srirupa. 2003. "Nuclear Frames: Official Nationalism, the Nuclear Bomb and the Anti-Nuclear Movement in India", in *Prisoners of the Nuclear Dream*, edited by M.V. Ramana and C.R. Reddy, Hyderabad: Orient Longman.

Rushdie, Salman. 1999. "Kashmir, the Imperilled Paradise", *The New York Times*, June 3.

Sahadevan, P. 1999. "Ethnic Conflict and Militarism, in South Asia", in *Kroc Occasional Paper No 16:OP:4*, Joan B Kroc Institute for International Peace Studies: University of Notre Dame.

Sahni, Varun 1996. "Going Nuclear: Establishing an Overt Nuclear Weapons Capability", in *India and the Bomb: Public Opinion and Nuclear Options*, edited by D. Cortright and A. Mattoo, Notre Dame: University of Notre Dame Press.

Saigol, Rubina. 2000. "Militarisation, Nation and Gender: Women's Bodies as Arenas of Violent Conflict", in *Women and Sexuality in Muslim Societies*, edited by P. Ilkkaracan, Istanbul: Women for Women's Human Rights.

Sakamoto, Yoshikazu, 1988. "Conditions for Peace in the Asia-Pacific Region", in *Asia: Militarisation and Regional Conflict*, edited by Y. Sakamoto: The United Nations University Tokyo & Zed Books London.

Samaddar, Ranabir. 2001. "Crossed Lines in Kashmir", *Security Dialogue*, 32 (1): 65–70.

Sapru, Abhay. 2004. "Diary of a Special Forces Officer", *Tehelka*, February 14.

Saraf, Pushp. 1990. "NC Bid to Regain Credibility", *Indian Express*, February 9.

Schaffer, Teresita, and Saigal-Arora. 1999. "India: A Fragmented Democracy", *The Washington Quarterly*, 22 (4): 143–150.

Schofield, Victoria. 2004. *Kashmir in Conflict: India, Pakistan and the Unending War*, New Delhi: Viva Books by arrangement with I.B. Tauris, London.

Sen, Amartya Kumar. 2006. *The Argumentative Indian: Writings on Indian History, Culture and Identity*, London: Penguin.

Sen Gupta, Bhabani. 1983. "Regional Security: The Indira Doctrine", *India Today*, August 31.

———. 1997. "India in the Twenty-First Century", *International Affairs*, 73 (2): 297–314.

Sharma, Dhirendra. 1983. *India's Nuclear Estate*, New Delhi: Lancers Publishers.

Sharma, Meera. 1990. "Why is Kashmir Burning?" *The Indian Express*, February 11.

Sidhva, Shiraz. 1990. "Brute Force", *Sunday*, March 13–19.

———. 1991. "We Will Have Our Own Country", *Sunday*, March 17–23.

———. 1991a. "Whitewash: A Press Council Report on Kashmir Clears the Army of Rape Charges", *Sunday*, August 18–24.

———. 1994. "Dukhtaranie Millat: Profile of a Militant, Fundamentalist Organisation", in *Against All Odds: Essays on Women, Religion and Development on India and Pakistan*, edited by K. Bhasin, R. Menon and N.S. Khan, New Delhi: Kali for Women.

Sills, David, ed. 1968. *International Encyclopaedia of the Social Sciences Vol. 10*, London: Collier Macmillan.

Simbulan, Roland G. 1988. "Militarisation in Southeast Asia", in *Asia: Militarisation and Regional Conflict*, edited by Y. Sakamoto, Tokyo and London: The United Nations University & Zed Books.

Singh, Sukhmani. 1990. "Protectors or Predators", *The Illustrated Weekly of India*, September 30.

Singh, Tavleen. 1990. "Srinagar: A War Zone", *The Daily*, January 23.

———. 1995. *Kashmir: A Tragedy of Errors*, New Delhi: Penguin.

Skjelsbaek, Inger. 2001. "Introduction", in *Gender, Peace And Conflict* edited by I. Skjelsbaek and D. Smith, London: Sage.

Skjelsbaek, Kjell. 1980. "Militarism, Its Dimensions and Corollaries: An Attempt at Conceptual Clarification", in *Problems of Contemporary Militarism*, edited by A. Eide and M. Thee, London: Croom-Helm.

Snow, Donald M. 1996. *Uncivil Wars: International Security and the New Internal Conflicts*, Boulder: Lynne Rienner.

Spivak, Gayatri C. 1988. "Can the Subaltern Speak?" in *Marxism and the Interpretation of Culture*, edited by C. Nelson and L. Grossberg, Basingstoke: Macmillan.

Steans, Jill. 1998. *Gender and International Relations: An Introduction*, Cambridge: Polity.

Surendran, C.P. 1991. "Should We Give Up Kashmir?" in *Secular Crown On Fire: The Kashmir Problem*, edited by A.A. Engineer, Delhi: Ajanta.

Suresh, Apu Esthose. "Barbed Wire Mentality", *The Daily Etalaat* (Srinagar) http://etalaat.net/english/index.php?option=com_content&task=view&id=3422&Itemid=2. Accessed January 23, 2008.

Suri, Kavita. 2006. "Women in the Valley: From Victims to Agents of Change", in *Kashmir: New Voices, New Approaches*, edited by W.P.S. Sidhu, B. Asif and C. Samii, Boulder: Lynne Rienner.

Praveen Swami. "Through the Valley of the Shadow of Death", http://www.atimes.com/atimes/South_Asia/EAD9Df02.html. Accessed November 16, 2004.

Thee, Marek. 1980. "Militarism and Militarisation in Contemporary International Relations", in *Problems of Contemporary Militarism*, edited by A. Eide and M. Thee, London: Croom-Helm.

Tickner, Anne J. 1997. "You Just Don't Understand: Troubled Engagements Between Feminists and IR Theorists", *International Studies Quarterly*, 41 (4): 611–632.

Tilly, Charles. 1985. "War and the Power of Warmakers in Western Europe and Elsewhere, 1600–1980", in *Global Militarisation*, edited by W. Peter, J. Galtung and C. Portales, Boulder: Westview Press.

Turpin, Jennifer E, and Lois Ann Lorentzen. 1996. "Introduction: The Gendered New World Order", in *The Gendered New World Order: Militarism, Development and the Environment*, edited by J.E. Turpin and L.A. Lorentzen, New York & London: Routledge.

Udayakumar, S.P. 2001. "Introduction", in *Handcuffed to History: Narratives, Pathologies and Violence in South Asia*, edited by S.P. Udayakumar, London: Praeger.

Vagts, Alfred. 1959. *A History of Militarism*, New York: Free Press.

Vardarajan, Patanjali M. 1993. "Kashmir: Extra-judicial Executions, Rape, Arbitrary Arrests, Disappearances and other Violations of Basic Human Rights by the Indian Security Forces in Indian-administered Kashmir". Paris: Federation Internationale Des Ligues Des Droits De L'Homme.

Viswanathan, Shiv. 2001. "The Patriot Games", in *Out of the Nuclear Shadow*, edited by S. Kothari and Z. Mian, New Delhi: Lokayan and Rainbow Publishers.

Walker, R.B.J. 1990. "Security, Sovereignty and the Challenge of World Politics", *Alternatives*, 15 (1): 3–27.

———. 1993. *Inside/Outside: International Relations as Political Theory*, Cambridge: Cambridge University Press.

Widmalm, Sten. 2002. *Kashmir in Comparative Perspective: Democracy*

and Violent Separatism in India, London: Routledge Curzon.
Wirsing, Robert G. 1994. *India, Pakistan and the Kashmir Dispute: On Regional Conflict and its Resolution,* New York: St. Martin's Press.
Wolpin, Miles D. 1986. *Militarisation, Internal Repression and Social Welfare in the Third World,* London: Croom-Helm.
Younghusband, Francis Edward. 1917. *Kashmir,* London.
Zalewski, Marysia. 1995. "Well, What's the Feminist Perspective on Bosnia?" *International Affairs,* 71 (2): 339–356.
Zia, Ather. "Kashmiri Women: Concerns, Milestones & Solutions". http://www.kashmiraffairs.org/Zia_Ather_Kashmiri_women.html. Accessed February 28, 2007.

Index

about the author

Seema Kazi is an internationally regarded expert on development, militarization, feminism, human rights, and violence against women around the world. She is a recipient of the Dorothy Marchus Senesh Fellowship and a grant from the International Peace Research Association. Kazi lives in New Delhi, India, where she is a Fellow at the Center for Women's Development Studies.

about women unlimited

In Kashmir was originally published by Women Unlimited (an associate of Kali for Women), India's first and oldest feminist press. Women Unlimited facilitates an essential space that amplifies and centers the voices of marginalized women in the continuous global struggle for gender equity. You can learn more by visiting www.womenunlimited.net.

about south end press

South End Press is an independent, nonprofit, collectively-run book publisher with more than 250 titles in print. Since our founding in 1977, we have met the needs of readers who are exploring, or are already committed to, the politics of radical social change. Our goal is to publish books that encourage critical thinking and constructive action on the key political, cultural, social, economic, and ecological issues shaping life in the United States and in the world. We hope to provide a forum for a wide variety of democratic social movements, and provide an alternative to the products and practices of corporate publishing.

From its inception, South End has organized itself as a collective with decision-making arranged to share as equally as possible the rewards and stresses of running the business. Each collective member is responsible for editorial and administrative tasks, and earns the same base salary. South End has made a practice of inverting the pervasive racial and gender hierarchies in traditional publishing houses; our collective has been majority women since the mid-1980s, and at least 50 percent people of color since the mid-1990s.

Our author list—which includes bell hooks, Andrea Smith, Arundhati Roy, Mumia Abu-Jamal, Noam Chomsky, Vandana Shiva, Winona LaDuke, and Howard Zinn—reflects South End's commitment to publish on myriad issues from diverse perspectives.

community supported publishing (CSP)

Community Supported Agriculture (CSA) has helped independent, healthy farming become more sustainable. Now there is Community Supported Publishing (CSP)! By joining the South End Press CSP movement you ensure a steady crop of books to change your world. Membership means you receive a book each month at no charge (every new book we publish while you are a member and selected backlist and best-sellers) and a 10% discount on everything else.

By becoming a CSP member you enable us to continue and expand the ways we serve and support radical movement. CSP members are crucial to our ongoing operations. It is your regular support that allows us to keep your shelves, and the shelves of the other thinkers and actors in the community and the academy, stocked with books that are important (even if they aren't on the *NYT* bestseller list).

Just as real change comes about from sustained grassroots organizing and people joining together, we know it is modest support from a broad range of people that allows South End Press to survive and grow. Subscriptions start at $20/month. Email southend@southendpress.org for more information.

related titles

Noam Chomsky

After the Cataclysm: Postwar, Indochina & the Reconstruction of Imperial Ideology (in collaboration with Edward S. Herman)

The Culture of Terrorism

Pirates & Emperors, Old & New: International Terrorism in the Real World

Rogue States: The Rule of Force in World Affairs

Year 501: The Conquest Continues

Roxanne Dunbar-Ortiz

Blood on the Border: A Memoir of the Contra War

Dana Frank

Bananeras: Women Transforming the Banana Unions of Latin America

bell hooks

Ain't I a Woman: Black Women & Feminism

Feminist Theory: From Margin to Center

INCITE! Women of Color Against Violence

Color of Violence: The INCITE! Anthology

Joanna Kadi (editor)

Food for Our Grandmothers: Writings by Arab-American & Arab-Canadian Feminists

Winona LaDuke

All Our Relations: Native Struggles for Land and Life

Miriam Ching Yoon Louie

Sweatshop Warriors: Immigrant Women Workers Take On the Global Factory

Oscar Olivera (in collaboration with Tom Lewis)

¡Cochabamba!: Water War in Bolivia

Vijay Prashad & Teo Ballvé (editors)

Dispatches from Latin America: On the Frontlines Against Neoliberalism

Arundhati Roy

The Checkbook & the Cruise Missile (with David Barsamian)
An Ordinary Person's Guide to Empire
Power Politics
War Talk

Vandana Shiva

Staying Alive: Women, Ecology, & Development
Earth Democracy: Justice, Sustainability, & Peace

Jael Silliman & Ynestra King (editors)

Dangerous Intersections: Feminist Perspectives on Population, Environment, & Development

Andrea Smith

Conquest: Sexual Violence & American Indian Genocide

Frank B. Wilderson, III

Incognegro: A Memoir of Exile & Apartheid